T0373331

THE POLITICS OF MEMOIR
AND THE NORTHERN
IRELAND CONFLICT

The Politics of Memoir and the Northern Ireland Conflict

Stephen Hopkins

Liverpool University Press

First published 2013 by
Liverpool University Press
4 Cambridge Street
Liverpool
L69 7ZU

Copyright © 2013 Stephen Hopkins

The right of Stephen Hopkins to be identified as the author of this book has been asserted
by him in accordance with the Copyright, Designs and Patents Act 1988.

All rights reserved. No part of this book may be reproduced, stored in a retrieval system,
or transmitted, in any form or by any means, electronic, mechanical, photocopying,
recording, or otherwise, without the prior written permission of the publisher.

British Library Cataloguing-in-Publication data
A British Library CIP record is available

ISBN 978-1-84631-942-6 cased
ISBN 978-1-78694-014-8 limp

Typeset by Carnegie Book Production, Lancaster
Printed and bound by CPI Group (UK) Ltd, Croydon CR0 4YY

Dedication
In memory of my father
John Brian Hopkins (1938–2006)

Contents

Acknowledgements

There are many people who have helped to shape the ideas contained in this book, and many others who have encouraged and supported me along the way. In professional terms, I am grateful to the staff and students of the Department of Politics and International Relations at the University of Leicester, many of whom have discussed the politics of Northern Ireland with me (sometimes reluctantly, perhaps). I am particularly thankful for a period of study leave in 2010, which enabled me to begin work intensively on the book.

I am also grateful to the UK Political Studies Association (Irish Politics Specialist Group), and the Political Studies Association of Ireland, as well as the British Association of Irish Studies and the European Federation of Associations and Centres of Irish Studies, all of whom hosted conferences at which many of the ideas in this book were first aired. The participants at these conferences helped influence my thinking in numerous ways, and provided the opportunity to discuss and argue about the politics of Northern Ireland and the politics of memoir-writing, in a serious but also enjoyable social environment.

As an outsider, with no particular ties to Northern Ireland, several people were very helpful to me at various stages of my education in the complexity of political life there. I am grateful to the Donnelly family in Lisburn, who first showed me the hospitality for which the region is rightly renowned; Liam and Edie, and Paul, were generous to such a naive 'blow-in' in 1987. A number of other friends and colleagues were instrumental in improving my understanding of Northern Ireland, and the politics of memoir: Dr Richard Dunphy, Professor Henry Patterson, Paddy Gillan, Dr Paul Dixon, Dr Graham Dawson, Dr Cillian McGrattan, Dr Robin Wilson, Jo Dover, Dr Lesley Lelourec, Dr Gráinne O'Keeffe-Vigneron, Professor Jon Tonge, Professor Jim McAuley, Dr Eamonn O'Kane, Dr Alan Greer, Dr Marisa McGlinchey, Professor Kevin Morgan, Dr Matt Worley, Dr Billy Gray, Dr Aaron Edwards, Dr Kevin Bean, Professor Tom Hennessey, Dr Connal Parr. Julian Coman and David Thomas have both been very good friends and comrades down the years. I have also been very lucky to have enjoyed the friendship and conversation of the drinkers and dreamers at Babelas in Leicester and the Flat Iron in Liverpool.

Thanks are also due to Alison Welsby and the staff at Liverpool University Press, and the two anonymous reviewers of the manuscript.

Some of the material in Chapters 4, 9 and 10 has been developed and substantially adapted from previously published work: earlier versions appeared in M. Busteed, F. Neal and J. Tonge (eds.), *Irish Protestant Identities* (Manchester University Press, 2012); *Nordic Journal of Irish Studies*, Vol. 10 (2011); L. Lelourec and G. O'Keefe (eds.), *Ireland and Victims: Confronting the Past, Forging the Future* (Peter Lang, 2012).

My love and thanks go to Mum, and Martin, Rachel, Polly, Alexander and Rowan. In a book about the politics of memory, it is also fitting to remember the influence of my Dad, who would have reminded me of Uncle Trevor's maxim: *Use your discretion, Bri!* I also greatly miss John Mohan, Edie Mohan, and Kathleen Hirst. During the lengthy period of writing this book, Cath has been a bedrock of love and support. Keep the faith littl'un …

Stephen Hopkins
Leicester, March 2013

Chapter 1

The Study of Political Memoir and the Legacy of the Conflict in Northern Ireland

Introduction

The purpose of this book is to examine and evaluate the political memoirs written by some of the many individuals who were engaged in or affected by the conflict in Northern Ireland in the period 1969–1998. Much scholarly attention across several disciplines has been devoted to the interlocking series of issues that, taken together, constitute efforts to address the complex legacies of this conflict. At least since the Belfast (Good Friday) Agreement of 1998, questions concerning how society should remember the 'Troubles' have been at the forefront of both popular and academic debate. The nature of the conflict, its genesis, its prosecution, and its outcome, if indeed it can be said to be definitively over, are all key aspects of this urgent, though often unfocused, attention. In an emerging, though still fragile, post-conflict environment, 'dealing with the past', whether in terms of a mooted overarching truth and reconciliation process, or through piecemeal attempts to uncover hitherto disputed or neglected aspects of the violent conflict, has become a critical arena within the contemporary political life of Northern Ireland. These are inevitably fraught and unsettling processes, often accompanied by ongoing ideological and political confrontation. The Consultative Group on the Past report (2009) is probably the most comprehensive attempt to date to put in place a systematic process for revisiting the contested past in Northern Ireland. However, the report was effectively shelved, largely as a result of controversy generated by its recommendation of a 'recognition payment' for all those bereaved as a result of the Troubles.

All sides to the conflict recognise that Northern Ireland is in a period of transition, but *from* what and *to* what is the subject of intense debate and confusion. Many of Northern Ireland's weary and traumatised inhabitants might be expected simply to be thankful for a period of relative peace, after the intensity of the violence. However, this is a deeply politicised society, for better or worse, and there is little realistic prospect of erasing the Troubles from collective memory, even if moving on from a *tabula rasa* does have its attractions to some.[1] Many individuals in Northern Ireland (and outside) have to live with the consequences of the Troubles on a daily basis, and the notion that they could, even if they so desired, simply forget, silence their memories and restart their lives from scratch, makes little sense. However, it is also the case that many experiences and emotions associated with the political violence have remained unspoken up to now, whether consciously or sub-consciously pushed to one side, due to their traumatic character. These lacunae and silences may also contribute to a culture of denial, in which erstwhile protagonists do not feel sufficiently confident to acknowledge all elements of their role in the conflict.

This study begins, therefore, with the observation that individual and collective commemoration or memorialisation of the Troubles is often unavoidable. If the potential exists for such remembrance to contribute to the forging of a consensus (or at least the minimising of polarisation) in post-conflict societies, then it is also possible, perhaps probable, that it will serve to deepen existing divisions. There has been a great deal of debate recently in Ireland, both north and south (though much less in Great Britain) regarding the 'decade of centenaries' that will stretch from 2012 until 2023. During this period, many of the foundational events in forging British-Irish relations over the last century will be remembered and commemorated. Such commemoration may involve a sincere effort on the part of protagonists to move beyond the sterile antagonisms of the past, to subject previous shibboleths and commitments to a robust critique, and to engage in a thoroughgoing self-criticism of long-held attitudes and policies. This kind of approach to the past may allow for the development of a culture of tolerance to take root in a hitherto pervasively divided society. Divisions based upon competing national identities and allegiances, reinforced by religious sectarianism, did not emerge for the first time fully formed in 1969. It is a misnomer to characterise Northern Irish society as 'peaceful' prior to the Troubles; rather, there was something akin to a 'cold war', characterised by communal distrust and the memories of previous sporadic violent confrontations, with both 'sides' engaged in a constant manoeuvring for perceived advantage. If a mooted post-Troubles societal reconciliation amongst Protestant and British unionists and Catholic and Irish nationalists is therefore too grand an aspiration, given the depth of inter-communal and ethno-national segregation and conflict that has characterised Northern Ireland, then perhaps some degree of mutually beneficial co-existence could be hoped for and worked towards. As Marie Breen Smyth has argued,

> a truth recovery process can perform a number of functions. It can undermine the denial about the past; provide access to discourses of the 'other'; create potential disincentives to violence; explore the distribution

of damage caused by the conflict; attempt to synthesise the polarised discourses of the past; contribute towards creating a common, inclusive history; educate the public about the impact of the conflict; address the issue of impunity; examine unsolved killings; challenge stances of moral superiority; address issues of reparation and compensation; acknowledge the suffering of victims and the responsibility of perpetrators; shed light on the role of institutions and civil society in the past and address the issue of forgiveness.[2]

However, although evidence in the Northern Ireland case can be adduced to support the existence of an inclusive and placatory approach to the past, nonetheless this must be recognised as a minority trend. More often than not, even in the absence of violent physical conflict, commemoration of the Troubles has involved a 'pitched battlefield of opposing ideologies, more divisive and triumphal than healing and celebratory.'[3] As Shirlow and Murtagh have argued, 'there appears to be a common tendency in societies emerging from conflict to present the future as utopian, shared and equal. Such naivety undermines the potential for history, victimhood and new forms of violence to reappoint the desire among most to remain attached to separate ideas, beliefs and practices.'[4] In this interpretation, a continuing antagonism towards traditional enemies is likely to be accompanied by ongoing distrust of the 'other' side's future intentions. This combination of an aggressive and defensive posture involves a large measure of self-justification concerning the actions of one's 'own' side, and an effort to use the debate about the past as a proxy weapon in an unending struggle for supremacy, or at least to avoid 'defeat'. Competing and exclusive interpretations of the Troubles may also comprise attempts to wrest control of the narrative telling and retelling of the conflict, shaping the future historical understanding of the nature of the meta-conflict. Smyth recognises the 'perceived risk that truth recovery will reopen wounds, reactivate old grievances and re-stimulate the desire for revenge', but on balance, her view is that these dangers should not invalidate the search for a comprehensive approach to the legacies of conflict.[5] A more cautious note is sounded by Paul Arthur, who warns that 'collective memory can be seen as a major obstacle in the business of trust-building.'[6] He cites Padraig O'Malley's judgment that Northern Ireland (in the aftermath of the 1980–1 hunger strikes by republican prisoners) had become a 'victim-bonded society in which memories of past injustice and humiliation are so firmly entrenched in both communities' that escaping the 'helplessness' this engenders will prove hugely difficult. Shirlow and Murtagh go further, stressing that 'the decrease in politically motivated violence over the past decade has been accompanied by an intensified process of claiming and "owning" victimhood.'[7] Even if such a logic is bound to undermine political stability and progress towards 'normalising' society, nonetheless both sides have a tendency to adopt discursive strategies that seek to 'claim the totem of having been the most persecuted community [...] Remaining blameless thus remains a key component in the perpetuation of sectarian atavism in Northern Ireland.'[8] Evaluating the report on 'ways of dealing with the past' of the Northern Ireland Affairs Committee of the United Kingdom's House of Commons (delivered in 2005), Arthur notes that the effort to tackle the 'politics and administration of "healing" [...] is an immensely complex and traumatic process that has to proceed in terms of decades rather than months.'[9] This study engages with this broader debate through a detailed analysis of memoir-writing, a hitherto neglected dimension of this subject.

The Politics of Memoir: Establishing the Parameters of Study

The increasing willingness of erstwhile protagonists of political life in Northern Ireland to publish their stories of the Troubles has become a significant element in the public engagement with the politics of the past in Northern Ireland. And yet this area of study has been under-researched in the academic treatment of this complex subject in the post-ceasefire era. This relative neglect stems from a number of factors: one is the surprising dearth of interest among scholars from a range of disciplines in the genre of memoir or autobiography in the Irish (and Northern Irish) context more broadly conceived; a second is the understandable scepticism with which historians and political scientists have tended to approach the unverifiable aspects of life-writing, even taking into consideration the 'biographical turn' in the social sciences in recent times; a third reason relates to the problematic nature of defining the parameters of the genre of 'memoir' or 'autobiography', a difficulty which is no less apparent in the sub-genre of 'political memoir'. All in all, the intrinsically inter-disciplinary nature of 'memory studies', including the study of political memoir-writing, may also help to explain the relative dearth of scholarly interest in this field.[10] Here, it is argued that, notwithstanding this lack of critical attention, the study of these sources can help to illuminate hitherto shadowy aspects of the wider issue of a societal reckoning with the past. Equally, a key advantage of studying the legacies of conflict through the life-writing of some of the major protagonists is the opportunity offered to understand in real depth the multi-layered relationship between the roles played by the individual and the politics of the collective and communal. Furthermore, this focus can potentially permit researchers to grasp the genuine complexity of the lived experience of the Troubles, and the efforts made to address their difficult personal and social aftermath. Borrowing from the frustratingly under-developed concept of 'structures of feeling' advanced by Raymond Williams, it is possible to argue that the study of memoir-writing permits an appreciation of the myriad reactions in Northern Ireland to the traumatic effects of violent conflict, which help to condition a series of negotiations with its legacies.

Terminology can present something of a difficulty in this area of study, but this is not merely a question of semantics. Rather, it reflects a substantive problem: how should the parameters of the study of political memoir be drawn? And what insights can be gained from a range of academic disciplines and diverse literatures? Several writers analysing life-writing have attempted to define the key distinction between memoir(s) and autobiography, but there is no consensus. According to one important historical survey of the genre, 'memoir' and 'autobiography' have tended to be used interchangeably, comprising 'a book understood by its author, its publisher, and its readers to be a factual account of an author's life.'[11] However, this apparently clear position is immediately qualified, in terms of the period of a life that such a book covers: the 'one clear difference is that while "autobiography" or "memoirs" usually cover the full span of that life, "memoir" has been used by books that cover the entirety *or* some portion of it.'[12] Another scholar, studying the ambivalence of life-writing, situates the genre between fact and fiction, and between literature and history: 'autobiography is arguably the most underhand of all literary genres, consistently avoiding the definitions fashioned for it and eluding the genre boundaries expected of it.'[13] Autobiography or memoir-writing is perhaps best understood, following George Egerton, as a 'polygenre'. The difficulty in 'classifying memoir in tidy categories, however, should not stand as an argument for diminishing its significance or impeding the development of a helpful body of criticism.'[14] Memoir and autobiography may be understood as being at opposite ends of a continuum of life-writing, based upon 'whether the focus is primarily inward, on the development of the self, as in the case of autobiography, or more external, on others, on events and deeds, as with memoir.'[15] Of course, it may well be difficult to assign a particular place on that continuum for any individual text, and ultimately it must be recognised that no hard and fast definitional boundaries are likely to prove robust, given the inherently hybrid nature of this kind of writing. Many, if not all, 'memoirs' involve this complex combination of both inward-looking self-reflective material, which concentrates upon the presentation of an individual psychology, alongside or bound up with externally oriented discussion of the socio-historical context in which that individual life is inscribed. For my purposes, it may be argued that although many of the memoirs studied below undoubtedly contain some autobiographical reflection, they tend to be more clearly oriented towards the public life of the writer and the public events he or she has witnessed or taken part in; therefore, this work will generally use the term 'memoir', rather than 'autobiography'.[16]

The memoirs studied in this volume display many of these hybrid qualities, being produced in an environment in which the changing influences of historical and political context are never far from the surface. Some of these sources are obviously 'political', in the sense that they have been authored by individuals who have played more or less prominent roles in the political life of Northern Ireland, whether as conventional elected representatives or as paramilitary protagonists of the conflict. However, in a society like Northern Ireland, one which has been saturated with bitter political and violent division, there is an authentic sense in which virtually *all* memoir-writing may be interpreted through a 'political' prism. Just as no-one who lived in Northern Ireland through the years of the Troubles can have emerged entirely unaffected (although some have been much more radically affected than others), so no memoirist of this period could ignore the political and historical effects of the conflict, both on the self and the wider society of which he or she forms a part. In his report regarding how best government and civil society could address the needs of 'victims' of the conflict, Ken Bloomfield recognised that 'there is, in a sense, some substance in the argument that no-one living in Northern Ireland through this most unhappy period of its history will have escaped some degree of damage.' However, in a partial understanding that such an inclusive definition would cause problems for the targeting of public policy at the most needy sections of society, he went on to argue that the Northern Ireland Office's Victims' unit (which was to be set up as a result of the report) must 'aim its effort at a coherent and manageable target group', namely the surviving injured and those who care for them, together with close relatives who mourn their dead.[17] In a parallel move, this volume will concentrate upon a restricted set of 'political memoirs', though this is not to deny that almost all memoir-writing from Northern Ireland during the course of the last twenty years or so has had a more or less explicit political dimension.

The Construction and Narration of Exemplary Lives

One significant way in which these political memoirs can be interpreted is in terms of their perceived *representativeness*. Certain individuals in arenas of conflict may well come to be understood, through their experiences as recounted in the writing of their life, to embody a collective political identity. In a society like Northern Ireland, which remains deeply segregated in terms of religious and political communal identities, many prominent individuals (whether strictly speaking political representatives or not) come to be viewed as *exemplary*, and their life-stories, as narrated and constructed in their memoirs, as emblematic of the wider experiences of their communities. The status of such individuals may be understood as unassailable, both within their communities, and by outside observers of the conflict. Equally, the same individuals may be understood, from the 'other side', as uniquely malevolent bogeymen, who exemplify everything that is 'wrong' with the other community. Part of this book engages in a critical reading of these claims, and interrogates the political function of this broadening of the genre. At its most basic, memoir-writing by such prominent individuals can offer the researcher information and opinions regarding a wide-ranging series of political and organisational issues, alongside the expected subjective insights into the personal role and retrospective judgment of conventional memoir. However, in a more profound sense, some of these memoirists have been highly important in shaping the nature of subsequent efforts to narrate the conflict. In this sense, certain memoirs have exercised a powerful grip on the public imagination, and they have helped to spawn several imitators. At this stage, one example will suffice: Gordon Wilson was badly injured in the Irish Republican Army's (IRA) Enniskillen bombing in 1987, and his 20-year-old daughter, Marie, was killed. In the immediate aftermath, Gordon Wilson spoke movingly of his daughter's last moments, and his desire that there should be no retribution from loyalists, and in favour of an end to all violence. He also specifically spelled out his refusal to bear the bombers any ill will, although he did not directly use the term 'forgiveness', as is often believed. While he expressly refused to see himself as a 'spokesman' for either the victims or survivors of Enniskillen, or any broader community of victims of violence, nevertheless many subsequent victims and survivors, who went on to become memoirists, did explicitly acknowledge the influence and example of Wilson's published memoir (and tribute), *Marie*.

Notwithstanding the problems in defining memoir and autobiography, and the distinctiveness of each, there has been a remarkable growth in publications of this type in recent years. As Leigh Gilmore has noted, 'memoir has become *the* genre in the skittish period around the turn of the millennium.'[18] This fascination among readers shows no sign of abating, and this is even the case when, in several high-profile incidents, some supposed 'memoirs' have been exposed as decidedly 'fictional'.[19] There is no reason to suppose that political memoir as a sub-genre has been immune to this trend, and in recent times a range of well-remunerated former statesmen have been tempted into print. Indeed, as Andrew Gamble has noted, 'the political memoir has become an expected rite of passage for political celebrity, and also a highly profitable one.'[20] Despite these general trends, which show no sign of diminishing, the academic study of political memoir remains under-developed, and this also holds true for political memoir in the specific context of the Northern Ireland conflict. As we have observed, there are several related dimensions to this critical neglect: one is in part a reflection of the broader neglect of Irish autobiography and memoir, which Liam Harte has referred to as a 'Cinderella genre'; a second is that this complex hybrid genre has rarely been adequately considered, precisely because it does not fit easily into the prevailing disciplinary traditions of academia. Harte argues that 'when weighed against the welter of scholarship on Irish poetry, drama and fiction, the critical literature on life writing seems remarkably slight, in quantity if not quality.'[21] He bemoans the absence of a systematic book devoted to the study of Irish autobiography, and the cursory mention of the genre in encyclopedia and companions of Irish literature. The former gap has been addressed to some extent with the publication of Claire Lynch's monograph, which builds upon Harte's work; she accepts the notion of Irish autobiography as a 'Cinderella genre', but points out that like fairytales, autobiography works through a 'blurring of expectations', drawing on both memory and imagination. She cites the critic James Olney's contention that 'when talking about autobiography, one always feels that there is a great and present danger that the subject will slip away altogether, that it will vanish into thinnest air, leaving behind the perception that there is no such creature as autobiography and that there never has been.'[22] As far as the second dimension is concerned, Lynch makes the case that, while the study of autobiography and memoir in the Irish context cannot be shoe-horned into prevailing literary categories, it does fit well with the cross-disciplinary and multi-layered approach of 'Irish Studies' as an arena of enquiry into, among other questions, aspects of Irish national identity. While acknowledging the force of this insight, it is worth noting that, in the context of the Northern Ireland conflict, in which violent confrontation has turned precisely around competing ethno-national identities, it is necessary to acknowledge the problematic character of such language, which can appear to posit a reductive interpretation of Irishness and nationality.

Within the social sciences there has been an even clearer dearth of research focused upon the politics of life-writing, at least until relatively recently. Despite the behaviouralist research agenda that grew in popularity from the 1960s, it can be argued that efforts to confront the complexities associated with the concept of 'agency' in political studies are still rather piecemeal. There are two significant and related dimensions to the study of life-writing, as an instance of this wider question: firstly, it generally involves an effort, on the part of both the author/subject and the researcher, to grapple with the complexities of the individual's relationship to the social and political context in which the life has been lived; secondly, the perennial question of truthfulness and authenticity in memoir-writing has coloured the social scientific reception for this type of source material. The emphasis upon the intertwining of individual and societal stories and histories as a constituent element of life-writing takes the subject beyond the usual boundaries of either literature or history. Instead, alongside Roy Foster and Lynch, it can be argued that this study should be embraced as 'part of a wider cultural system, explicable through historical and geographical circumstances to create a formulation in which autobiography is a type of writing or indeed thinking about the self which is directly dependent upon the time and place from which its author drew influence.'[23] The insistent incorporation of an historical and political framework for the writing of Irish lives means that social scientists and historians should perhaps try more assiduously to overcome what Lynch characterises as their fear of 'the unverifiable nature of literature'.[24]

It is perhaps understandable that historians and social scientists, or at least more traditionally minded practitioners of these disciplines, are concerned that the integration of the study of life-writing into their fields of enquiry may affect the purity or integrity of their endeavours. Nevertheless, the parameters of these disciplines are necessarily porous, and increasingly open to the challenges presented by taking life-writing seriously. From the perspective of those embedded in the study of autobiography as a literary genre, the challenges are also pertinent, and potentially destabilising. To suggest that the study of memoir and autobiography is 'not limited in scope to the life of one individual is both rational and disturbing'.[25] No individual's life is lived as completely under one spotlight as the 'pure' notion of autobiography may suggest, and rather than producing a record of individuality, autobiography and memoir-writing highlight instead a complex web of interconnections, some at the familial level, and others at the broader communal or national level. This is especially the case for emblematic or exemplary individuals, whose life-stories and life-writing need to be analysed both in terms of individual agency, but also in terms of the light they shed on the political institutions and collective organisations of which they are key figures. In the context of the historiography of the international communist movement, Kevin Morgan has persuasively argued that taking seriously the biographical dimension of political analysis, particularly in avowedly collectivist and conformist political movements, is 'subtly disintegrative of more structured causation'.[26] Furthermore, critics of this focus upon the biographical dimension have tended to emphasise the dangers inherent in 'abstracting the individual from the social' or, alternatively, 'imbuing this discrete "life" with a wholeness, coherence and narrative logic that are illusory'.[27] But defenders of this approach would stress the significance of trying to 'recover' the memories of social actors, and their motivations and experiences, from becoming lost in the construction of grand narratives. As with communist autobiography or memoir, the study of narratives of the Northern Ireland conflict is marked by the pervasive power of group identities, and the question of how individual life-histories can be related to this encompassing, and sometimes claustrophobic, presence of the group. There are perhaps some echoes to be found here of the question Jochen Hellbeck asks, in his provocative study of Soviet diarists in the Stalinist era: 'what is meant by writing the word *I* in an age of a larger *We*?'[28] The politics of interpreting these narratives therefore resides in their blurring of boundaries, whether between autobiography and biography, or history and memory. Ultimately, of course, the potential for the blurring of fact and fiction is yet another critical aspect of this field of enquiry.

The History of an Individual's Soul:
Truth and Memory in Life-Writing

Ben Yagoda addresses the question of truth and falsity in memoir-writing, and persuasively argues that debate over the authenticity and credibility of the genre as a whole (as well as particular accounts) is as venerable as life-writing itself. Many memoirs have been intended (or interpreted) as 'didactic entries' in ongoing political arguments, where there is a powerful temptation for the author to operate on an 'ends justify the means' basis, foregoing any fundamental concern with the literal truth of their story, in the overwhelming desire to further their ideological purpose. Yet, it is also important to recognise that '"true" testimony is always powerful ammunition in a political debate.'[29] There is thus a premium on establishing the essential 'truth' of such writing, even as authors are often tempted to embellish or invent aspects of their narrative for the purpose of their overarching political vision. In this view, life-writing becomes another important weapon in the struggle for hegemony amongst competing versions of conflicting social interests in the here and now, and also competing accounts of the recent past. As a result of this battle in the realm of personalised history, 'one side will be at least tempted to exaggerate or fabricate; [while] the other side will respond with an effort to debunk or expose.'[30] Yagoda illustrates this argument with reference to memoirs pertaining to the debate over slavery in the United States in the first half of the nineteenth century, where claim and counter-claim regarding the accuracy and authenticity of published accounts meant that the competition to establish (or demolish) the credibility of the witness testimonies of fugitive slaves became a crucial battleground. With highly charged subjects, where political instrumentalisation of individual life-stories is almost unavoidable, any demonstration of falsity could prove fatal for the cause, although it should be recognised that for less controversial subjects, embellishment or downright invention does not necessarily mean that a memoir will be renounced by the readership. In a number of cases where memoirs have been exposed as hoaxes, the 'charlatanry' involved has not necessarily been greeted with shocked howls of protest from the public, and sales have often been unaffected.[31] Ultimately, these vexed problems of authenticity are likely to be decided by the court of public opinion, although on occasion the actual courts have become involved in a formal process of determining disputed truth claims.

However, this does not capture the full complexity of the question of 'truth' in memoir-writing. One of the key difficulties that may arise in this debate over truthfulness involves judgments regarding the *motivation* or intentions of the memoirist. The substance of any exercise in memoir-writing, and the 'facts' that are presented to the reader, may be exposed as false in two distinct ways: there could be a deliberate attempt to deceive, based upon the political advantages that might accrue through the invention of testimony and the manipulation of the evidence (or the omission of inconvenient truths); on the other hand, there is the inevitable fallibility of memory, recognised by autobiographers as long ago as Rousseau. In the latter interpretation, the 'facts' as presented may not be accurate or correct in every detail, but the memoirist may try to excuse such oversight. This may be done through the claim (with Rousseau) that the key to interpreting these texts is understanding how the author *felt* or experienced the events he lived through, rather than a supposedly 'objective' account of the events themselves. Yagoda cites the *Confessions* to illustrate the point: Rousseau begins by insisting that he has relied only upon his memory, and while certain events remain absolutely clear to him, others are confused, provoking the observation that in his memories

> there are voids and lacunae, too, which I can fill only with the aid of anecdotes as confused as the memory that remains of them. I may sometimes, then, have made mistakes and may do so again over trifling details [...] but in what truly concerns my subject, I am confident of being precise and faithful, as I will try always to be in everything.[32]

Even if certain facts are later proved incorrect, Rousseau insists that he 'cannot be mistaken about what I felt, nor about what my feelings led me to do [...] It is the history of my soul that I promised, and to relate it I require no other memorandum; all I need do [...] is to look inside myself.'[33] This is strikingly similar language to that used by Sinn Féin President, Gerry Adams, in the preface to his second volume of memoirs, where he argues that, 'it is not my business to offer an objective account of events or to see through someone else's eyes. Nor is it my responsibility to document these events. My intention is to tell a story. It is my story. My truth. My reality.'[34]

Equally, another type of defence entails a frank admission that the story as recounted may not conform to the facts in every particular, but that this should not impede an acknowledgement that the *overall* intention of the author is to put forward a truthful testimony. The memoir-writing of 'Spanish Red' Jorge Semprún, who was incarcerated at Buchenwald during 1944–5, is a case that illustrates the wider point: he reconstructs a conversation between former prisoners of the concentration camp, held soon after their liberation, in which discussion centred upon whether and how it would be possible for them to bear witness to their experiences. The problem was how to talk about such experiences in a fashion that would be believable given their horrific, almost unimaginable, nature: one survivor argued that the story must be told just as things were, 'with no fancy stuff!' Semprún disagreed, arguing that the story must be well told, 'so as to be understood. You can't manage it without a bit of artifice. Enough artifice to make it art.' He summed up his position: 'How do you tell such an unlikely truth, how do you foster the imagination of the unimaginable, if not by elaborating, by reworking reality, by putting it in perspective? With a bit of artifice, then!'[35] In another characteristic aspect of his writing, Semprún tells and retells different versions of certain stories that the reader is led to believe are autobiographical (or at least inspired by his own experience). For instance, he has told the story of his initiation and registration at Buchenwald in a number of subtly different variations; these may be understood as an implicit commentary upon the fallibility of memory, or perhaps the relative insignificance of apparently trivial details, faced with the overwhelming requirement to capture the essential 'truth' in a powerful and convincing testimony. In a similar vein, Susan Suleiman cites Charlotte Delbo's witness account of her imprisonment at Auschwitz, in which she provides the epigraph: 'Today, I am not sure that what I wrote is true. I am certain it is truthful.'[36]

Some memoirists have insisted upon posthumous publication of their testimonies, in an effort to reassure readers of their frankness. For example, Mark Twain specifically prefaced his memoirs by stating: 'I speak from the grave rather than with my living tongue for a good reason. I can thus speak freely.'[37] From Twain's perspective, any attempt to publish a genuinely honest account whilst the subject is alive is doomed to failure. Interestingly, in the context of Northern Ireland, a key project dedicated to the collection of personal 'stories' of the Troubles appears to start from a similar premise: the Boston College Oral History Archive has recorded and transcribed the memories of several significant IRA and Ulster Volunteer Force (UVF) personnel, but access to this rich resource is severely restricted. Indeed, Boston College is contractually obliged to sequester the tapes and transcriptions until either the interviewee expressly permits their release, or they are dead.[38] In the latter case, journalist Ed Moloney has edited the oral testimonies of two key individuals who were interviewed as part of the project: Brendan Hughes (who died in 2008) was a central figure in the Provisional republican movement, whilst David Ervine (who died in 2005) was latterly a politician representing the Progressive Unionist Party, and had previously served a jail sentence for his activities in the UVF during the 1970s. According to Moloney, the project was predicated upon the idea that collecting the stories of paramilitary protagonists in the conflict would provide an unsullied primary source for future historians of the Troubles. If these stories were not told now, they would be lost, 'distorted or rewritten, deliberately by those with a vested interest, or otherwise by the passage of time or the distortion wrought in the retelling.'[39] As the preface makes clear, these interviews were conducted by academic researchers, but with roots in the republican and loyalist communities from which the paramilitaries sprang, and they took place after 2001, when it was judged that the 'peace process', though fragile, was very likely to endure. In such circumstances, the project was based upon the belief that interviewees would be willing to 'open up candidly and comprehensively not only about their own lives and activities but about others' as well.'[40] Whilst these precautions may well have permitted the reader a degree of confidence regarding the reliability of these testimonies from Hughes and Ervine, the *political* purpose of their recollections is still a critical issue to be examined and evaluated. For instance, at the time of his interviews for the archive (in 2001/2002) Hughes was no longer supportive of the direction taken by the mainstream republican movement, and he was particularly scathing about the role of his erstwhile close comrade (and SF President), Gerry Adams. Hughes used his memories to launch a bitter attack upon Adams, especially his oft-repeated claim that he had never been a member of the IRA:

> Gerry was a major, major player in the war, not just in Ireland, but in the decision to send Volunteers and bombs to England. I'm totally disgusted. I mean, there are things you can say, and things you can't say. I'm not going to stand up on a platform and say I was involved in the shooting of a soldier or involved in the planning of operations in England. But I'm certainly not going to stand up and deny it.[41]

Ultimately, therefore, interpreting Hughes's testimony requires an understanding of his contemporary political perspective; the use to which he puts his memories is crucially shaped by his feelings of betrayal, both personal and political. In this regard, posthumous publication may allow for frankness, but it is authorial motivation that we really need to interrogate, and that still requires a hermeneutic approach. This particular case is discussed in greater depth in Chapter 3, which analyses memoir-writing by 'dissident' republicans.

The notion that how we remember is based upon a more or less conscious reconstruction of events (in the light of our contemporary purposes at the time of remembering), rather than any mechanical reproduction of those events, is now well established. In this sense, insights from psychology suggest that memory is itself a 'creative writer': it proceeds through 'cobbling together "actual" memories, beliefs about the world, cues from a variety of sources, and memories of *previous* memories to plausibly imagine what might have been [...].'[42] The design of autobiographical writing is usually predicated upon a construction of memory that will permit an individual to preserve the essential integrity of their sense of self, including a continuity with their past commitments and actions. The full complexity of 'historical truth' may be too rich for any single individual memory to retain, but that does not invalidate those recollections. Even where 'memories' of particular events or conversations can be demonstrably shown to be inaccurate or false, that does not mean that they are useless for researchers: they may still shed light on the thinking or motivation of the protagonist. There is a range of ways in which memories may be flawed, whether through sincere misremembering or deliberate manipulation, or a combination of both.

Within the discipline of political science it has been argued that 'some think political scientists should be like detectives, searching out the one true account of what happened.'[43] Indeed, where memories are uncorroborated, or can be shown to be inconsistent with other facts that have been established through documentary sources, then careful scholarship may expose these errors. Notwithstanding the insight from humanities and literary studies that there may be many different and competing perceptions of the same event, and that 'reality' is constructed and experienced in a number of diverse ways, it remains the case that political memoirs should not simply be studied as a branch of 'poetics and fiction – metaphors of self, novels of self-exploration'.[44] Even if Gamble is correct that 'determining what *actually* happened in any final sense is an aspiration impossible to achieve', it is still worthwhile making an attempt to 'clear the ground', in the sense that memoirs *can* provide valuable sources of evidence. This is particularly the case where much political activity has been conducted in a conspiratorial fashion and within a clandestine environment; for example, much of what we now recognise as the accepted wisdom of the history of the conflict in Northern Ireland has been gleaned from personal accounts. In these circumstances, the careful 'sifting' and interpretation of political memoir and autobiography, alongside other related techniques such as oral history and diaristic writing, are crucial potential resources for painting a fuller picture of the experience and conduct of protagonists of the Troubles. As George Egerton has convincingly argued, 'with all the distortions to which this type of personal historiography is prey, the potential for honesty, accuracy and insight remains; for historians "truthfulness", however old-fashioned, ultimately stands as a fundamental critical concern in the evaluation of memoirs.'[45] Of course, even when memoirists are tempted onto the 'paths of vindication, exculpation and the byways of personal interest', the critical reader can determine a good deal from the 'deliberate gap in the narrative: the momentous elision, the leap in the story'. If 'instruction is to be found also in the evasions and omissions which feature all too prominently in most memoirs', then 'the memoirist is almost inevitably self-betrayed into the hands of the later historian.'[46] There are important insights in these considerations of how memoir should be studied in the Irish context, but there are also significant and problematic issues that arise.

Making a related point, Roy Foster has argued cogently that 'the elision of the personal and the national, the way history becomes a kind of scaled-up biography, and biography a microcosmic history, is a particularly Irish phenomenon.'[47] However, although the 'individual's experience as a kind of national microcosm comes up too insistently in Irish history and fiction not to be worth examining [...]. This process can conceal [...] very large and untested assumptions; it can also run the danger of collapsing alternative history into anecdote and psychobabble (or anecdotal psychobabble).'[48] Claire Lynch picks up this insight, and argues that 'an artificial narrative structure must be applied to histories of all scales – personal and national – in order that they become meaningful.' Writing memoir or autobiography inevitably involves compiling 'the multiple histories of the self, others, cultures and contexts into a workable narrative structure'.[49] Lynch provides valuable support for the idea that 'the concept of the nation refuses to keep out of Irish autobiography, irrespective of the precise historical backdrop of the author's life, supporting the approaches of those who use history as a password to unlock Irish autobiography.'[50] However, whilst it can be agreed that many Irish memoirists have been as concerned with representing the group as with representing the self, it is clear that Lynch has at the forefront of her enquiry the growth in Irish nationalist/republican life-writing, particularly in the tumultuous period of political revolution and the struggle for independence from the United Kingdom (approximately from the 1890s through until the 1920s). This genre, uniquely concerned with problems of identity construction, seemed ideally suited to the cultural ferment of this era: the autobiographical form was a 'drawing board on which writers improvised new concepts of Irishness'.[51] One of the speculations of this work might be to ask whether one could argue something similar for *Northern* Irishness after a similar period of conflict, political upheaval and uncertainty. In the contemporary political life of Northern Ireland, it could be argued that prospects for societal reconciliation depend, at least in part, on some such process of identity construction. On the other hand, there is ample evidence for those who wish to argue that memoir-writing is as likely to reopen wounds, or even inflict new wounds upon the body politic, as it is to foster mutual understanding.

Lynch acknowledges that these blueprints for the subsequent development of a tradition of Irish autobiography were built upon both ambiguous and plural visions of the future (and the past) of 'the nation'. This influence of the 'nation' as a predominant category in Irish life-writing (which has been dominated by writers working within an avowedly *nationalist* framework) leads Lynch to argue that the conventional distinction between memoir and autobiography is 'not applicable' in the Irish case 'as autobiographies from across the century shape themselves around the history of the nation to such an extent that it has become a standard element of the genre, on a par with first-person narration and therefore only notable if absent.'[52] From this perspective, memoir or autobiography becomes not merely the collecting and reporting of historical facts, but instead the internalisation of these concerns of the wider nation or community as an organic dimension of the individual's lived experience. In this sense, the argument presented here is that the conflict (and *meta-conflict*) concerning Northern Ireland's constitutional future is similarly an unavoidable 'presence' in memoir-writing of this political generation.

In my view, the argument put forward by both Lynch and Foster for the crucial importance of the 'national' in memoir-writing in the Irish context is compelling. In the same vein, the critical significance of the 'communal', as both an element of division, and as a dimension of belonging, is evident in memoir-writing in the Northern Irish context. As part of the complex web of connections that are highlighted in many Irish, and Northern Irish, life-stories, the interweaving of the individual's path through life, and the construction of the wider national/communal identities is usually accorded a privileged place. And yet, both the concept of 'Irishness' and that of the 'nation' are themselves deeply contested on the island of Ireland, and there is insufficient recognition of this complicating factor in Lynch's book. The sheer pervasiveness of divisions along ethno-national and communal lines in Northern Ireland (but also in the Republic of Ireland after partition) is not explicitly addressed by Lynch, but this is surely of primary significance for a full understanding of the way in which the individual 'I' has been pluralised in this section of the territory (however we define it politically).

The book begins with a section devoted to the memoirs of (ex-)paramilitaries, analysing writing from within the Provisional republican movement (Chapter 2), the so-called 'dissident' republicans (Chapter 3), and from loyalist groups (Chapter 4). It continues with a section devoted to memoirs by constitutional politicians, analysing unionists (Chapter 5), nationalists (Chapter 6), and a case study of memoir-writing devoted to the power-sharing Executive of 1974 (Chapter 7). Chapter 8 examines the memoirs of British Secretaries of State for Northern Ireland, Chapter 9 discusses the memoirs of journalists who have covered the conflict, and Chapter 10 deals with the publications of victims or survivors of the violence. This work makes no claim to analyse exhaustively *all* recent memoir-writing in the context of Northern Ireland. For instance, the growing number of memoirs by former members of the police or security forces is not treated in depth here,[53] nor are memoirs by politicians from the Republic of Ireland. However, the intention is to analyse some of the critical (ex-)protagonists from the ranks of those who have shaped the cultural memory of the Troubles to date.

Chapter 2

Provisional Republican Memoir-Writing

Introduction

There has been a great deal of both academic and popular literature devoted to the involvement of the Provisional republican movement in the peace process since the Irish Republican Army (IRA) ceasefire of 1994. This attention has been concentrated upon the ideological and strategic transformation wrought by the leadership group, based around the Sinn Féin (SF) President since 1983, Gerry Adams. This chapter analyses a hitherto neglected dimension of these developments: the significance of political memoir-writing by Provisionals, which has provided both an insight into the movement's role and objectives during the prosecution of its 'armed struggle' in Northern Ireland, as well as its efforts to control the narrative telling of the conflict. Moreover, the memoirs studied here, particularly those authored by leadership figures, often seek to transmit and interpret the dramatic changes that the movement has lived through, in order to make sense of this evolution for both an internal constituency of activists and sympathisers, and an external audience of sometimes sceptical or hostile onlookers. The formation and shaping of the republican movement's collective memory of the Troubles and its self-presentation owe a good deal to the memoir-writing of some of its key personnel, not least Gerry Adams.

Some authors who have worked on the collective memory of the republican movement have argued that 'personal memoirs' may help us to understand the motivations and the 'narrative interpretations' that members have developed to explain their beliefs and actions to themselves and others.[1] However, very often these arguments stress the unreliability of such sources, and the 'mechanisms of denial' that characterise them; Rogelio Alonso, for instance, makes the case for 'the existence of a group mentality [amongst Irish republicans] which results in the ideological convergence of its members and their adherence to an accepted "official explanation" for their conduct.'[2] This chapter seeks to argue that the memoir-writing of key exemplary individuals has been of critical significance in constructing this ideological convergence, and shaping the 'official explanation' of the movement's past. It is also the case, however, that such a convergence, inspired as it was by the perceived requirement for unity and self-discipline within the republican movement, has at times 'masked underlying division'.[3] Memoirs that capture these dissenting voices, or those that have stood against the prevailing orthodoxies within the movement, will be the subject of the following chapter.

This chapter does not seek explicitly to compare the memoirs of the 'peace process' era with those of earlier generations, but it is interesting to note a number of common themes, and some continuities in the republican movement's self-presentation over the course of its long existence. In the aftermath of the civil strife and guerrilla warfare of the revolutionary period (1916–23), an earlier generation of republicans, such as Dan Breen, Tom Barry and Ernie O'Malley did a great deal to develop the tradition of memoir-writing by (ex-)protagonists of violent conflict in Ireland.[4] It is also the case that in recent years, with what appears to be the definitive ending of the Provisional IRA campaign, a number of former IRA activists, ordinary foot-soldiers rather than leadership figures, have decided to venture into print, publishing sometimes revealing accounts of the operational details and the internal political life of volunteers in the republican movement. As has been argued in this work, the 'elision of the personal and the national, the way history becomes a kind of scaled-up biography, and biography a microcosmic history, is a particularly Irish phenomenon.'[5] The memoir-writing of Provisional Irish republicans shares a number of important characteristics with the life-writing of previous generations of republican and nationalist activists.

One of the key points of comparison is the complex relationship between the military and political roles played by diverse protagonists within the overall movement. Clearly, this question of how best to interpret the relationship between the IRA and SF is a subject beyond the scope of this work, but nevertheless it is, both implicitly and on occasion explicitly, a core theme of much of the memoir-writing under consideration here. In general terms, this chapter follows the prevailing view espoused by most, if not all, academics who have investigated the republican movement, in its various incarnations; namely, the IRA and SF have been enmeshed in an integrated movement, with close 'organic links' between the political and military 'wings'.[6] As a leading Provisional strategist of the 1980s and subsequently a writer and memoirist, Danny Morrison, has made plain, there was a significant degree of overlap between the memberships of the two wings of the movement, and this was true at both the base and the apex of the organisations: 'the fortunes of Sinn Féin and the IRA are inextricably linked: they have the same cause and ultimate objectives and their memberships are drawn from the same pool of support.'[7] However, this was not a relationship of equal partners: the IRA enjoyed the upper hand historically, even if the basis of this relationship may have changed considerably in the last decade. Indeed, as English argues, SF was a 'creature' of the IRA, with only a very circumscribed capacity for autonomous action.[8] At various junctures, it has suited the purposes of both wings of the movement to deny the true nature of this symbiotic relationship. For instance, Gerry Adams, in his second volume of memoir, argued explicitly that in the period after the 1985 Anglo-Irish Agreement, 'the thought processes within the two organisations, that is Sinn Féin and the IRA, were quite independent and jealously guarded, particularly by the army. Contrary to popular opinion, there was no integrated strategy.'[9] However, such denials have tended to lack credibility amongst close observers and analysts of republicanism. One commentator sums it up as follows:

> clearly the political party and the terrorist group were not independent entities. The alleged separation of both wings was a fiction that their members have often tried to maintain over the years, albeit unsuccessfully given that it has been proved beyond doubt that certain leaders, such as Gerry Adams and Martin McGuinness, were simultaneously members of the top executive bodies of both organisations.[10]

As far as the credentials of Gerry Adams are concerned, he has obstinately maintained his denial of ever having played a leading role in the military wing, the IRA, or indeed of having been a member at all; this chapter will critically assess this claim with specific reference to Adams' memoir-writing.

Over the course of the long history of the Irish republican movement, and certainly since the late nineteenth century, there has developed a tradition of personalised narrative construction, produced especially by exemplary individual leaders. These individuals have closely identified their own personal trajectories with that of the collective organisation, and they have often been recognised, both inside and outside the ranks of republicanism, as the embodiment of the political, social and cultural essence of the movement. There have been some important elements of continuity in the movement's self-presentation and a self-conscious conformity to an established political tradition or identity, and this has also been evident in the memoir-writing of Irish republicans. One example will suffice here: the experience of incarceration in British jails has often provided an opportunity for republicans to reflect on the political direction of their struggle, and strategic or organisational questions regarding its future development. In addition, several leading figures have utilised the space provided by imprisonment for personal writing (whether diaristic or in the form of memoir). From the Fenian movement of the 1860s, through the revolutionary era of the Anglo-Irish War and the Irish Civil War, and on into the era of the modern Troubles, republicans have regularly published their prison memoirs.[11] Such writing has served to provide unifying narratives for the movement emphasising self-sacrifice, revolutionary discipline, and a countervailing discourse capable of challenging the establishment or 'official' attempts to criminalise the republican movement. In these circumstances, there has been an ongoing 'struggle for memory', incorporating competing narratives, with the 'official' canonical version of the national story provoking alternatives and resistances. Key players in this struggle for hegemony are the 'memory entrepreneurs' who seek to provide, often through memoir-writing, social recognition and political legitimacy for their communal rendering of the past.[12]

Smith convincingly argued that this Irish republican tradition involved *inter alia* the belief in an unchanging British colonial attitude towards Ireland; a commitment to vanguardism and military elitism within the national movement; a revolutionary absolutism, which disdained both reformist piecemeal advances towards the ultimate objective of Irish unity and, specifically, electoralism; a rhetorical embrace of secularism and anti-sectarianism, at the same time as the movement was actually marked strongly by Catholic religious identity and social thought; and, ultimately, a 'staunch belief in the utility of the military instrument [which] has helped elevate the concept of physical force to the high ground of republicanism.'[13] Smith also demonstrated the teleological character of the republican movement's ideology; despite a number of significant strategic shifts over the years, the movement maintained a commitment to viewing Irish history as having a pre-determined end-point, namely Irish unity and independence: 'Irish republicans cannot tolerate any thought that their goal is receding or may never be reached. There may be setbacks and wrong turnings but these are occasional and temporary and will not stop the march of progress.'[14] However, as he presciently recognised, writing in the immediate aftermath of the IRA's 1994 ceasefire, such an emphasis upon traditional continuities in thought should not be confused with an immutable immobilism in the republican movement's politics.

And yet, in the period since Smith published his analysis, republicans and, in particular, memoirists from within the movement, have had to adjust their sights, and their strategies of remembrance, as critical elements of their erstwhile ideology and identity have been subject to dramatic, sometimes disorienting, upheaval. As Smith concluded, 'if a psychological pebble is dislodged, it may start a landslide.'[15] For some of the memoirists considered below, a central objective of their writing has been to shore up the republican movement's sense of continuity, and reconstruct the 'wall' from which some of the pebbles have been removed, or alternatively, to deny that they were removed in the first place. On the other hand, there is an increasing tendency for some republicans to question this narrative, and to cast a critical, or dissenting, eye over the orthodox accounts. The struggle for Irish republican memory of the Troubles is being played out not only in the commemorative practices of the movement (e.g. in the competing public rallies associated with various factions of the movement, at Bodenstown in Co. Kildare at the grave of Wolfe Tone, and in numerous other cemeteries across Ireland), but also in the publishing houses, from which the memoirs of activists are starting to flow.

Becoming a Provo: Narratives of Belonging

In many memoirs by political leaders and activists, the recounting of the subject's life-story follows certain well-established patterns. Beginning with an account of the origins of an individual's commitment to the political path they espoused, the memoirist usually offers a detailed discussion of their conversion to the cause, and their early initiation as a supporter or sympathiser, followed by their graduation to become a fully-fledged member, activist, and perhaps eventually, a leader of the movement/organisation. This pattern is often followed by two more standard tropes in the unfolding of the life-story: first, the experience of trial or struggle, during which the commitments and beliefs of the subject are tested, often through their involvement in war or imprisonment; and, second, as a result of this life-changing period, either the individual emerges with a renewed commitment, or alternatively they may engage in a form of self-criticism, which can on occasion lead to a permanent separation from the movement. In the former case, the memoirist may reveal a sense of self that is even more deeply immersed in their feeling of belonging to a broader collective; they are organically linked to the political movement, and their memoirs 'narrate and reflect upon the process by which political beliefs and commitments become imbricated in the process of [personal] identity formation, thus belying the commonly held belief that intimacy and ideology are lived out in separate spheres.'[16] In the latter case, the memoirist often reflects upon their previous commitment, which has been tested to destruction, and the rationale for their dissent from the 'master narrative'. These master plots of political life-writing may have clear parallels with the trajectories associated with religious memoirists, but it is argued here that Irish republicanism can also be studied in comparison with other forms of *revolutionary* political movement. In particular, as was pointed out in the opening chapter, the study of political memoir in the context of the Communist movement may shed significant light upon the life-writing of Irish republicans.[17]

There are several repeated themes in Provisional republican memoirs with regard to the individual's formative experiences, and their decision to join the movement. One of the key elements that recurs in many of the memoirs studied is the influence of close-knit family and kinship groups in the socialisation of many of the early Provisionals. For example, Brendan Hughes (born in 1948 in the Lower Falls area of Belfast, and later a charismatic and highly effective operator, and officer commanding the Belfast Brigade of the IRA) argued that his father Kevin's influence, as a long-standing supporter of republican and socialist politics, was highly significant in furthering his political education.[18] This was in spite of the fact that his father rarely spoke openly about his experiences in the republican movement during the 1930s and 1940s, when he had been interned alongside Gerry Adams senior: 'my father, as I say, was an old Republican; he did time in prison but very seldom would he tell us any stories about his involvement. He never talked about any operation he was on, even though I know he was on operations.'[19] Perhaps more unusually, Hughes's mother, and at least two of his grandparents had also been involved in the IRA. Clearly, even though he didn't recall much overt republican political discussion at home, nonetheless as a teenager in the mid-1960s (during what was a fallow period for the movement after the defeat of the Border campaign of 1956–62), Brendan Hughes absorbed an understanding of the movement's history and its place within the Catholic community in Belfast. He argued that 'there was a kind of dormant Republican tradition in West Belfast during the sixties.'[20] The 1966 commemoration at the fiftieth anniversary of the 1916 Easter Rising helped to provide a new impetus for the republican tradition, but for Hughes and a number of others who came from well-established republican families, there was a predisposition towards joining the movement: 'I was so sort of romantically involved with the IRA, even before I joined it. It was just something that I believe I was destined to be, and I don't think my father actually directed me towards this, consciously [...].'[21]

There are several similar stories of family, and particularly paternal, influence on youthful Catholics. For instance, when Richard O'Rawe was arrested in early 1972, he was interned on the prison ship, the *Maidstone*, harboured in Belfast Lough, and as he was being escorted on board, he thought of his father's uncannily similar experience: 'I couldn't help but remember a saying my father had: "Show me the father, and I'll show you the son." Because of his involvement with the IRA, he had been interned aboard the *Al Rawdah*, a prison ship that had been anchored in Strangford Lough in 1940.'[22] For Gerry Bradley (from the Unity Flats near Belfast city centre), his experience was one of shock and surprise when he discovered that he came from a republican family with 'an impeccable pedigree'.[23] Although his father, Willie, had been arrested following a bombing in England during the 1939 IRA campaign, and served a ten-year sentence, the young Gerry (who was twelve when his father died in 1966) knew nothing of his activism and imprisonment. According to Brian Feeney, who co-wrote Bradley's memoir, such ignorance was not unusual amongst the sons and daughters of Belfast republican families in the mid-1960s: 'the IRA and republicans in general were discredited and shunned [...] In this atmosphere of defeat and depression, Bradley's mother had not tried to inculcate any republicanism in him or his brother. It seemed there was no future in it. It was over.'[24]

As with so many other aspects of republican memoir-writing and its conventions, the role of Gerry Adams, and his approach to autobiography, is critical in providing a template, and a sense of validation, for subsequent memoirists. As with the autobiographies of a number of West European Communist Party leaders, Adams' writing can be interpreted as a 'personalised form of official party history'.[25] In *Before the Dawn*, Adams' first volume of writing that is explicitly

presented as autobiographical in form, the determining influence of Adams'
belonging to an historic republican clan (the Adams and Hannaway families
were both steeped in the movement over the course of several generations) is
made plain. Adams was partly brought up by his paternal grandmother, a woman
from the Lower Falls who 'had witnessed two generations of political opposition
and who knew full well the hardships of struggle'.[26] Her husband had been
active in the Irish Republican Brotherhood, and several of her six surviving sons
(including Gerry Adams senior) had joined the IRA; in 1942, as a sixteen-year-
old, Adams' father had been shot and wounded in an exchange of fire with the
RUC on the day after another IRA teenager, Tom Williams, had been hanged
in Crumlin Road jail for his part in the killing of a policeman. Gerry Adams
senior received an eight-year sentence, and in police reports, it was noted that
he came from a notorious family, and that his actions were an 'endeavour to
uphold the republican family traditions'.[27] As has been demonstrated elsewhere,
this pattern of recruitment at a very young age into the republican movement
(whether directly into the IRA, or through *Na Fianna Éireann*, the republican
youth organisation) is a 'dominant feature in the sociological profile' of the
Provisional movement.[28] This is evident amongst both those with historic family
ties, and those with no such background, suggesting that in this respect it was
the politicised milieu in Catholic areas (particularly urban Belfast and Derry),
and the cataclysmic events associated with communal conflict, as much as the
direct influence of family, that help to explain such early commitment. Even
for those, like Adams, Hughes and O'Rawe, who were steeped in the tradition
of the movement, there is no clear evidence from their memoir-writing that
they were any more ideologically advanced than their fellow teenage recruits, or
that they joined the movement with a fully-formed belief system, or a mature
understanding of the IRA's goals and programme.

As with Brendan Hughes, Adams insists in his memoir that he was not
indoctrinated by members of his family; indeed, he argues that due to her painful
experiences associated with commitment to the republican cause, his grandmother
'may have actively discouraged me from taking an interest in politics'.[29] On
his mother's side, the Hannaways were at least as strongly identified with the
republican movement; Adams' great-grandfather had been a Fenian in the late
nineteenth century, his grandfather a socialist republican who had worked
alongside James Larkin and James Connolly in the early years of the twentieth,
and his uncle Liam was involved in the IRA's D Company of Belfast Brigade.
Another key figure in the leadership of the Provisionals in the late 1970s and
through the 1980s was Danny Morrison, who has also proved a prolific writer of
novels, plays, a prison diary, assorted journalism and memoir.[30] Morrison's uncle,
Harry White, had been a long-standing IRA man, and instructed young recruits
in the use of explosives (one of whom was the future playwright and memoirist

Brendan Behan, who was arrested in Liverpool on a bombing mission in 1940, aged sixteen). Arrested by the RUC in 1946 and handed over to the Garda Síochána, Harry was charged with the killing of Detective George Mordaunt in Dublin in 1942; he was sentenced to hang, but his appeal was successful, and the sentence was reduced to twelve years for manslaughter. As with the other examples discussed above, Morrison acknowledges his pride in the unimpeachable republican heritage that he has imbibed.[31]

The important point to note here is that these cases illustrate that, for many of the early Provisionals, there is no explicit conversion narrative in their memoir-writing. Instead, a republican belief system was absorbed almost as a process of osmosis. In this sense, there was no necessity for an epiphanic 'awakening' or a 'second birth', as in the memoirs of a number of religious figures. However, it is clear from their memoirs that, notwithstanding the impeccable republican credentials of Brendan Hughes, Gerry Adams, Danny Morrison, Richard O'Rawe and Gerry Bradley, they required a specific catalyst to become politically committed and active in the movement. Before this seminal event, their republicanism was largely a matter of affinity, rather than a conscious choice: as Adams put it, 'I had absorbed an ethos of Republicanism while growing up, even though I had taken no great interest in politics.'[32] Their sense of belonging and entitlement were largely uncontested by their peers; notwithstanding Feeney's note of caution with regard to the parlous state of republicanism in Belfast in the mid-1960s, these individuals were highly likely to be attracted to republican ideas and organisations later on, when the catalyst of the civil rights movement (and the reaction of unionists to it) produced increasing communal tension, rioting and street confrontations with both the police and loyalists.

Of course, subtle differences exist in the respective trajectories of these memoirists: for Gerry Adams (born in 1948 and therefore slightly older than many of those who joined the Provisionals as teenagers in 1969–70), it was the experience of the 1964 parliamentary election campaign that propelled him into joining the local SF branch. As a sixteen-year-old schoolboy, Adams recalls that he noticed the 'tension, the charged atmosphere' that had been provoked by the RUC's decision, at the insistence of Protestant firebrand Ian Paisley, to remove the Irish tricolour from the electoral office of Liam (Billy) McMillen, the SF candidate.[33] The incident, which involved a minor fracas between republican supporters and the RUC, pricked the curiosity of the young Adams and, 'with some initial encouragement from my father', he began to work for McMillen during the campaign; his 'political appetite was whetted. All kinds of little things fell into place.' Even though he joined SF only weeks after the Divis Street disturbances, Adams insists that 'despite my firmly republican family background, I had not really formed any definite political views' at that stage.[34] Critical biographers of Adams have hinted that perhaps he was more closely connected with SF, and the rioting, than he was willing to acknowledge in his memoir.[35]

For Brendan Hughes, also born in 1948, there is no similar emphasis upon this incident, partly because he had acquired broader horizons than West Belfast. In the mid-1960s, after the death of his mother, he had joined the Merchant Navy in order to ease the burden on his father, left with six children to raise. Hughes states that 'in the late sixties I didn't have any Republican philosophy or Republican ideas.'[36] The critical change that determined Hughes' subsequent trajectory was the inter-communal violence of August 1969; home on leave, he was part of the crowd that confronted Protestant rioters in the vicinity of Divis Street and Dover Street on 14 August when the IRA opened fire over the heads of the oncoming crowd (although a Protestant was also shot and killed by republicans that night).[37] Interestingly, in recalling these events for the Boston College archive, Hughes remembered his involvement with some ambivalence, as he recognised the sectarian implication of such confrontations, and having been raised in a 'mixed' district (near the Grosvenor Road), he was perhaps more aware than some other young Catholics of the Protestant perception of events. After a short spell in jail for 'fighting with cops', Hughes states that he joined the IRA in late 1969, partly on the recommendation of his cousin. Whilst the specific catalyst was an Orange march on the Grosvenor Road, Hughes argues that 'I just didn't become a rebel in 1970. I didn't become a gunman in 1970. I didn't become a revolutionary in 1970. That process was being built up over the years, and years of seeing privation, years of seeing exploitation, years of hunger and sadness and love.'[38] Hughes was sworn into the movement by Joe Cahill (who later became Chief of Staff of the Provisionals), who had known his father, and who accepted Hughes' *bona fides* immediately.

As with Communist movements, individual republicans could be ranked, and were encouraged to rank themselves, in terms of a 'continuum of graded purity'.[39] In this understanding, when judging activists, all starting points and family origins might be considered legitimate, but it was simply much easier to both join and be accepted in the ranks of the republican movement if one came from an 'historic' family known for its fidelity to the cause over one or more generations. For someone who aspired to be a Communist, if one began life as an incontrovertible proletarian, then much less work was required with regard to self-fashioning, in order to reach the required standard for entry to the movement, than would be the case for someone from a bourgeois background. The latter had to prove their commitment, and demonstrate a degree of self-transformation, that was considered unnecessary for the proletarian. So it was with Irish republicans: an individual with the 'right' family background, and/or from a known republican district, might be welcomed into the republican movement more readily than a 'blow-in', who could be expected to 'prove' themselves before suspicions would be put to one side. As with Communist parties, in circumstances where republicans were working in clandestine conditions, and felt themselves to be under siege from the hostile forces of the state and unionists, such conspiratorial attitudes were understandable, but they also tended to produce a rather enclosed, inward-looking organisational culture. In discussing the involvement of republicans in the civil rights campaign, Gerry Adams argued that the 'breakdown of republican isolation', and the opportunities presented for political exchange, was of critical importance: 'the traditional internalisation of republican activities and their restriction to a chosen few now seemed a thing of the past.'[40]

Ultimately, however, for many early supporters of the Provisionals, whether from historic republican families or not, it was the increasingly violent civil conflict of 1968–9 that proved the catalyst for their decision to join the movement. Often this occurred at a specific moment, creating the 'spark' that ignited a commitment to action. The testimonies gathered by many oral histories of the movement, as well as the memoirs already mentioned, display a consensus (among those from Belfast, in particular) that defence of Catholic districts and communities that were perceived to be under attack (or were threatened) by loyalists and/or the RUC in the summer of 1969, was a primary motivation for those hundreds of very young recruits who flooded into the republican movement in the days and months that followed. Many of these individuals formed the founding cadre of the fledgling Provisional movement, after the split from the Officials in late 1969. There is not space here to analyse this period in depth, but it is clear that the sectarian confrontations of this era, and the sense that neither the state of Northern Ireland (in the shape of the Unionist government at Stormont), nor the Westminster administration, could be relied upon to protect the Catholic nationalist people, were uppermost in the minds of those who looked to the republican movement. There are countless references in memoirs to the 'ashes of Bombay Street', the 'turning point' of August 1969, the 'pogroms' allegedly directed against vulnerable Catholic districts, and the necessity to form an organised, disciplined force that was capable of responding.[41] A prevailing view was that, whether or not one was 'converted' to republican ideology in any meaningful sense, nevertheless this was a time to 'stand up and be counted', and the only realistic vehicle for such communal defence was the IRA, even if it was in a parlous state to deliver on its historic role of providing protection for the beleaguered Catholics of Northern Ireland.

Such a 'standard republican narrative' has been subjected to critical scrutiny by a number of commentators, but for my purpose the key aspect of this interpretation is how deep-rooted it has become in the Provisional movement's collective memory of the essential causes of the conflict (and the very birth of the movement itself).[42] What a close reading of these memoirs tends to confirm is the significance attached to this narrative, and whether we choose to characterise it as a 'myth' or not, is unlikely to cut much ice with the Provisionals' own story, or the determination with which they maintain this version of events. As so often, in Gerry Adams' memoir, we can read a subtle account of this period: whilst he is at pains to stress the paucity of the IRA's preparations (thereby appearing to share the critique of the Dublin leadership, later accused by Provisionals of abandoning the Catholics to the 'pogrom'), and its inability to respond to the threat of violence from loyalists and the RUC, he also remembers arguing against those who were pressing for republicans to 'militarise the situation, to bring the IRA in to it and to engage the RUC on their own terms'.[43] Still, 'even though the IRA's armed intervention throughout Belfast was an extremely limited one', Adams goes on to pay tribute to the courageous 'IRA actions in the Falls area [which] were crucially important in halting the Loyalist mobs at decisive times.'[44] Through such a nuanced account, Adams attempts to identify himself both with the heroism of the local Catholic community, which had repelled the concerted attacks upon their areas, largely without organised republican action, and the subsequent Provisional narrative that the IRA's 'rebirth' was necessary and legitimate.

Different Worlds of the Troubles:
Locality and Internal Republican Politics

One dimension of the Provisional movement's experience upon which memoir-writing by protagonists can shed significant light is the geographical and territorial aspects of the organisation's political activities. It is now commonly accepted that physical separation and segregation of communities in Northern Ireland is so deeply ingrained that it is unlikely to be broken down in the short to medium term, even if 'peace' continues to hold sway. For Shirlow and Murtagh, 'segregated places aid the fashioning of community belief and the certitude of mutual solidarity and spatial control.'[45] However, segregated urban spaces are not always as socially or politically homogeneous as they may at first appear; the differences 'within' ethno-sectarian communal spaces can sometimes be obscured by the apparently overwhelming character of the difference 'between' any such space and the 'other side'. If 'Belfast remains not as a city but as an assemblage of "villages" within which detachment from other places is crucial', then it is also the case that diverse republican (or Catholic nationalist) districts exhibit distinctive features, and that researchers should always be careful to recognise the complexity of the *internal* politics of these areas.[46] Significantly, Gerry Adams' first book-length publication was *Falls Memories: A Belfast Life* (1982), which is part memoir, part local history, and part semi-fictional recreation of one such Belfast 'village', known variously as the Pound Loney or the Lower Falls (but christened ironically the 'Lower Wack' or 'the Dogs' by some republicans).[47] Although the precise boundary of this district is 'much disputed', Adams' narrative mines the collective memory of the local community. As Zwicker has argued, his intense sense of place is thoroughly politicised; Adams' early writing 'demonstrates the intimate imbrications of politics with streetscapes in Catholic West Belfast.'[48] In this view, the very streets and stones of this district have been 'made, and changed, and made again by the Troubles', with paving stones and cobbles used as weapons against the police during rioting, and later against the British Army patrols in the area.

As we have seen, whilst it is true that the foundational myth of Bombay Street has been critical to the broader Provisional narrative, and has been replayed for subsequent generations within the movement, it is also the case that relationships within republicanism have often been characterised by a localism or even parochialism, with suspicion and distrust between republicans from different cities and townlands, and even between those from different districts of the same town, often within walking distance of each other. Even in the cages of Long Kesh internment camp, a form of 'clannish' self-segregation existed, with internees from diverse geographical areas choosing not to occupy the same cage: 'Derry people stuck together and even within that grouping Waterside people stuck together. And you had other groupings, Tyrone, Belfast and that. So although it was all republicans together it was very much segregated.'[49] On occasion, there were clearly objective differences in the social environments in which republicans were operating. For instance, it has been widely recognised that sectarian attitudes were more prevalent in the intensely divided patchwork of Belfast, rather than in Derry, where Catholics were in a clear majority: Eamonn MacDermott recounted that Derry republicans were 'very clear on who the enemy was, it was the state. We didn't have to worry so much about the Orangemen. There's the old story about the Belfast Republican faced with a Brit, a cop and an Orangeman – he would shoot the Orangeman first! We didn't have to make those sorts of choices.'[50]

Equally, a recurring theme in internal republican politics has been a tension, and sometimes a genuine mistrust, between those based in the Republic of Ireland (and in particular the leadership in Dublin) and those in Northern Ireland (the 'occupied territory'). There are numerous examples of this phenomenon, but one will suffice: Seán MacStíofáin (who would become the Provisionals' first chief of staff after the split with the Officials) travelled to Belfast after the August rioting, to meet with some of those who had expressed no confidence in the Goulding leadership; in his memoir, he recounted that 'I was coolly received. After a while I was told, "You're the only effing [sic] one of that Dublin crowd we want to see up here. If it had been anyone else from HQ he'd probably have been shot"'.[51] Interestingly, later on, Gerry Bradley reported attending a large gathering of republicans during the short-lived 1972 ceasefire, which was addressed by MacStiofáin, who was on a visit that was supposed to raise morale. Bradley found him 'uppity and obnoxious, full of himself'.[52]

From the perspective adopted here, a key criterion for judging the utility of these memoirs is an author's willingness or capacity to place their experiences within a broader *political* framework, and to what extent they attempt to interpret the conflict beyond the narrow confines of their immediate geographical area. Some of these memoirs have been written by 'foot-soldiers', individuals who often operated within a comparatively restricted environment which they knew intimately, but whose recollections deal primarily with the minutiae of paramilitary life and activities, engagements with the 'enemy' and so on. This may be the case due to a conscious decision to concentrate upon these 'bottom-up' accounts, or simply that for these individuals, their experience of the conflict was played out at a local level, and they may not have had a well-developed wider appreciation or knowledge of the broader political canvas on which their particular dramas took place. For example, Gerry Bradley conveyed a very strong impression of the enclosed world of a Provisional operator during the 1970s and 1980s. Bradley's story revolves around the claustrophobic world of IRA activities in the strongly republican, but vulnerable, enclave of Unity Flats, near Belfast city centre, cheek by jowl with the fiercely loyalist Lower Shankill. Although the Flats were demolished in the 1990s, the social world inhabited by Gerry Bradley and his comrades is vividly recreated in his memoir, and for this reason, amongst others, his book is a valuable primary resource.

One of the striking aspects of his memoir is its effort to bring into the public domain the experience of a long-standing IRA activist, and the daily life of a highly committed operator, planning and co-ordinating attacks upon the security services, and ensuring the organisational and logistical support for the IRA's campaign in this particular area. Bradley's account starts with his being 'propelled spontaneously into the conflict to defend his district' in early August 1969, when he was fifteen.[53] Besieged by Protestant rioters, the area was, like the Short Strand in East Belfast or Ardoyne further north, especially exposed, and this produced a very different mentality amongst its beleaguered Catholic residents than that which existed in 'safer' republican parts of the city. Bradley joined the IRA in the summer of 1971, and by the time he was nineteen, he had become the Officer Commanding 3rd Battalion of the Belfast Brigade (which included the relatively isolated republican areas of North Belfast, as well as the Markets in the city centre, and Short Strand), a huge responsibility for such a young man. Although later on Bradley would become familiar with other districts and the different characteristics of the IRA organisation in diverse areas of the city, nevertheless his effectiveness as an operator depended upon his 'intimate knowledge of his own locality'; he freely acknowledged that there were parts of

Belfast where he 'hadn't a clue', and 'everywhere else outside Belfast was "the country", *terra incognita*'.[54]

The Boy from Ballymurphy

The history of Gerry Adams as a published author may be used, alongside a more conventional analysis of his political trajectory, to trace the development of his critical influence upon the character and structure of the Provisional republican narrative of the Troubles. In terms of political leadership, Adams' regular re-election as President of SF since 1983 makes him unmatched in terms of political longevity in Northern Ireland, at least since the retirement of Ian Paisley (who remained at the helm of the Democratic Unionist Party from 1971–2008). In addition, Adams was an abstentionist Westminster MP for West Belfast from 1983–2011 (with the exception of the period 1992–7, when the seat was won for the SDLP by Joe Hendron), building a huge majority, and making the constituency one of the safest in the UK. He recently vacated this seat, in order to fight (and win) a seat in Co. Louth in the Republic of Ireland, and he has taken up a seat in Dáil Éireann. Adams has spent almost forty years as one of the key strategic thinkers in the Provisional movement, and he has certainly been the dominant individual in SF during this period. Although it might be an exaggeration to argue that Adams was, at all times, the 'undisputed leader' of the movement, it is hard to quarrel with the judgment that he has expertly managed the tricky task of remaining at the helm of what had been viewed as a notoriously fractious movement.[55] He has gained a reputation as a shrewd, intelligent politician, capable of inspiring devotion from his supporters. Although he has accomplished this feat with the constant support of a small, self-perpetuating leadership group (including Martin McGuinness, SF Deputy First Minister in the Northern Ireland Executive since 2007), it is around Adams himself that a 'cult of personality' has developed.[56] In 2008, in the aftermath of disappointing election results in the Republic, Adams' leadership credentials were subjected, perhaps for the first time, to close scrutiny, and not just by 'dissidents', but also by some hitherto devoted supporters. Anthony McIntyre, commenting on criticism of Adams in the usually compliant *Andersonstown News*, argued that Adams 'now stands increasingly isolated as the sole remaining dinosaur of Northern Irish politics […] an antediluvian figure from the 1980s'.[57] However, as so often in the past, Adams has proved astute at navigating through the storm, and in the wake of impressive SF results in the 2011 Dáil election, his position once again seems impregnable.

To return briefly to the comparison with the Communist movement, it can be argued that, as with the political memoirs associated with the leaders of several West European Communist parties, Adams' memoir-writing has had an emblematic significance for his movement. The authorised Communist master-narratives, produced on occasion by party committee, involved a deep-rooted anti-individualism, which was easily overlooked by observers who tended to stress the 'cult of personality' within such parties. Indeed, the life-story of the leader was subsumed within the Party's collective identity, its ethos and values being enshrined in the exemplary figure of the General Secretary. In this schema, anything that might set the leader apart from the Party, or might single him out, was renounced. The leader was assimilated to the bureaucratic 'persona' of the collectivity, and very often the first person singular (the autobiographical "I") was eschewed in favour of the plural.[58] In these 'socialist realist' autobiographies (such as Maurice Thorez's *Fils du peuple*), the 'mildest deprecation of self or party' was taboo, and 'not human frailty or temptation but a steely self-control was expected, and party lives had to be exemplary in the mass, and at the peak bore an almost symbolic significance.'[59]

In this respect, although Gerry Adams' memoir-writing bears a number of important similarities, it can also be understood differently. Firstly, Adams is certainly the author of his own narratives (including his memoir-writing) in a way in which Communist Party leaders have not always been. Although he does recognise the advice and editorial input of some key individuals, notably SF's long-standing public relations chief, Richard McAuley, and Steve MacDonogh, his editor at Brandon/Mount Eagle, nonetheless it is clear that Adams himself is the genuine author of his works. Secondly, Adams utilises self-deprecation (or even self-mockery) as a subtle device, and acknowledges his personal frailties as a badge of authenticity. In discussing Adams' writing as a 'refutation of the stereotype of the terrorist', Zwicker attempts to analyse what she refers to as his use of 'discursive disarmament', or 'oblique strategies of rebuttal'.[60] In this view, Adams is able to successfully undermine the British establishment's effort to characterise both him and the wider republican constituency as 'criminal'; he employs 'humour, self-effacement, legend and myth in order to structure an anti-stereotypical community'.[61] We can perhaps question the degree to which this strategy has been successful, or indeed whether its success would be cause for celebration, but there is little doubt that this is, in fact, Adams' purpose. More critical commentators would point out the folksiness and affected simplicity of Adams' recollections, especially those of his childhood and family, but could agree that they serve a determinedly political purpose. Adams makes no pretence of being a paragon of revolutionary virtue; instead, he presents himself as sharing the same hopes and dreams as the 'plain people' of Ballymurphy, and he exhibits the same positive characteristics (and suffers from the same faults) as the ordinary rank-and-file, salt-of-the-earth republicans who constitute the heartland of the movement. This approach may also be understood as a reflection of a less deferential era, when any attempt to portray the leader as a virtuous incarnation of all that is 'pure' within the movement is likely to stretch credulity, even in an authoritarian political movement.

Interestingly, Gerry Adams is also ready to acknowledge the critical distinctiveness of particular districts, and their diverse experiences of the Troubles. But, Adams' purpose in discussing his home district of Ballymurphy masks a much more strategic, even cunning, political intent than, for instance, Gerry Bradley's. Initially, Adams is at pains to describe Ballymurphy in terms of its generic characteristics as a working-class area; he commends the area's hardworking families, determined to make the most of their limited economic opportunities, and interprets the district in terms that emphasise its ordinariness: 'In my travels over the years, I have seen Ballymurphys everywhere. In Britain, across Europe, in cities throughout Ireland, in the USA and in South Africa.'[62] Adams characterises life in republican West Belfast as an intimate patchwork of familial connections, with each discrete district enjoying its own particular character. In Ballymurphy, in contrast to Unity Flats, Adams could grow up 'barely conscious' of the existence of unionists, and 'naive about sectarianism, partly because I didn't encounter it in my everyday life, and partly because I didn't always recognise it when I did meet it'.[63] Gerry Bradley illustrated a significant diversity within the movement in respect of attitudes towards the Protestant population, and the IRA's nuanced approach to the vexed question of sectarianism:

> None of the third batt [...] ever got to brigade staff because they [the IRA's Belfast Brigade leadership] thought we were sectarian, but it *was* one of our jobs to hit back at loyalist attacks. It was okay for first and second batt to talk, but places like Andersonstown only had the Brits to worry about. The loyalists were always having a go at us.[64]

Even though Adams was beginning to think much more strategically about the republican struggle, he claims that at the time of the split in the IRA, the complexity of the ideological, geographical and personal dimensions of the growing divisions within the movement went over his head; 'To a large extent, my political world was Ballymurphy. I was busy enough there without worrying about the rest of the struggle.'[65] Whether we should take this claim at face value is certainly questionable, but Adams' presents himself, uncharacteristically, as reticent and without a settled political position. There were two potential reasons for Adams to stress his immersion in the local political world at this juncture, one historical, and one decidedly contemporary. The historical controversy concerns Adams' position with regard to the looming split in the republican movement; by denying his engagement with the broader issues that were dividing the movement, Adams perhaps hoped to escape a close scrutiny of his ambivalent stance at the time. There are a number of competing accounts of his position, but Adams himself is only willing to acknowledge that 'I was in a strange position, one of a small cadre with contacts in both factions.'[66] In contrast to some of those older republicans who formed the leading organs of the Provisionals after the split (including the first Chief of Staff, Seán MacStíofáin, and men like Billy McKee, Joe Cahill and Jimmy Steele), Adams was not obviously ideologically opposed to the left-wing rhetoric and socialist direction being pursued by the Goulding leadership in Dublin; indeed, Adams favoured the leadership's proposal for the development of a National Liberation Front, in which the republican movement would work with other anti-imperialist forces to confront British interference in Irish affairs.

However, despite this ideological disposition towards the leadership, Adams claims in *Before the Dawn* that after August 1969 he had little confidence in the local Belfast leadership of Billy McMillen; 'there needed to be major changes in Belfast, but I had had neither the opportunity nor indeed the inclination to work these out.'[67] Ultimately, Adams sided with the Provisionals (along with the bulk of the wider Adams/Hannaway clan, with the notable exception of his sister, Margaret), but his memoir remains unrevealing about the reasons for his decision, or how he weighed up the various factors involved. He claims not to have been present at either the IRA convention or the SF *ard fheis* that formalised the split into Official and Provisional wings of the movement.[68] By emphasising his essentially *localised* political activity at this time, Adams may believe he can avoid awkward issues with regard to a painful episode for the wider republican family, and probing questions with respect to his own role. One of these questions concerns the uncertainty that surrounds Adams' suspension from his 'local leadership role' in the Ballymurphy SF after a car crash in November 1969 in which a fellow activist, Liam McParland, suffered fatal injuries. Adams offered no clear explanation for his suspension, and some commentators have speculated that by joining the Provisionals in the split which followed the next month, Adams was therefore able to avoid the disciplinary proceedings that were hanging over him.[69]

The second, contemporary, political purpose which explains Adams' determination to 'see things purely in the perspective of his mother's back window', was a desire to offer reassurance to the republican grassroots that he had not abandoned the movement's fundamental principles, despite the ideological and strategic somersaults that accompanied the 'peace process' of the early-mid 1990s.[70] Publishing his memoir in 1996, Adams was at pains to convince the republican heartlands (including Ballymurphy) that the movement's revolutionary struggle had not been defeated, despite the IRA's 1994 ceasefire, and that all of the communal hardship and sacrifice in sustaining the 'war' had been worthwhile. By grounding his memoir in the familiar environs of West Belfast, it is easier for Adams to achieve his self-appointed task, namely to subsume his personal story into the heroic collective resistance of the republican population, his own people.

This effort to identify himself as a leader who was at one with his supporters, as a 'man of the people' who shared their hopes and fears, served an important function in denying the arguments of dissidents, who had begun to claim that the leadership was out of touch, and was pursuing a secret agenda, which effectively involved an unacknowledged renunciation of the republican armed struggle and its objectives. Faced with scepticism, and subsequently outright hostility, from key figures like Brendan Hughes (and eventually from 'foot-soldiers' like Gerry Bradley), Gerry Adams needed a strategy to insulate his leadership from this potentially powerful internal critique. Roy Foster rightly points out that the account Adams puts forward suggests 'his most passionate commitment is to the narrow world of West Belfast, a self-justifying and tightly knit community later replicated in the republican wing of internment prison.'[71] But Foster does not analyse the specific strategic purpose behind this commitment. In contrast to Adams' disingenuously parochial image, he in fact commands worldwide exposure: in marketing terms, 'as an Irish product, Gerry Adams has name recognition rivalling Guinness or Waterford Glass'.[72] He purports, however, to be a 'very shy person', explaining: 'I find other people are much more relaxed in dealing with public events. I mean, I wouldn't be running about to banquets or balls or fancy suppers. It's nothing to those who lost their lives [...] or lost loved ones, but I think the loss of anonymity is a big thing.'[73] Adams' target audience in Ireland and, especially, the USA is again invited to see him as a grounded politician who understands them and their community.

'My intention is to tell a story. It is my story. My truth. My reality'

It is important to start this section by saying something about fact and fiction in Adams' writing. His two volumes of memoir were preceded by *Cage Eleven* (1990), a book based on his 'Brownie' articles written while he was an internee and then a convicted prisoner (after a failed escape attempt), and published in *Republican News* between 1975 and 1977. Although Adams gives the real names of some of his fellow internees in the book's introduction, he later claims that 'the main characters are fictional, but they and their escapades are my way of representing life as it was in Long Kesh.'[74] Steve MacDonogh characterises his literary development (at least before his memoirs were published) as a gradual move away from factual writing towards fiction. Introducing Adams' *Selected Writings* (1994), he explains that while *Falls Memories: A Belfast Life* (1982) has 'qualities of fiction', and *Cage Eleven* 'hover[s] between fact and fiction', *The Street and Other Stories* (1992) is 'more decidedly fictional'.[75] In *Before the Dawn*, however, Adams' propensity to blur the margins between fact and fiction provoked controversy when he 'tried to capture in a short story something of the harsh reality of the campaign waged by the IRA against Britain's armed forces as they patrolled the streets of my home town' in the early 1970s.[76]

Although this 'story', presented in the third person, which recounts the internal moral questioning of a Provo sniper before he shoots a member of a British Army patrol, is written in italics, it is not explicitly presented purely as fiction, the product only of imagination rather than experience. Zwicker has argued that this is 'one of the craftiest examples' of a two-pronged strategy deployed by Adams: whilst Adams' IRA affiliation is an 'open secret', he cannot explicitly acknowledge this fact, because to do so would pave the way for legal proceedings. On the other hand, he must not disavow this affiliation openly either, if he is to retain the confidence of the movement.[77] Hence, according to Zwicker, Adams is able to subvert the official attempt to label him as a 'terrorist', and he is able to 'straddle the boundary between the said and the unsayable with relative ease'. However, the argument that Adams cannot admit to his IRA involvement without running the risk of incriminating himself has been undermined by the willingness of other leading Provisionals (not least Martin McGuinness) to publicly recognise and discuss their roles in the 'army'. There may well be some 'sneaking regarders' who know full well that Adams has lied about his past, but are willing to indulge him, or even admire his brazen decision to 'tough it out'. But, both outside, and more significantly, inside the movement, this devious evasion has caused Adams considerable embarrassment and political difficulty. Whatever the more general interpretation of Adams' discursive strategy, Fintan O'Toole criticised another more specific dimension of evasiveness in Adams' story of the IRA sniper, 'Seán': 'it is striking in itself that the IRA campaign on the streets of Belfast is not represented by bombs tearing civilians apart in restaurants, by children blown up on their way into the Falls Road baths or by "informers" having nail-studded clubs aimed at their flesh.'[78] Although this criticism could hardly be expected to move Adams, nevertheless the strength of the critical reaction that greeted this aspect of his 'story' seems to have had an impact; certainly, no similar episode appears in his second volume of memoir, *Hope and History*.

Although Gerry Adams is willing to use personal anecdotes to supplement and further his political purpose, this nevertheless makes any perceived dissimulation on his part more damaging. Of course, Adams is by no means alone in utilising what Aughey has described as 'the art of political lying'; as McIntyre has pointed out, the idea of the 'revolutionary lie' has been used by many organisations that accept the logic of the ends justifying the means.[79] Adams wished to identify himself in *Before the Dawn* with the heroic communal sacrifice and struggle of the republican community and its 'army', but this identification inevitably led him into an ambivalent position as far as the actual campaign of violence was concerned. His position was complicated by his strategic purpose at the time of publication (1996): first, he wanted to distance the political 'wing' of the Provisional movement from the military, arguing against all the evidence that they are in fact entirely separate organisations; Adams' oft-repeated argument was that the former deserved to be involved in all-party talks because of its electoral mandate alone. One way to achieve this was for Adams to deny ever having played a prominent role in the IRA, or indeed having been a member at all. Secondly, with the benefit of hindsight, we can speculate that he wished to prepare the ground for the definitive abandonment of armed struggle, but he could not state this openly, for fear of provoking a serious split in the movement. Subsequently, however, a number of Adams' closest erstwhile comrades, such as Brendan Hughes, vented their fury at such subterfuge:

> Gerry was a major, major player in the war, not just in Ireland, but in the decision to send Volunteers and bombs to England. And to hear people who I would have died for – and almost did on a few occasions – stand up and deny the part in history that he has played [...] the part in the war that he directed, and deny it, it is totally disgusting and a disgrace to all the people who have died.[80]

To summarise, Adams' credibility on this issue has been undermined by a succession of biographers and commentators, and there is virtual unanimity amongst academic researchers:

> between April/May 1971 and March 1972 Gerry Adams was OC of the Provisionals' 2nd Battalion in Belfast; in the latter year he became Adjutant for the Belfast Brigade as a whole; by the time of his arrest on 19 July 1973 he had become OC of the entire Belfast Brigade [...] Adams was released from prison in 1977 and in the same year became an Army Council member, a position which he was to hold for a long time.[81]

Most accounts also agree that Adams was, for a short period at the end of 1977 until February 1978, the PIRA's Chief of Staff.[82] Nevertheless, as O'Toole has observed, *Before the Dawn* 'almost entirely glossed over' Adams' IRA career, a view endorsed by Foster, who claims that he is 'unnecessarily coy' about the IRA and likens his memoir to 'a biography of Field Marshal Montgomery that leaves out the British Army'.[83] The political subtext was clear to all, however. The context of the developing peace process, and the perceived requirement to maintain Adams' position as the Provisionals' unchallenged leader, capable of delivering an IRA ceasefire and committing (at least the vast bulk of) the movement to this new strategy, meant that 'these incredible assertions were allowed to pass with no more than mild expressions of skepticism.'[84] If Adams was to be accepted locally and internationally as a genuine agent of peace *and* compromise, then it suited the purposes of governments in London, Dublin and

Washington, as well as republicans and even pro-Agreement unionists, to collude in this necessary fiction.

However, as O'Toole noted, 'the danger has always been that the tacit agreement to ignore the IRA past of the SF leader would encourage a larger and more profound act of denial. If Adams did not have to account for his involvement with the IRA, then perhaps the IRA itself could remain unaccountable.'[85] In the period since the signing of the Good Friday Agreement, this issue of accountability for past actions has taken on a central importance for the shape of Northern Ireland's political future. Adams must have been more aware than most of the likely reaction to his address at the SF-sponsored March for Truth Rally (August 2007), in which he called for full disclosure of the British state's role in 'violence and collusion' with loyalist paramilitary 'death squads' during the Troubles. Entirely predictably, Adams was roundly condemned from many quarters for his apparent hypocrisy; a senior political source at Stormont was quoted as saying, 'It's a case of "be careful what you wish for" because the whole truth and nothing but the truth would have far more serious consequences for Adams and co. than anyone else.'[86] Families and victims of alleged state collusion, who may well have legitimate grievances that deserve to be investigated impartially, must also surely recognise that recruiting Gerry Adams to publicise their case will inevitably lead to accusations that they are willing pawns in a party political game, where the 'truth' is merely harnessed to party calculation at any given moment.

The motifs of communal endurance and resistance are repeated at virtually every turn in Adams' memoirs, and he consciously adopts an omniscient stance, seeking to symbolise and embody this spirit. Adams readily eulogises the republican base's stubborn refusal to buckle under enormous pressure, despite the tough conditions that it had to endure whilst sustaining the guerrilla conflict. However, one of the consequences of prosecuting the war, according to Adams, is that it helped to create an under-developed political consciousness within the movement's heartlands. The implication, though not explicit, is that only he (and a few other perspicacious members of the leadership coterie) was aware of the broader context within which the Provisionals' heroic resistance was played out, and only this hand-picked close-knit group can fully appreciate the newly-changed political circumstances. Ordinary activists and foot-soldiers are conceived as incapable of this sort of deeper strategic and political thinking, and are therefore almost completely reliant on the wisdom and far-sightedness of their leaders. Again, the parallels with Communist parties, and their intolerance of internal questioning and dissent, are strikingly clear. This may have been convincing within the Provisional movement whilst SF was making steady electoral progress, but as a result of more recent setbacks (particularly in the general election in the Republic of Ireland in 2007) increasingly questions were being asked, and perhaps Adams' hitherto unchallengeable position would begin to appear less secure.

If Adams' memoir writing is guarded and opaque, this is explicable in terms of his perception of the *political* imperatives of the republican movement at that particular juncture, though this does not of itself render such an approach justifiable to a wider readership. Foster acknowledges that 'since the Adams story is a small part of the story of modern Ireland, so the fact that it supplies – yet again – a narrative of evasions is only appropriate.'[87] O'Toole notes that 'political autobiographies should be written when the hurly-burly's done. They should tell a story whose ending is known, reflect on something that has actually been achieved.'[88] There is a clear parallel here with the Communist memoirs we have mentioned (Harry Pollitt's was published when he was aged fifty, yet he still had another sixteen years to serve as Communist Party of Great Britain leader; Thorez's was first published when he was only thirty-seven, and still had twenty-five years to come at the apex of the French Communist Party). But, the end of Adams' story remains unpredictable (he was only forty-eight when his first volume of memoir came out) because, as he recognises in the foreword to *Before the Dawn*:

> I am also conscious that the elements of conflict remain today and retain their potency. For this reason I must write nothing which would place in jeopardy the liberties or the lives of others, so I am necessarily constrained. It is probably an invariable rule that the participants in any conflict cannot tell the entire story until some time after that conflict is fully resolved.[89]

These words were written in February 1996 when, with the end of the IRA's ceasefire at Canary Wharf, it was the Provisionals' actions rather than Adams' text that was taking lives, and not merely jeopardising them. Even today, Adams would no doubt take the view that the conflict has yet to be 'fully resolved'. Indeed, it is arguable that when Adams talks of the conflict requiring complete resolution before he could tell 'the entire story', the only circumstance that would satisfy his criterion is the creation of a united Ireland, or at least SF in government across the island. Again, just as there is a teleological core at the heart of Adams' thinking, the parallel with the Communist view of the necessary conditions for the ending of class conflict is striking.

Despite the absence of discernible movement towards a united Ireland, in 2003 Adams brought out a second volume of memoir.[90] However, *Hope and History: Making Peace in Ireland*, came no closer to offering a 'real and fully truthful autobiography'.[91] Rather, it presented the author's version of the process leading up to the successful negotiation of the Agreement in April 1998, and while there is a perfunctory final chapter outlining some of the problems it has encountered in subsequent years, Adams has conceded (again) that the narrative remains unfinished: 'there is a natural third book [...] but apart from noting that in my head, I have no plans, notions, ambitions to even think about writing it at the moment'.[92] Moreover, he insists that since the 'story' of the peace process is 'still unfolding, still sensitive, still fragile [...] it is not my business to offer an objective account of events or to see through someone else's eyes. Nor is it my responsibility to document these events. My intention is to tell a story. It is my story. My truth. My reality.' The rationale for publication at this particular time, therefore, seems to be that 'a happy ending' – the signing of the Agreement – is 'more important than a tell-all story'.[93]

Once more, Adams also conflates his 'personal journey' with the communal story. The peace process in his eyes is presented as a morality tale, where selfless nationalists – notably John Hume of the SDLP and Catholic clerics such as Fr Alec Reid – and republicans consistently urge the British government and the unionist parties to address 'the underlying causes of conflict', as if these are self-evident, uncomplicated and uncontested. He places enormous emphasis upon his dialogue with Hume and the quest for pan-nationalist unity in the early 1990s, and the need to press the Dublin and Washington administrations to adopt the 'Irish peace initiative', with no apparent recognition that, without a balancing input from the Westminster government, no serious negotiation with *any section* of unionism would be feasible. Indeed, the unionists as an autonomous force hardly figure at all in Adams' narrative. Interestingly, his later overtures to unionism are revealed as merely a rhetorical device:

> the mess within unionism is inherently part of any process of change. Unionism *at its best* is quite a conservative, reactionary philosophy [...] I've been reading recently Faulkner's memoirs, different bits and pieces of writings by unionist leaders [...] and you'd almost think that some of the senior British officials, some of the NIO people, are using a script written in the 1920s or 1970s.[94]

But does not Adams' presentation of his political thought imply that his own 'script' remains fundamentally unaltered? From this perspective, the 1993 Downing Street Declaration is seen as no more than 'a significant development', though an alternative reading would suggest that without it there would have been no potential for progress towards genuinely inclusive talks. Republicans had to be provided with an alternative to 'armed struggle' before peace was possible, says Adams, but the unanswered question remains: what happens if the republican movement maintains its evolution into a party 'like all the others', with the military wing entirely dismantled, and the 'struggle' pursued solely through the democratic process, but the outcome is not Irish unity, at least not any time soon? The teleology inherent in Adams' narrative means that he cannot entertain such an outcome; a 'proper' democracy, in his view, is defined as leading inexorably to a sovereign, united Republic.[95] Even today, there is no adequate answer to this question, but it is becoming starker for many ordinary republicans in the run up to 2016, and the centenary of the Easter Rising.

Chapter 3

Departing the Republican Movement: Memoir-Writing and the Politics of Dissent

Introduction

As the previous chapter argued, the Irish Provisional republican movement, and more specifically its leadership group based around SF President Gerry Adams and Deputy First Minister Martin McGuinness, has jealously guarded the collective memory of the movement's historical evolution, including in the field of life-writing. This close attention to control of the master narrative of the Provos' story of the conflict has proceeded in parallel with the importance attached to maintaining the grip of the leading group over the political, strategic and internal processes by which the movement has discussed and interpreted its past. The leadership has also been engaged in a, mostly successful, effort to keep the Provisional movement united behind their contemporary political strategy, despite the highly significant departures from previously orthodox republican beliefs that have characterised the movement's trajectory since the late 1980s. To enumerate only a few of these ideological somersaults can give an indication of how sweeping such change has been, and it can be imagined how disorienting this process has proved for many members and sympathisers of SF and the IRA: in 1986, the movement abandoned its historical policy of abstention from Dáil Éireann (or Leinster House to republicans), the seat of the Republic of Ireland's parliament, which had hitherto been dismissed scornfully as a 'partitionist assembly'[1]; in 1994, the IRA agreed to call a unilateral ceasefire, so the movement could gain entry to all-party negotiations (the 'peace process'), thereby abandoning a central demand of the post-1975 period, that the IRA would only suspend its campaign *after* a British government declaration of intent to withdraw from Northern Ireland; in 1998, SF signed up to the Good Friday Agreement, which effectively entailed a commitment to the principle of majority consent within Northern Ireland for any putative constitutional reunification, and moreover signified a return to an internal Northern Ireland-based devolved assembly (Stormont), albeit with cross-border institutions and, more importantly, SF in a strong electoral position; during the decade after the signing of this Agreement, the Provisional movement also shocked some observers (and many of its own supporters) by endorsing the leadership's arguments in favour of the decommissioning of IRA weaponry (begun tentatively in 2001, and completed in 2005, to the satisfaction of the Independent International Commission on Decommissioning), and the movement's support for the Police Service of Northern Ireland (the replacement for the hated RUC).

However, although the Provisionals have generally proved rather adept at rationalising these departures from traditional doctrine, and maintaining the movement's hegemony within republican politics, there has been consternation in the ranks, and some internal disharmony, at various junctures in this process of jettisoning what had often been understood as core tenets of republican ideology. Perhaps this was particularly the case for those policies, such as decommissioning, where the leadership had, until shortly before the announcement of the new departure, rubbished reports that such change was in the offing. In these circumstances, it is unsurprising that there have been a number of defections over the course of the 'peace process', and several attempts to create rival organisational centres that could challenge the continuing centrality of the Provisionals as the standard bearers of republican ideology and memory. There has been sporadic paramilitary action from groups such as the Continuity IRA (CIRA)[2], the Real IRA (RIRA)[3], *Óglaigh na hÉireann* and other offshoots or 'micro-groups' as SF has disparagingly called them. Many of those engaged in such activity are ex-Provisionals, who decided to depart the mainstream movement in despair at the political direction being followed by the Adams/McGuinness leadership, although increasingly these groups have also sought to recruit disaffected younger members of the Catholic nationalist community. Equally, there is an important constituency of ex-Provisionals who have not been persuaded of the merits of continuing republican activism: 'disillusion and apathy with the Republican project in general and its Provisional incarnation in particular became widespread among IRA members [...] Worn down in this way, many became inactive or left altogether, leaving behind a Provisional movement reduced to a pliable corps of loyal followers.'[4]

However, there is also a growing number of those who have withdrawn from the Provisionals over the course of the last twenty years who remain critically engaged, and willing to run the risk of antagonising the Provos' leadership through a sustained critique of what they perceive as the neutering of the movement's revolutionary vocation. Notwithstanding the alternatives on offer, they have argued that either there is insufficient support to sustain a renewed armed campaign, or alternatively that such a strategy has no realistic prospect of success in the short to medium term. A number of individuals and loose organisations have put forward critiques of the Provisionals and, in particular, their support for the Good Friday Agreement. For instance, the Republican Network for Unity, and Éirigí (usually translated as 'Arise'), a socialist republican grouping, have both sought to portray themselves as taking up the revolutionary mantle allegedly laid down by SF. In a number of formats (both periodical and on-line), publications such as *The Blanket* (subtitled 'a journal of protest and dissent', and associated in particular with the ex-IRA 'Blanketman' Anthony McIntyre[5]), or *Fourthwrite* (the forum of the Irish Republican Writers' group, one of whose key figures has been ex-IRA man and hunger striker, Tommy McKearney) have sought to provide a space for an eclectic band of critics of the Provisionals to debate the way forward for Irish republicanism, but also to develop a sustained critique of the leadership's attempts to control the historical narrative of the 'struggle'. Perhaps unsurprisingly, it is from within the ranks of these non-aligned ex-Provisionals that some of the most interesting and sophisticated memoir-writing has emerged in recent years. This might be termed 'intellectual dissidence', and it has exercised a growing influence in the post-1998 era, even though the leadership has often dismissed its significance, and sought to isolate its protagonists from the 'mainstream' movement.

Individual critics and members of this diversity of competing groups tend to be treated as a cohesive bloc by the print and broadcast media, and are routinely referred to as 'dissident republicans'; indeed, this has become the standard nomenclature. The use of such terminology may be arguable, given that many of those involved in the public activities of RSF or 32CSM have insisted that they are merely upholding and propagating the 'orthodox' doctrine previously espoused by the Provisionals. They also dispute that their politics involves any 'deviation' from real or true republican principles and objectives. However, the use of the term 'dissident' has come to be understood in popular parlance as encompassing those republicans who remain wedded to the military instrument. In fact, the ideological and strategic complexion of those who have parted company with the Provisionals is a good deal more convoluted than this one-dimensional account allows.[6] The study of memoir-writing by those 'dissidents' who have left the Provisionals, at various junctures over the course of the Troubles, can shed significant light upon both the overall trajectory of the movement, and the specific internal debates and disputes that have followed upon such deep-seated ideological and organisational change.

Explaining the Break: Dissent or Disavowal?

Some useful distinctions may be drawn with regard to the type of 'dissent' which can be identified amongst (ex-)Provisional memoirists. A key question here relates to the motivation behind an individual's break with the mainstream movement.

Firstly, there are those who may be interpreted as **essentialist** in their motivation. The 'dissident' may believe that they have the best interests of the movement at heart, and that they remain genuine bearers of the republican cause and identity. In such cases, the 'dissident' is likely to retain a strong commitment to either the professed goals of the republican movement (i.e. a '32-county socialist republic' or 'a united Ireland') and/or the traditional methods to achieve such goals (i.e. the utility of 'armed struggle', or a belief in the principle of 'abstentionism'). For such individuals, the primary motivation for their eventual departure from the movement (or, as they might argue, the movement's departure from them!), which was only confirmed after much soul searching and with a heavy heart, was their belief that its leadership and direction had traduced the 'authentic' movement, and there was no realistic prospect for the movement to be re-established on the 'correct' footing. There are several instances of memoir-writing that could be largely understood in such terms, and it is unsurprising that this kind of writing has been especially prevalent in the post-IRA ceasefire and peace process environment.

Indeed, after the completion of the process of weapons decommissioning, and the effective standing down of the Provisional IRA in 2005, for this kind of 'dissident' the priority often became the shaping of the historical narrative of the movement.[7] Alongside challenging the 'official memory' of the Provisionals (as formulated in Gerry Adams' memoir-writing), such 'dissidents' remain fiercely proud of their erstwhile membership of the movement, and in particular of their fallen comrades, and have used their writing to express this pride, often accompanied by a bitter regret that, in their eyes, the 'struggle' has been 'sold out'. For these memoirists, the prevailing question, in the light of their belief that the revolutionary struggle has been definitively abandoned or usurped, is 'What was it all for?' There is a plaintive, poignant tone to much of this writing: for example, Brendan Hughes talked in his interviews (published posthumously) about his personal commitment to the leadership (especially Gerry Adams), and his acute sense of betrayal, once it became clear to him that 'the revolutionary socialist direction that [...] I was fighting for has been dropped. And all Sinn Féin have done, all the IRA have done is just to become another SDLP.'[8] For Hughes, who became a key symbolic figure for many of the dissidents discussed here, there was a genuine sense that he was heartbroken at the turn of events that saw his estrangement from the Provisional movement and his erstwhile comrades. In terms of both socialist and nationalist objectives, Hughes was scathing with regard to what had been achieved through the 1998 settlement; he told Anthony McIntyre that he was demoralised and disillusioned by 'the futility of it all. From a nationalist perspective alone what we have now we could have had at any time in the last twenty-five years [...] And in the process we have lost much of our honesty, sincerity, and comradeship.'[9] However, the psychological cost of breaking with the movement would be enormous, and not all of those republicans who were profoundly unhappy with the direction being charted by the leadership were willing or able to translate this sentiment into concrete action. In other words, dissidence is often an intensely personal journey, one that is undertaken at a varying pace, and with a great deal of soul searching. In answer to a question concerning the leadership's attitude to 'democratic republicanism', Brendan Hughes replied that the response had always been 'a plea to stay within the army line. Even doing this interview with you generates a reluctance within me. The republican leadership has always exploited our loyalty.'[10]

Another variant among 'dissident' memoirs consists of a more explicitly **ideological** motivation for the break from the mainstream movement. To give one example, Tommy McKearney, whilst imprisoned in the H-Blocks of Long Kesh, was among a small group of prisoners who were opposed to what they viewed as both the increasing drift towards parliamentarianism within SF, and the abandoning of socialist/Marxist ideological positions by the leadership. After a period of uneasy co-existence, this small group (or the bulk of it) resigned from the Provisionals in 1986, and founded the League of Communist Republicans.[11] Significantly, although Hughes, Bradley and other more recent memoirists may also have an ideological rationale for their opposition to the leadership, they remained loyal and committed members during earlier waves of 'dissidence', and it was not until *after* the definitive ending of the IRA's campaign that these individuals felt able to make a stand, even if they had been out of sympathy with the Provisionals' line of march for much longer. McKearney, and others including members of RSF like Ruairí Ó Brádaigh, had had the courage of their convictions at an earlier stage. In this important sense, the *timing* of public dissidence is very significant. There are several factors inhibiting the breaking of ties with the mainstream: there are the very strong bonds of comradeship, and the profound attachment to the republican 'resistance community' that would be lost in the event of a leavetaking; second, there is the concomitant fear of ostracism and being 'cast adrift' by the erstwhile 'republican family'; and, third, there is the related fear of intimidation, threats and ultimately physical violence or expulsion, if the 'dissident' has the temerity to publicly denounce the Provisionals.

Nonetheless, despite these powerful inhibiting factors, there is sometimes a particular event or narrative that acts as a catalyst for the 'break', and which pushes the 'dissident' out into the open, despite the real risks that are involved in such a decision. For instance, for Gerry Bradley, the event that pushed him towards publishing his revealing memoir of his life as an IRA 'operator' was the revelation in 2005 that Denis Donaldson, a senior SF leader who had run the party's Stormont office, had acted as an informer within the movement for twenty years. Ordinary IRA foot-soldiers like Bradley were profoundly depressed and disoriented by the revelation (and several other prominent scandals of a similar kind):

they had been risking their lives for years, confident in the belief that the republican leadership, though they made mistakes, were immune from British influence and were directing the struggle against the British presence in Ireland with the purest of motives. By the early years of this century, no one could be sure of any of that [...] It led many IRA members to question what they had been ordered to do during the campaign, why they had been doing it and who exactly had wanted it done.[12]

Another Provisional who became a 'dissident' after a prolonged period of soul searching is Richard O'Rawe, a former IRA 'Blanketman' and public relations officer for the hunger strikers in Long Kesh/HMP Maze during 1981. In two volumes of memoir, O'Rawe has defended the incendiary claim that a small leadership group (based around Gerry Adams), unbeknownst to the IRA's formal leadership (the Army Council), deliberately prolonged the hunger strike between July and October 1981 (after the deaths of four republicans, but before six others died), despite the fact that the leadership of the prisoners believed a deal could be reached with the British authorities.[13] Ed Moloney has argued in the foreword to *Afterlives* that O'Rawe's decision came after a lengthy period of imposed silence, due to his guilt at allowing himself to acquiesce in what he knew to be a false historical narrative of the events. Interviewed by Anthony McIntyre for the Boston College archive, O'Rawe broke down, 'as if a dam had finally burst'.[14] O'Rawe was determined that he wished to publish his account of the hunger strikes and he went ahead though Moloney tried to dissuade him, suspecting correctly that he would be vilified by his former comrades for his pains. He addressed the question of his silence on this hugely controversial topic in the prologue of *Blanketmen*: 'Some may ask why I am writing about these things now? Why did it take twenty-four years for me to tell this story?' The answer is that when O'Rawe raised his concerns in private with the leadership in 1991, he was told in no uncertain terms that 'I could be shot for opening my mouth.' Revealingly, he was still reluctant 'to expose certain individuals in the leadership of the republican movement to the possibility of criticism, while other IRA Volunteers were giving their lives in the same armed struggle for which my ten dead comrades had died'.[15] Alongside the commitment to his jail comrades, O'Rawe also appeared to retain an unshakeable faith in the republican ideals which led to the sacrifice of the hunger strikers, even if he came to believe that these ideals had been besmirched in practice, due to the conduct of the Adams group at the time and subsequently.

With the ending of the armed struggle, O'Rawe was finally willing to confront the 'duplicity that has surrounded the hunger strike'.[16] However, he attempted to soften the impact of his decision to publish by insisting he bore no grudge against the republican movement, or any individual within it; if this restated commitment to the movement was designed to forestall the ostracism and character assassination that he must have suspected was likely to follow, then it was a forlorn hope. In *Afterlives*, O'Rawe also extended his critique of the Adams cabal, arguing from a more explicit ideological perspective that this leadership had offered 'little resistance' to British efforts to reinforce the 'unionist veto' through the mechanism of the peace process.[17] The complexity and ambivalence of O'Rawe's published accounts are a very revealing illustration of the personal costs involved in embarking on such a course. Many other Provisionals, or former members, were drawn into the increasingly bitter dispute between O'Rawe, and his small band of supporters (some of whom were already publicly associated with dissident views and/or organisations), and the mainstream leadership. One example will suffice: O'Rawe had shown a draft of *Blanketmen* to his cellmate during the hunger strikes, Colm Scullion, who had privately endorsed O'Rawe's version of events. However, he 'made it clear he did not want to be publicly drawn into the inevitable controversy that would result from its publication, saying he was "friends with everyone". I respected the delicacy of his position and replied that I had no intention of dragging him into the dispute against his will.'[18] This proved a naive hope on both their parts, for Scullion was visited by Brendan McFarlane and Danny Morrison on behalf of the leadership, and O'Rawe belatedly recognised that

> the pressure likely to be heaped on to him would be nearly impossible to resist, and I have little doubt that he would have been told that my account of the hunger strike was damaging to the reputation of Gerry Adams – which was true – and that, consequently, the peace process could be at risk because Adams represented the first line of defence against those republicans who, mistakenly in my view, believed a military victory over the British was achievable.[19]

Ultimately, to protect his vulnerable position, O'Rawe decided to clandestinely tape a telephone conversation with his erstwhile comrade, which could be used to substantiate his account, if Scullion was ever induced to publicly renounce O'Rawe's position. This almost came to pass in an exchange of letters in the *Irish News* in 2008, yet according to *Afterlives* O'Rawe refrained from releasing the tape; given 'what Colm and I had come through in the H-Blocks, that would have been a tragedy for us both'.[20] This episode exemplifies the existential issues at stake for republicans in choosing how to remember the contested past in Northern Ireland, and the critical significance of 'truth-telling' about that past for the contemporary republican movement and wider community.

Thirdly, a number of memoirists over the course of the period since the formation of the Provisionals may be understood as having written narratives of **disavowal**. The life-stories of these individuals revolve around their decision to join the republican movement, their experiences whilst they were members (often involving their engagement in political violence, and their arrest and imprisonment for these activities) and, ultimately, their renunciation or disavowal of these previous commitments. The regularity of this trajectory of early conversion to the cause, trial or struggle in its pursuit, and sometimes de-conversion as a result, means that these memoirs are usually bookended in terms of arrival and departure from the movement. The motivation and timing of these decisions to break from the movement is clearly crucial. This leavetaking is often experienced as a difficult and highly emotional wrench, but on occasion can also be felt as a relief. The decision to renounce the movement may be primarily the result of an explicit rejection of republican ideas and/or methods; on other occasions, the motivation for leaving can be characterised in more personal, rather than ideological, terms.

Shane Paul O'Doherty's *The Volunteer* (1993) is a good example of this type of memoir, which has often been conceived as a cautionary tale, a warning to others who might be tempted along a similar path to the author.[21] After joining the Provos as a teenager in Derry during 1970, and having participated in an intensive period of violent activities, O'Doherty turned his back upon the 'armed struggle' early on during his long period of imprisonment in English jails (which lasted from 1975 until 1989), which he served for his part in a campaign of letter bombing. He argued that whilst the Catholic nationalist community's anger that fuelled the IRA's campaign was understandable, the violent response was counter-productive and ultimately immoral, from a Christian standpoint, which he had come to embrace. O'Doherty was angered by the republican movement's refusal to publish in *Republican News* (without censorship), a letter he had written outlining his rationale for abandoning the use of violence. In early 1978, he sent the letter to his local newspaper, the *Derry Journal*, where it made the front page, and was picked up by many other media outlets. As a result, O'Doherty was ostracised by many fellow republicans, but as he tellingly pointed out in his memoir: 'those who reacted bitterly to my call for Republican engagement with the political process some years later meekly accepted the Republican Movement's decision to take part in elections to the British and Irish parliaments.'[22] O'Doherty's memoir was only written and published after his release from prison in 1989, which coincided with the start of the peace process. However, his message was not met with any more receptivity within the republican movement, thus proving the adage that in authoritarian political movements, one cannot be right against the party, even when the views expressed are subsequently embraced to some degree.

A very early instance of this kind of memoir can be seen in Maria McGuire's *To Take Arms: A Year in the IRA* (1973), in which she outlined her role as a rather unusual IRA recruit who rapidly won the confidence of senior figures on the Army Council during 1971–2. McGuire began to doubt the efficacy of the armed campaign in early 1972, and the catalyst for her decision to leave the movement, and expose its internal workings in her memoir, was the 'mindless, senseless killing' of Bloody Friday in Belfast in July 1972.[23] Although she denied that she had 'gone over to the British', and claimed to still support the aims of the republican movement, she no longer believed in the 'sterile and murderous' campaign being waged under the auspices of the leadership of Seán MacStíofáin. Her book, which she recognised would be viewed as a betrayal by many republicans, represented a sustained critique of the leadership of MacStíofáin. As M. L. R. Smith has pointed out, this account needs to be treated with caution, and the 'title itself is misleading since it is evident that McGuire never saw any combat with PIRA.'[24] McGuire's status within the movement was rather unclear, but she certainly did manage to get close to its leadership, and Dáithí O'Conaill in particular. Smith rightly argues that MacStíofáin's memoir[25], written after he also had left the movement (although he was effectively ousted by his rivals in the leadership, after he abandoned a hunger strike), is 'utterly unreflective, with no hint of any kind of introspection'.[26]

It is especially instructive to contrast these two accounts of this critical period in 1972, at the height of the Provisionals' violence, in order to understand in greater detail the balance between the fully-fledged military campaign and the political immaturity of the movement at that time. According to McGuire, O'Conaill (along with Ó Brádaigh), 'saw that ultimately the struggle would have to be translated into political terms, and that how successfully they managed to do this depended on the size of the movement they built up and the basis for unity it had'.[27] This insight foreshadows the later trajectory of Adams and the younger generation of Northern Provos, and their tentative critique of the movement's inherent military elitism. At this juncture, it was MacStíofáin and the Belfast Brigade leader, Seamus Twomey, who remained wedded to the military instrument, and its logic of 'one more push', and disdained almost any political strategy worthy of the name.

Equally, the alleged sectarian attitude towards Protestant unionists displayed by MacStíofáin also brings to the fore another key dimension in the subsequent evolution of the movement. MacStíofáin's conservative Catholicism is acknowledged by almost all commentators on the period, but McGuire's allegations went significantly further, when she recalled his comments after civilians had been killed in a car bombing in May 1972: '"What does it matter if Protestants get killed" MacStíofáin had raged. "They're all bigots, aren't they?"'[28] MacStíofáin was moved to respond directly to this accusation in the foreword to his own memoir, in which he expressly denied any sectarian motivation, either personally or with regard to the Provisional movement as a whole. According to MacStíofáin,

McGuire's invented testimony had damaged his credibility with Protestants, and that of the entire movement: 'Fact, fiction and "black" material were plausibly interwoven in the "revelations". Anyone who knew the game could see their purpose immediately. It was simply another attempt to discredit the leadership and encourage disunity in the movement.'[29] According to the biographer of Ruairí Ó Brádaigh, McGuire's allegations had long-term consequences in that 'for years, journalists and academics accepted without question her portrayal that leading Republicans, especially Seán MacStíofáin, were openly anti-Protestant.'[30] Whilst ascertaining the accuracy of these exchanges is problematic, nonetheless these testimonies can help researchers to evaluate the state of the Provisional movement at a critical juncture, in what became the bloodiest year of the Troubles. Unlike the spate of memoir-writing from within the ranks of republicanism in the post-ceasefire period after 1994, these examples were published whilst the conflict was still raging, although the personal involvement of these authors had been curtailed, whether voluntarily or not. Clearly, there are significant differences in terms of authorial motivation, and the likely reception for these sources, if they are conceived and published as specific interventions in an ongoing politico-military struggle, rather than as a contribution to what has become an historical debate surrounding the character of a conflict that is perceived as over and done. The debates and disputes at the apex of the movement in the period 1973–5 were partly inspired by differences concerning strategy and tactics, particularly with regard to the utility or otherwise of maintaining the 'armed struggle' in the post-June 1972 ceasefire era, but they were also the result of personality clashes and mutual distrust. In interviews conducted for his biography, Ó Brádaigh does confirm that there was tension between himself and Dáithí O'Conaill on one side, and MacStíofáin on the other, and that the latter did institute a 'court of inquiry' on foot of allegations that Ó Brádaigh had misappropriated some of the movement's funds.[31] So, at least some of McGuire's memoir is borne out by other protagonists in her story.

Ultimately, she recognised that she had burned her bridges with the movement; indeed, she began her memoir with the arresting sentence: 'I am, I suppose, a defector. I have left my family, my friends and the movement I believed in – the Provisional IRA.'[32] But, in contrast to Cold War defectors, McGuire argued that she had no sanctuary, and was effectively a 'stateless person'. She reiterated that even though the republican movement would undoubtedly regard her as a traitor (she claimed that MacStíofáin had publicly threatened court-martial and the possibility of 'execution'), she did not see herself as having 'gone over' or been 'turned' by the British. After a lengthy period out of the spotlight, McGuire was briefly back in the news in 2008 after it became known that she was living in Croydon, Surrey, as Maria Gatland, and had reinvented herself as a local councillor for the Conservative party.[33]

A further variant of the narrative of disavowal can be seen in the memoirs by self-confessed **informers** or agents acting on behalf of one or other branch of the state's security forces. These were often individuals who had either joined the IRA/SF with the explicit motive of undermining its activities, or who had been loyal members of the republican movement, but had for various reasons been 'turned'. An important example of this particular sub-genre is Sean O'Callaghan's *The Informer* (1998), which detailed his years as an IRA operator and leading member of SF, and his growing disillusionment with the movement.[34] O'Callaghan was born in Tralee, Co. Kerry in 1954, into a republican family; his father's family had taken the anti-Treaty side during the Irish Civil War, and the folk memory of both the War of Independence and the civil war was very strong, even two generations on. O'Callaghan had joined the Provisionals after the inter-communal violence in Northern Ireland in 1969, as a 15-year-old, and within a couple of years was effectively a full-time volunteer. He served a six-month sentence in Mountjoy jail, after explosives he had been mixing blew up at the family farm. According to his memoir, on his release O'Callaghan threw himself once more into activity for the IRA, and became 'active' in Northern Ireland. He was involved in IRA attacks in Co. Tyrone in 1974 which led to the deaths of a woman Ulster Defence Regiment (UDR) officer and an RUC Inspector.[35] He rose through the ranks and became a leading figure in the strongly republican area around Carrickmore. However, O'Callaghan increasingly questioned the nature of the Provos' campaign; in Tyrone he witnessed the deep-seated character of local sectarian hatreds at first hand: 'it was becoming clear to me that the Provisional IRA were in reality representative of the Catholic "defender" tradition […] No matter how I looked at it the reality stared me full in the face: this was a war between Catholics and Protestants, not against the British.'[36] O'Callaghan began to realise that, not hailing from Northern Ireland, he was not 'soaked in the pathological hatreds and half-truths about the "other side" […] The truth is I had come to Northern Ireland abysmally ignorant of the realities and yet prepared to kill and bomb.'[37] This excerpt gives a flavour of O'Callaghan's subsequent ideological renunciation of the Provisional movement, and explains his decision to turn informer, and work for the Irish state, in order to damage an organisation he believed was engaged in a squalid, sectarian conflict.

In 1975, when the IRA was engaged in a lengthy and debilitating ceasefire, O'Callaghan was asked to reorganise the IRA in west Fermanagh, but instead he returned to Tralee and wrote his letter of resignation:

> I knew that I had devoted five years of my life to something that was evil […] I realised that joining the Provisional IRA had been the biggest mistake of my life. One way or another the disgustingly stupid things I had been involved in would haunt me for years to come.[38]

After a spell in England, during which he had met and married his wife, O'Callaghan returned to Kerry, with the express purpose of re-joining the IRA, and attempting to subvert its activities, through working on behalf of 'Irish democracy'. In his account, the IRA's bombing of Mountbatten in 1979, and the deliberate killing of civilians that this entailed, was the final straw which determined O'Callaghan to act. He rationalised this 'frightening decision' on the basis that he needed to make amends for his earlier commitment to 'armed struggle'.[39] For the next seven years, O'Callaghan lived a double existence, and much of his memoir dealt with the tribulations of this life. He claimed to have risen to become head of the IRA's Southern Command, and a central figure in the movement (although this has been denied by republican critics). Of course, the ethical dilemmas for the state authorities in protecting the cover of agents who may be engaged in criminal activity, and for informers themselves, make this world extremely morally ambiguous. O'Callaghan's self-confessed role in the death of an alleged informer, John Corcoran, in Co. Cork in March 1985, which he subsequently withdrew in his memoir, has been the subject of intense debate.[40] What is known for certain is that O'Callaghan fled from Ireland later that year, but in 1988 handed himself into a police station in Kent, and confessed to his role in the murders of Eva Martin and D. I. Peter Flanagan in 1974, as well as numerous other charges. He was sentenced to life imprisonment, but was released on foot of royal prerogative in 1996. Subsequently, O'Callaghan played a highly public role as a media commentator on Irish republican politics, and also acted as an adviser to the Ulster Unionist leader, David Trimble.[41]

These sources are notoriously difficult for outsiders to judge, given the doubly clandestine nature of the activities recounted, and the obvious interest of the author, the state and the Provisionals in manipulating the public reception of such testimonies. The political motivation for some of these memoirs was explicit, with the aim of inflicting maximum damage upon the Provisionals, even after the author's subterfuge had been exposed and they had been withdrawn from Northern Ireland for their own protection. This was the case for Martin McGartland, Raymond Gilmour and O'Callaghan, who published their memoirs of infiltrating the IRA (on behalf of the RUC in the first two cases, and the Garda Síochána in the latter) within a couple of years of each other at the time of the Good Friday Agreement.[42] It might be argued that this particular sub-genre of memoirs are uniquely untrustworthy, and certainly some of them are sensationalist in tone, and produced by downmarket commercially driven publishers (reminiscent in this respect of the growing lists of 'true crime' exposés or first-hand accounts of British military personnel). Nevertheless, the potential for honesty and insight should not be discounted in all cases. It was perhaps instructive that the mainstream republican movement did not simply ignore this rash of works in the late 1990s, but went to considerable effort to refute the allegations of O'Callaghan and McGartland, and sought to dismiss these authors as deluded fantasists and/or mentally unstable.[43]

These categories for analysing the memoirs of 'dissidents' are not meant to be understood as rigid; indeed, the example of Eamon Collins' *Killing Rage* (1997) illustrates the extent to which these works may straddle the typology outlined above.[44] Collins joined the Provisionals in the Newry area during the winter of 1979–80, when he was in his mid-twenties, but even before this, in 1971 at the outbreak of the Troubles, as an impressionable teenager, he acknowledged that, 'Republicanism both energized and frightened me: "*Eiróimíd Arís! Tiocfaidh Ár Lá!*" "We will rise again; our day will come." But I was young, and the idea of political violence began to work its way into my mind. I had a sneaking regard for the IRA, a gut sympathy.'[45] Collins' journey towards joining the republican movement took several years, however, and although there were specific incidents that might have provided the catalyst for becoming a fully-fledged convert to political violence, he remained unconvinced for most of the 1970s. Reflecting upon this period, Collins argued that he was not persuaded by the Provisionals' analysis and rationale for the use of 'armed struggle', partly because he believed a measure of justice for Northern Ireland's Catholic population was achievable without recourse to a violent campaign. This attitude survived the murder of three 'unarmed youths' in Newry in October 1971, and even a British Army raid on the family farm, during which Collins was arrested, along with his father and brother.[46] By his account, it was the unionists' destruction of the power-sharing Executive, through the Ulster Workers' Council strike in May 1974 (with the complicity of the Westminster government, according to Collins), that sowed the seed for his reappraisal of the efficacy and potential of republican violence. However, Collins attempted to describe something of the complexity of the responses within the Catholic community to the question of the morality of such violence: he termed it a 'schizophrenic condition': 'many Catholics even today [1997] can offer varying degrees of sympathy to the IRA while honestly saying they do not support the organization if they personally do not carry out any physical acts of support.'[47] This ambivalence, allied to an unfocused and immature embrace of ultra-leftist Marxist ideology (under the tutelage of an English member of the Revolutionary Communist Group, who he had met during his time as a law student at Queen's University in Belfast), made Collins suspicious in the eyes of the local IRA commander, whom he had approached about joining the movement.

Collins gravitated towards the IRA in the late 1970s as part of a personal search for belonging, and as a result of his sympathy for the growing mass movement that was campaigning for 'political status' for republican prisoners. Support for the 'Blanketmen' in Long Kesh/HMP Maze, and the republican women incarcerated in Armagh jail, was waged by a 'broad front' of nationalists/

republicans and socialists, and organised through the Relatives Action Committees and, later, the National H-Block/Armagh Committee. Collins was impressed at the scope of this movement, and in particular the apparent willingness of the Provisionals' new leadership to embrace both a much more clearly defined socialist ideological message, and a broader strategic approach involving a new emphasis upon community mobilisation and street politics.[48] After he secured a job working as a customs officer, he was to serve a two-year 'apprenticeship', during which time he provided intelligence information to the local IRA unit, before reaching the point of no return, and effectively becoming a full-time, fully-fledged terrorist operator. His job enabled him to provide intelligence on local members of the UDR and the police, and in the early 1980s Collins built a growing reputation within the South Down/North Louth border district.

Collins' information helped to target a number of security force personnel for murder, and his book provides harrowing details of the process by which the IRA conducted its campaign. In *Killing Rage*, the mythic and supposedly heroic dimension of the 'armed struggle' to remove the British from Ireland, is exposed as a litany of 'dirty little deeds', involving betrayal, lies and a heartless extremism that Collins embraced as proof of his revolutionary zeal. His capacity to fully embrace this 'vocation' as a dedicated and ruthless 'operator' made him a prized asset of the movement. Looking back upon his IRA 'career', Collins portrayed himself as skilled and totally committed:

> I felt that I was moving towards a terrifying state of efficiency [...] I was getting better all the time. I had no illusions about the nature of my work: I never lost sight of the awfulness of what I was doing, yet I felt this savagery was the necessary price of our struggle to create a more just society.[49]

However, Collins could not remain unaffected by his immersion in the business of targeting and effectively consigning to death members of the RUC and UDR; despite his insistence that he recognised the 'awfulness' of his acts, it is difficult to read Collins' detailed descriptions of his cold, brutal approach, without reflecting upon the sordid and dehumanising character of much of the campaign of assassination. Indeed, Collins does acknowledge the brutalising effect of his commitment:

> We were involved in a war of attrition and even then I knew that my participation in that war had changed me: I knew I no longer existed as a normal human being [...] I knew that a change had taken place within me but at the time I felt I had changed *for the better*. I was becoming a true revolutionary.[50]

By suppressing any vestige of compassion for his victims, Collins believed at the time that he was shedding the bourgeois morality of his upbringing.

Largely responsible for an upsurge in IRA attacks in the Newry area during the early 1980s, Collins became a key figure in the local hierarchy, and was eventually promoted to work with the IRA's internal disciplinary unit, tasked with rooting out suspected informers. By 1984, Collins had been identified as an active and ruthless operator by the security forces; his life became highly complicated, and the pressures he had worked under began to tell on him. In his memoir, he suggested that by this time disillusionment with his life as a full-time Provo had begun to gnaw at him, but he was also determined to fight this growing sense of the futility of continuing violence. Interestingly, according to his reconstruction of events, Collins began to wrestle with his growing sense that the 'armed struggle' was leading nowhere, but he resisted the logic of this realisation, and determined to apply himself with even greater vigour to the cause in an effort to still his doubts.

From this point on, the memoir recounts a double dissidence: in the first place, Collins became a militarist critic of the increasing influence of Sinn Féin in the internal political life of the republican movement; he writes, arguably with the benefit of hindsight (given the trajectory of the movement between the mid-1980s and the IRA ceasefire of 1994), that he began to view the leadership of the movement as engaged in a long-term strategy to effectively neuter the 'cutting edge' of the IRA's violent campaign. Collins disagreed with the majority decision of the Provisionals to end abstentionism from Dáil Éireann, which had been dismissed as an illegitimate, 'partitionist Assembly' up until then. He was clear-eyed about the likely effects of this shift by the movement, in terms of the inevitable downgrading of the 'armed struggle', as the electoral fortunes of SF came to weigh more heavily than the IRA's continuing capacity to wage the 'war'. According to Collins, 'Republicans outside of Belfast had begun to suspect that had it not been for the influence of Derry republican leader Martin McGuinness, the armed struggle would have been called off long ago.'[51] And yet, he remained wedded to the movement for a further year or more, based upon his forlorn hope that the 'brutal and ruthless volunteers of South Armagh might show us the way forward by stopping the rot that had set in. But in my heart I knew this was an impossibility. I knew that the IRA's so-called "long war" was built on foundations of sand'.[52] He even met with hardliners from the South Armagh district, including the then 'quartermaster general', who sought to recruit him for a rearguard action against the Belfast leadership; Collins was asked to 'take over Newry Sinn Féin and run it as an extension of the IRA'.[53] The purpose here was to prevent the growth of SF as an autonomous institution, and its evolution as a 'normal' political party; instead, the IRA needed to reassert its control over the movement as a whole, and return SF to its 'rightful' place as a subordinate organisation. In what appears a prescient understanding of the probable future trajectory of the movement, Collins recounted an altercation he allegedly had with Gerry Adams, at the funeral of IRA Volunteer Brendan Watters (who had died in Newry when a grenade he was handling exploded prematurely in August 1984): Collins argued with SF stewards who had come down from Belfast and were trying to avoid confrontation with the RUC. This represented definitive proof for Collins that the 'war' was indeed over, as far as Adams was concerned, and he ended up accusing Adams of sounding like the 'Sticks' (the hated Official republican movement, who had called an indefinite ceasefire in May 1972). As Collins recognised, this was perhaps the greatest insult that could be levelled by one Provisional at another, and of course Adams was no ordinary member of the movement. If Collins had not completely burned his bridges at this juncture, his memoir made it plain that others believed he was no longer reliable; attending a meeting at the SF office on the Falls Road, Collins was greeted by a very hostile SF Director of Publicity, Danny Morrison, and was told by another leading Belfast figure, Tom Hartley, that he should 'reconsider [his] position within the republican movement'.[54]

Ultimately, within a few months, this is precisely what Collins did, though not in the fashion that Hartley had in mind. In the end, Collins argued that by 1985 all that held him to the movement was his 'emotional commitment to the memory of the dead hunger strikers', yet they had been expendable, as was he.[55] Eventually, after he was arrested as part of the police operation in the wake of an IRA mortar bombing of the RUC station in Newry (which had killed nine officers), Collins broke under interrogation. He recognised that once he began talking of his IRA role, and those associates and operations he knew about, he had 'crossed over into the enemy camp'. Collins argued that he had thought the RUC might release him to act as an informer, but in fact they hoped to use him as a 'supergrass' to testify against his former comrades. Although Collins agreed to this initially, after visits from his wife and brother, and intimations that if he retracted his evidence, he would be exonerated by the republican movement, he decided not to co-operate any further. He had been charged with murder, as a result of the information he had passed on. However, in his memoir, Collins described his disorientation during this period; he had stepped back from the brink by refusing to turn Queen's evidence, but he no longer felt any affinity for the republican cause, and he would be forever under suspicion from that movement. A measure of his desperation and confusion is apparent in his reflections on this period while he was on remand in Crumlin Road jail:

> although I felt shame at what I had done [collaborating with the state], I resisted [...] the urge to crawl on my knees in repentance for my sins against 'the republican family'. I knew that my breaking under

interrogation had not been merely a straightforward response to police pressure. I knew my collapse had taken place as a result of a long process of disillusionment.[56]

Collins found himself in limbo, not fully outside the republican 'family', but certainly not inside any longer.

When his case came to trial in 1987, Collins was found not guilty after the judge ruled his confessions inadmissible. Although he understood that the IRA had 'amnestied' him, nonetheless during his debriefing he continued to antagonise the IRA with his independence of thought, and he was ordered to leave the 'war zone' and live in the Republic of Ireland. He found work in Dublin as a community worker, but like many exiles, felt a strong desire to return home, particularly as his wife had continued to live in Newry. After some negotiation with the republican movement, Collins moved back to Northern Ireland, but the *quid pro quo* for this flexibility was that he effectively kept his head down, and did nothing further that would embarrass the movement. Ultimately, it was Collins' refusal to stay silent, and his decision to continue speaking out (not only did he publish his memoir and appear in a television documentary[57], but he also gave evidence against a key IRA figure in South Armagh during a libel trial), that consigned him to a violent death in January 1999.[58] It is a measure of the complexity of Collins' relationship to the republican movement that he was willing to acknowledge in *Killing Rage* that a part of him 'missed being in the IRA [...] Life outside the IRA could often feel terribly mundane'.[59] For several years after his release from prison,

> I still had ambivalent feelings towards the IRA tradition [...] I remember feeling an incredible visceral rage when the SAS shot dead three unarmed IRA members in Gibraltar in 1988 [...] emotionally I wanted to attend those funerals and – if I am honest – I wanted to see the IRA hit back.[60]

Killing Rage is difficult to read, especially in hindsight, given Collins' brutal murder, but this chronicle of a death foretold possesses a visceral quality which makes it one of the most powerful examples of dissident memoir-writing to have emerged thus far. Kevin Toolis, author of a provocative 'journey' into the heart of the IRA, recognised before the book's publication that Collins' releasing his memoir was an 'act of blind courage': 'perhaps the book and its coming impact will protect him from harm. I hope so.'[61] An anonymous neighbour of Collins, interviewed after his killing, put it slightly differently: 'I don't know if he [Collins] was more stupid than brave but he was trying to do the right thing by that book. A lot of people read it and were disgusted with the IRA. But after he wrote it, he should have stayed away.'[62] The complex political sensitivities surrounding such memoir literature may also be illustrated if we consider that the family of one of Collins' victims, Major Ivan Toombs, accused him of profiting as a result of the book, even though he apologised profusely for his part in the murder, and used his reflections upon it as a platform for a concerted assault on the IRA's whole rationale for 'armed struggle'.

These memoirs of (ex-)members of the movement can aid researchers in forming a fuller picture of the development of the Provisionals' internal political culture, and attitudes within the organisation towards 'dissent' (although some might argue for a term such as 'debate' or even 'democracy' here). In this regard, there are two competing trends discernible in the Provisionals' history (and arguably throughout the twentieth-century history of the republican movement): firstly, as a primarily clandestine and conspiratorial organisation, the movement was characterised by a military elitism which placed huge emphasis upon unity in action. This political culture stressed the necessity of a strong hierarchy of control in terms of internal discussion, with a firm commitment to discipline within the ranks, and a prevailing intellectual culture of conformity. The pressures on republican volunteers, both externally and internally, to loyally maintain this culture, and uphold the 'collective consciousness' of the republican community, were intense.[63] As Brendan Hughes acknowledged, a key factor in the repression of dissenting voices was the volunteer's sense that any dispute within the movement that was permitted to become public would only provide succour to the 'enemy'; thus, 'people stay quiet out of loyalty to the movement.'[64] Speaking publicly about the internal affairs of the movement, particularly the 'naming of names' whilst the armed struggle was ongoing, also ran the risk of undermining its capacity to act, and of jeopardising the liberty of other activists. This self-censorship was of course seized upon by the leadership, and exacerbated, so that anything other than silent acquiescence could be viewed as disloyalty. Doubts and questions were likely to be suppressed before they even appeared, thereby helping to promote the culture of unanimity. As Laurence McKeown made plain, ex-prisoners were highly suspicious of researchers seeking to probe into the movement's activities, both inside and outside the jail walls: '*because of the nature of their politics and the organisation they belong to*, any "outsider" approaching them for research purposes is first referred to the Republican Movement for clearance. Should the Movement advise against participation the research ends before it has even begun.'[65] Any decision to persist in either questioning or challenging this culture was likely to be met with hostility, ostracism, and ultimately with intimidation and the threat of violence or actual physical confrontation. In this respect, the evolution of a leadership-dominated narrative concerning contemporary political strategy, but also the movement's interpretation of its own history, should not come as a surprise.

On the other hand, there has been an important countervailing trend in the movement's internal political culture. Irish republicanism, despite (or perhaps because of) the strength of the centralising trend described in the above paragraph, has often been understood as a fissiparous movement prone to regular and debilitating splits, often based upon ideological or strategic disputes, but also as a result of clashes based upon personality or regional affiliation. Even in circumstances where the leadership has had some success in imposing central control and direction upon the movement, this has often only been temporary, before a renewed bout of disunity, accompanied on some occasions by feuding. Of course, the birth of the Provisionals occurred precisely as a consequence of such a complex combination of factors. Also, in the spontaneity of the Provisionals' early efforts to challenge the British government and its security forces, the centralised hierarchy of control implicit in the organisation's military elitism came under severe strain. As the previous chapter demonstrated, the insurrectionary, and to some extent improvised, character of the communal protest of the early 1970s also meant that the movement was 'relatively fragmented and localised' during this era.[66] As Tommy McKearney recognised, individual geographical areas developed a certain degree of autonomy in this period, responding to the conditions of the struggle 'on the ground': 'the IRA was almost like a federation of local armies.' In this interpretation, the movement's leadership could not entirely 'stifle critique', for 'debate and dissent did exist along with local initiative and responsibility.'[67]

Perhaps even more explicitly than the effects of this decentralisation, the significance attached to 'active republicanism' in the late 1970s seemed to be in tension with the notion of hierarchical control exercised from the 'top down'. McKeown's reconstruction of the experience of long-term republican prisoners in the period after the British government introduced its criminalisation policy (and removed the 'special category' or political status, in 1976), highlights the evolution of a critical revolutionary subject. Based upon the prioritisation of a collective educational programme, inspired by the radical non-hierarchical principles of theorists such as Paulo Freire, a substantial group of these prisoners developed an open and questioning approach to internal organisation and issues of discipline and dissent.[68] These important debates reflected the changing organisational culture inside the jail, where the conservative elitism associated with the leadership of David Morley was eventually defeated. However, it also helped to some extent to shape the wider culture of the movement outside the prisons. Perhaps ironically, in the light of their subsequent estrangement, two of the key 'dissenters' who pressed for a more 'open' culture, focused primarily upon political development and self-education (rather than an exclusive focus upon the rigid application of military discipline), were Brendan Hughes *and* Gerry Adams.

As they tried to respond to criminalisation, the 'Blanketmen' fostered a 'process of discussion and debate [during which] the prisoners radicalised their politics to the degree that they were often openly dismissive of orthodox republican beliefs or re-interpreted those beliefs in the light of new understandings.'[69] Although

McKeown argued that the prisoner community was characterised primarily by unity and solidarity, nonetheless he also recognised that this could, on occasion, mask underlying divisions. Generally, however, when such division threatened the basic values of unity, its effects were contained and minimised through the camp staff's commitment to an 'open democratic form of social organisation': their 'style of leadership and philosophy encouraged [...] all prisoners within the community to become involved in the decision-making and responsibility-sharing of the community.'[70] Within the 'experimental milieu' of the jail, such a vibrant culture of mutual criticism may have held sway, but 'whether this has permeated to other environments is debatable.'[71] McKeown himself acknowledged the limits of such openness outside the jail:

> the revelation of disagreement and schisms within the community of republican prisoners is something that many of them would abhor. The 'washing of dirty linen in public' is, after all, not something encouraged by any organisation and I knew that some aspects of my study would prompt opposition in some quarters.[72]

Eamon Collins also expressed an interest in examining the 'way in which prisoners' education in the H-Blocks had influenced and effected social movements on the outside.'[73] When he broached this idea for a doctoral thesis with SF, whose clearance he knew would be necessary to interview former prisoners, Tom Hartley 'shut that door in my face'.[74] It is ironic that some of the most articulate and vociferous critics of the direction of the post-1994 movement formed their views during this radical experience in the H-blocks. Men like Anthony McIntyre, Tommy McKearney, Brendan Hughes, Tommy Gorman and Richard O'Rawe have been at the forefront of recent 'dissidence', and would surely qualify as precisely the kind of self-conscious revolutionary cadre (or 'organic intellectuals', to borrow Gramsci's suggestive phrase) that the leadership purported to support.

In *Before the Dawn*, Gerry Adams made some oblique references to this tension within the cultural and organisational politics of the Provisionals, and his own ambivalent relationship to issues of 'dissent'. When he began to write his 'Brownie' columns for *Republican News* in 1975, Adams claimed he 'was very wedded to the principle that a leadership needed support, especially that of prisoners and others in positions of influence'.[75] For this reason, he was very cautious in his conversations in Long Kesh, although he felt he could be more open 'with old friends like the Dark' [Brendan Hughes]: 'it was only when I started to write that I began to be more openly critical. Even then I was always very guarded in my criticism; indeed sometimes my criticisms were so subtle that they weren't even picked up on.'[76] Unfortunately, Adams does not elaborate or provide any specific examples. He bemoaned the fact that the split from which his movement was created had 'robbed the republican struggle of many of its more political elements' (most of whom joined the Officials), and he has often been concerned in his writing to challenge a narrow conception of the movement *as* the Army, and nothing more: 'armed struggle had dominated the movement to the extent of being considered almost the only form of struggle. What I was arguing was that we must build a political practice, and that it must be open and public rather than conspiratorial.'[77] Adams is here referring to the late 1970s, an era when he was still committed to revolutionary politics, and when he was 'conspiring' with other younger, and mostly northern, members to oust the traditionalists. The crucial lesson he had taken from the experience of the 1969 split was not just the necessity for the leadership to maintain a firm grip upon the movement, and to preserve unity (or control) once it had been constructed, but also the significance of preparing the ground for change, of moving cautiously, keeping a tight rein upon the organisation's communications, both external and internal. The post-peace process 'dissidents', such as Tommy Gorman, have argued that as the Adams leadership of the Provisional movement progressively abandoned its revolutionary vocation in favour of a reformist and electoralist agenda, it became 'much more internally repressive the further it move[d] away from traditional republicanism and supposedly towards democratic values.'[78]

Chapter 4

Loyalist Paramilitarism and the Politics of Memoir-Writing

Introduction: A New Phenomenon?

As we have demonstrated in the chapters analysing memoir-writing from within the republican movement, there is a long tradition of Irish republican and nationalist writing that has conflated individual protagonists' lives with the 'story' of the nation. This personalisation of Irish republican history can be traced back at least as far as the nineteenth century, and this approach remains popular in the contemporary period. By contrast, it is difficult to discern a similar tradition within loyalist paramilitarism, at least until recently, even if republican efforts to 're-write the script' and control the narrative of the peace process have proved irksome.[1] With only a few exceptions, loyalists have seemed inarticulate and slow to react to this transparent republican strategy to control the narrative 'telling' of the conflict. Within Ulster unionism, the prevailing tradition of memoir-writing has been the ministerial memoir, firmly based upon the parliamentary arena, and mirroring the Cabinet reminiscences of Westminster politicians; Brian Faulkner's *Memoirs of a Statesman* (1977) is a classic in this sub-genre.[2] There is also a range of memoir-writing from within the wider Protestant working-class community, although these works are not always explicitly political in outlook.[3] Also, there is a fine tradition of autobiographically inspired writing for the theatre, specifically documenting the Belfast Protestant working-class experience.[4] Specifically in terms of using the loyalist paramilitary tradition as a subject for the theatre, there is also the recent work of playwright Gary Mitchell, who has vividly dramatised this enclosed world.[5] Whilst not belonging to any of the loyalist organisations, Mitchell was brought up and lived for many years in the loyalist stronghold of Rathcoole, in North Belfast. As an unemployed youth in a 'desolate claustrophobic environment'[6], dominated by the Ulster Defence Association (UDA), Mitchell has admitted that he 'wanted to join the UDA, I had a really strong desire to do it. There is a bravado associated with being in the organisation, you were tough if you got involved.'[7] The UDA was a legal organisation until 1992, although those of its members prepared to engage in terrorist violence were often recruited into the Ulster Freedom Fighters (UFF). This characteristic of the UDA placed it in a different category from the other main loyalist paramilitary group, the Ulster Volunteer Force (UVF), which had been declared illegal in the late 1960s. Mitchell was dissuaded from joining the UDA by his father, but he used his intimate understanding of the roots and culture of the UDA in places like Rathcoole as the location and subject for his dramatic works. In 2005, Mitchell's home was attacked and his car petrol bombed by loyalist paramilitaries, and he was forced to leave the estate. It was not absolutely clear why he became the target for such intimidation ('there is a feeling that certain people are jealous and feel that I am depicting them in a bad way'), but he has again used this experience as inspiration for an autobiographical play.[8]

With regard to loyalism and specifically self-writing from within the paramilitary milieu, there was until recently a paucity of material available. There have been several fictional attempts to imagine the world of the UDA and the UVF, some more successful than others; the neglected *Silver's City* by Maurice Leitch is a persuasive portrayal of an ageing loyalist leader.[9] There are several possible explanations for this relative lack of memoir-writing from within this community: sociologically, it could be argued that working-class Protestant culture in Northern Ireland and the social groups that formed the bedrock of loyalist paramilitary personnel did not set great store by literary forms of cultural presentation. In what is now considered something of a clichéd view, but one that nevertheless may contain some truth, working-class Protestant educational values placed greater emphasis upon craft, technical and scientific training than upon the arts and humanities. For loyalists, memoir-writing (and literary production more generally) was simply less likely to be considered as a vehicle for self-expression, or political articulation. This is one reason, apart from their dramatic energy, why Mitchell's plays, written from direct experience of loyalism, are so unusual. There has also been considerable debate concerning the alleged 'defeatism' and 'fatalism' within Northern Ireland's Protestant population and we can speculate that this may have inhibited the production of life-writing.[10]

Second, both unionists and loyalists felt less pressure than republicans to construct a personalised narrative of their history in which the political experiences of emblematic individuals could stand as symbols of their community's forbearance and suffering. After all, unionists had been in control of the machinery of the state through much of the twentieth century and thus had no need to develop a mythologised version of their historical fortitude. Many working-class loyalists, despite their precarious social circumstances, could also buy into this "official" history of Northern Ireland's elite. On a broader canvas, it was also the case that loyalists strongly identified with the British imperial grand narrative. Interestingly, in a study of the British military and its life-writing, it has been argued that recent memoirs about soldiering and war identify 'militarism and imperialism as central concerns of British national identity'.[11] There has been a significant growth in this type of memoir in the period since the Falklands conflict, and some of it has dealt specifically with the British Army's experience in Northern Ireland.[12] Arguably, we can also place the recent spate of memoirs by former police officers of the Royal Ulster Constabulary (RUC) in a similar sub-genre, and publishers clearly believe there is a similar market for this kind of narrative.[13] We can agree with Newsinger that these 'military memoirs are a literary form that has received little critical attention, at least in part, one suspects, because the experiences recounted are so uncongenial to most students of literary and cultural studies.'[14]

Third, as republican 'dissident' Anthony McIntyre has pointed out, 'in the world of publishing, loyalism is not the marketable commodity that has earned republicanism considerable capital in terms of public interest.'[15] In terms of 'popular' literature and journalism, in the aftermath of the Combined Loyalist Military Command's ceasefire of October 1994, some works have begun to rectify this gap: Jim Cusack and Henry McDonald have completed general histories of both the UVF and the UDA, and Peter Taylor has published a general survey of loyalist paramilitarism during the Troubles.[16] Other works by journalists such as Susan McKay and Geoffrey Beattie also include significant sections devoted to loyalist politics.[17] In academic research in the social sciences, particularly sociology and political science, the study of loyalism has made significant strides since the early 1990s in the work of Steve Bruce, Peter Shirlow, Colin Crawford, Jim McAuley, Ian Wood and others.[18] It is probably worth noting that some of this literature analyses the broader phenomenon of what might be termed 'political loyalism', and its often problematic relationship to the wider unionist family. Other works have been primarily concerned with the history of loyalist organisations within the paramilitary conflict, more narrowly understood. What is clear, however, is that recent studies of both the UVF and UDA have been preoccupied with the efforts of loyalists to adjust to an emerging post-conflict environment. The role of the Progressive Unionist Party (PUP), and the short-lived Ulster Democratic Party (UDP), have also become the subjects for academic study, although their capacity to build a sustained electoral presence has been significantly curtailed. This chapter seeks to place the study of loyalist life-writing within these broader parameters. Nonetheless, both in terms of academic and popular writing, 'the republican/loyalist imbalance shows few signs of being incrementally adjusted, loyalism [is] permanently locked in the catch up spot.'[19] Bearing in mind these potential explanations for the relative neglect of loyalist paramilitary memoir-writing, at least until recently, we turn now to an examination of contemporary writing about loyalist paramilitary actors and their political world.

A Line in the Sand? Authorial Motivation and Loyalist Paramilitary Memoir

On one level, it is not too surprising that there has been a growth in memoir-writing among loyalists in Northern Ireland. After all, memoir as a genre (and political memoir as a sub-genre) has been a publishing phenomenon in the latter part of the twentieth and the early years of the twenty-first century. Equally, there are specific causes of this increased output: as Northern Ireland moved tentatively towards a transitional, 'post-conflict' phase, some of the key protagonists of the thirty-five-year Troubles began to contemplate telling their stories to a wider public, explaining their interpretation of the conflict, its genesis and its outcome (if, indeed, the conflict could be said to be definitively over).

Since the turn of the century, several key individuals in the contemporary history of loyalism have either published autobiographical accounts or been the subject of biographies. From the ranks of the UVF, Roy Garland wrote *Gusty Spence* about one of the veteran members of the reformed organisation; as we will argue below, whilst this is clearly not a conventional memoir, there are good reasons to study this work alongside the others analysed here.[20] In a related fashion, there has been important auto/biographical work produced by and about David Ervine, a political leader and elected representative of this strand of loyalism, organised in the PUP.[21] Another interesting memoir by a former UVF man from Lurgan, Co. Armagh, Alistair Little, has received a great deal of coverage, partly as a result of his explicit embrace of a discourse based upon reconciliation, and partly due to his story having been adapted for a BBC television drama.[22] From inside the UDA, Michael Stone, the notorious Milltown cemetery loyalist terrorist, published a ghost-written memoir.[23] Another key individual in the UDA/UFF who has published a ghost-written memoir is Johnny Adair, from the Lower Shankill Road, West Belfast.[24] Chris Anderson wrote a biography (or perhaps *necrography*) of Billy Wright, the leader of the Loyalist Volunteer Force (LVF), a splinter group from the UVF.[25]

Two distinct trends can be observed in these works: on one hand, there was sometimes a sincere effort on behalf of the protagonist to draw a 'line in the sand', to move away from sterile ideological antagonism and inflexibility towards a self-critical reappraisal of previous commitments and shibboleths. On the other, the idea of a 'line in the sand' may, of course, be used in a more traditional loyalist sense also, summed up in the classic slogans of 'No Surrender!', 'What we have we hold!', and 'Not an Inch!' In the latter case, there was an effort to justify the protagonist's engagement with loyalist paramilitary violence, and to explain why such violence was considered necessary. There is probably clearer evidence of this trend in the memoirs under consideration here. Fionola Meredith, in an insightful interview with Richard English, author of a recent major academic study of the IRA based largely on interviews with republican activists, made a telling point with regard to the utility of these memoirs:

> Why then should we accept the 'authenticity' of their self-reflexive accounts as holding any more significance, insight or weight than a more 'objective' analysis? The experiential narrative offered by 'someone who's been through it' can be as duplicitous and untrustworthy as it is vivid. The truth-claim based on experience is often furthest from veracity.[26]

There may certainly be merit in this caution regarding the utility of memoir-writing, but equally the argument presented here suggests that one important way to understand the motivations and internal culture that sustained paramilitary organisations in Northern Ireland is to study the literary output of key individuals within them. Meredith went on to conclude that 'the most fundamental impulse in the stories of those who have committed politically-motivated violent atrocities will nearly always be self-justification. That's the difficulty with narrative accounts – their need for legitimacy means that the truths they offer are partial, loaded and incomplete.'[27] Again, this may well be the case for many of these publications, but there are also some that contain a genuine attempt to provide a self-critical appraisal of the past actions and affiliations of the author.

If it is the case that loyalists are keen to contest the republican version of the rights and wrongs of the Northern Ireland conflict, there may also be more prosaic (and less edifying) reasons for this recent spate of publications. Memoirs by well-known public figures, whether politicians, entertainers, sports stars, or criminal 'bosses', have all traded upon the celebrity of the individuals concerned, and can represent a significant commercial opportunity. This element of celebrity (or notoriety), allied with a widespread unease about the financial gains that erstwhile paramilitaries might make from writing sensationalist accounts of their exploits, has been the subject of lively debate in Northern Ireland. This trend towards the conflation of celebrity, violent crime and sensationalism is now well-established in mainstream British popular culture, as evidenced by the glamorisation of gangsterism in recent films and the growth in the 'true crime' genre.

In the context of Northern Ireland, it was probably inevitable, though nonetheless a matter of regret for many, that (ex-)paramilitaries would also haul themselves onto the bandwagon. A nationalist victims' group, Relatives for Justice, sought legal advice to try and prevent Michael Stone from profiting from the publication of *None Shall Divide Us*, but the Northern Ireland Office

(NIO) issued a statement indicating that the Proceeds of Crime Act 'does not cover the writing of a memoir, however profitable'.[28] In 2006, it was reported that Johnny Adair had signed up to publish his autobiography with John Blake Ltd. for a reputed advance of nearly £100,000. Adair argued that, 'when I look at my bookshelf, there are at least four books about me written by journalists. If they can make money writing about my life then why can't I do the same?' He betrayed some confusion regarding the motivation for his venture, however, stating that he wanted to 'tell it as it is, warts and all [...] I don't intend to hold anything back, and I want to expose these so-called loyalists [the UDA leadership that expelled Adair in 2002] for the gangsters, bullyboys and informers that they are.' In the same interview, he also admitted he would be taking legal advice to make sure 'I don't talk myself into any trouble when I look back at my past'.[29] John Reid (then Labour Home Secretary) announced in October 2006 that he would be seeking to introduce new legislation to prevent (ex-)criminals from indulging in this kind of profiteering. Expressing sentiments that are undoubtedly widely shared in Northern Ireland, Gail Walker excoriated Adair and others who had gone into print with their '250 pages of bold-type whitewash PR, with murder and mayhem thrown in to titillate the bloodlust of the reader.' She was disturbed by the fact that publishers liked 'to flog them as if they are contributing to the scientific knowledge of Ulster's war', but she was even more disconcerted at the 'large market for these "kill and tells" here'.[30]

Of course, emotions continue to run high in an atmosphere where ideological differences over past deeds are never far from the surface of political discourse. However, the tendency to dismiss these narratives, even though they may be on occasion untrustworthy and contemptuous of victims' sensitivities, is mistaken on at least two counts. First, the act of self-writing often tempts authors onto the paths of 'vindication, exculpation and the byways of personal interest', whether intentionally or subconsciously.[31] Whether being deliberately self-serving or manipulating the historical narrative for contemporary ideological purposes, 'the memoirist is almost invariably self-betrayed into the hands of the later historian.'[32] Second, professional political scientists or historians, accustomed to the rigorous demands of a disciplined historiography, have displayed an understandable tendency to downplay the significance of political memoir, but there is often a paucity of reliable documentary evidence with which to work. In these circumstances, reliance upon the historian's usual injunction to collect, collate and evaluate documentary material will not yield a complete picture. Indeed, it is in the nature of the Northern Ireland conflict, where a good deal of 'political' activity (particularly, but not exclusively, the use of violence for political ends) has been necessarily clandestine and conspiratorial, that much of what is now accepted by historians as 'conventional wisdom' has been gleaned from memoir and personal testimony, and the related field of oral history. For example, in possibly the most rigorous academic study of the UDA, Wood explicitly praises the biography of Adair by Lister and Jordan as 'compelling and meticulously detailed'.[33] It is therefore potentially instructive to compare this account with Adair's own presentation of his role and memories. So while these accounts must be treated with due caution, not least because they are often mutually contradictory and sometimes internally inconsistent, they ought to be recognised for their potential as a valuable resource for researchers.

A Confusion of Voices: Author and Subject in Loyalist Life-Writing

Alongside the question of the motivation behind some of the recent crop of loyalist life-writing, it is also important to consider the confused authorship of some of these works. In some cases, like the biography of Billy Wright, there is little room for doubt about the nature of the enterprise: after all, the subject of the biography could not co-operate in this project, having been killed inside the Maze jail by republican inmates in December 1997. In the introduction to their collective biography of Adair's UDA/UFF 'team' in the Lower Shankill, Lister and Jordan 'are at pains to stress that this is not an autobiography of Johnny Adair', which is a rather strange statement, given that Adair's name is not featured anywhere as an author of the book.[34] Adair himself was certainly interested in the project, but this is definitely not an authorised account of his life: 'During a lengthy interview inside Maghaberry Prison and a series of telephone conversations, Johnny Adair blew hot and cold. When the mood took him, he spoke freely and we acknowledge that contribution.'[35] However, it is clear that the authors wish to make it known that they received at least some co-operation from their subject. They lay bare Adair's instrumental approach to telling his life-story: 'In May 2003, during the first of many telephone conversations from the jail, he said he wanted to write his autobiography and offered to do this with the authors.'[36] Informed that this was not the plan of the biographers, Adair then asked for some share of the profits, if he was to co-operate further: '"What's in it for me? What am I going to get out of this?" he demanded. [...] The minute Adair realised there was no money in it for him, his interest died.'[37] At various points in the story, Lister and Jordan question the veracity of Adair's version of his life as he presented it to them. Another author who interviewed Adair on several occasions underlined the fact that he 'can be highly selective about what he wants to remember'.[38]

In Adair's own book, written with a Scottish *News of the World* journalist, he recognised that many would find it 'unpalatable' that he should have written an autobiography. Moreover, Adair acknowledged that 'there will be concerns I am exploiting the horrors of the Troubles for my own profit.'[39] Indeed, the front cover of the book, which featured a photograph of Adair in profile, holding a firearm, can surely only be interpreted as provocative and exploitative. In terms of motivation, however, Adair offered the justification that 'there have been countless versions and accounts of my life put into the public arena with no input from myself and it is time for me to tell my story.'[40] Of course, those who have read Lister and Jordan's biography, or Wood's history of the UDA, will be aware that this characterisation is questionable. One suspects that the foreword, written by a senior research fellow at the Centre for the Study of Terrorism and Political Violence (University of St Andrews), is an attempt by the publishers to provide a veneer of respectability for this venture, which was likely to be highly controversial. It may be agreed that loyalist paramilitarism went for years, 'largely unexamined, and this is why its significance continues to remain poorly understood'.[41] However, whilst 'understanding' and interpreting the backgrounds and motivations of paramilitaries may be important for a fuller picture of the conflict to emerge, this may indeed 'come with an uncomfortable price'.[42] The moral misgivings that many might harbour regarding Adair's memoir-writing do not necessarily mean that, as researchers, there is nothing to learn from a careful reading of this material.

Michael Stone's memoir is presented *as if* Stone himself had written it; his name alone appears on the cover and title page. However, in the introduction, journalist Karen McManus claims some sort of authorial status: 'to my critics, of whom I expect there will be plenty, I would say just one thing: I do not intend this book to be a glorification of the life of Michael Stone. I do not intend this book to glamorise his life as a paramilitary.'[43] It is not unusual for autobiographies to be 'ghosted' by sympathetic journalists, of course, though such works tend to have celebrities or sportspeople as their subject, or individuals not otherwise known for their literary dexterity. It is also usual for this relationship between 'author' and ghost-writer to be made plain to the reader. As Malachi O'Doherty shrewdly recognised, 'this is not a psychological portrait of a killer, but it is the raw material from which such a book might be written. Everywhere there are stories which an astute reader will understand better than the writer and his assistant have done.'[44] Both Stone and Adair claim that one of the purposes in their decision to write memoirs was to avoid any attempts to drag Northern Ireland back towards renewed conflict. However, as we shall see, such sentiments were expressed in a highly ambivalent fashion, and we can speculate concerning the role of their respective ghost-writers and publishers, who must have recognised the likely storm of criticism that such memoirs would provoke.

In his biography of Gusty Spence, Roy Garland is both personally and politically close to his subject, and much of the material in the book consists of edited transcripts of the men's 'conversations', a word he uses advisedly, arguing that '"interview" seems much too formal a description of our many discussions.'[45] The copious use of this first-person testimony, and the relative lack of interpretive text from Garland, means that the reader is constantly encouraged to read this book as if Spence himself were the author. Garland's obvious admiration for his subject does not prevent him from stating that 'in writing this book it has not been my intention to glamourise or lionise Gusty Spence, nor would he want this', and it is certainly no hagiography.[46] A key interviewee for Garland was the leading PUP figure David Ervine, the subject of Henry Sinnerton's biography, which adopts a similar approach, and is also based upon the active collaboration of the subject. However, it could be that greater critical distance between biographer and subject would ultimately have left less room for ambiguity concerning who was really directing and narrating the project. As far as Alistair Little was concerned, whilst his collaboration with Ruth Scott contained none of the sensationalism apparent in the books by Adair/McKendry or Stone/McManus, nonetheless it is not always clear how the 'storytelling journey' (that Scott describes it as) was being directed, or ultimately who decided upon its parameters.[47] However, there is certainly less room for ambivalence concerning the overarching purpose of Little/ Scott, which is based upon their professional involvement with peace-building. In the case of Stone, Adair and Spence, the authentic 'voice' of the subject has clearly been mediated or filtered by a journalist/biographer. What is more difficult to discern is the precise nature of the relationship between mediator and subject. Who is really in control of the structure and content of the narrative? Who speaks through whom? Paradoxically, it does seem as though Spence and Ervine might enjoy a greater degree of influence over the narrative structure of their 'biographies' than Stone or Adair do over their own memoirs.

An Enclosed World? Localism and Loyalist Memoir-Writing

A key criterion when judging the historical utility of these memoirs is the authors' willingness or capacity to place their individual experiences within a broader *political* framework. However much controversy they have generated, and however disputed their accounts of life within the loyalist paramilitary milieu, they do differ significantly in their attitude to this wider context. Ultimately, some of these memoirs are of limited interest to the contemporary political historian in that they are primarily concerned with the minutiae of paramilitary activities and personalities, engagements with the 'enemy' and so forth. This may well be the result of a deliberate authorial or publishing decision to highlight these aspects, often with an eye on sales and the sensationalist appetites of populist audiences, or it may be that these 'foot-soldiers' have a relative lack of concern, knowledge or even understanding of the broader framework within which their particular dramas were played out. These works are useful nonetheless in pointing up the diverse experiences of the 'different "worlds"' that exist in Northern Ireland in relation to the Troubles.[48]

For instance, some of the works studied here show how defiantly parochial the experience and interests of many loyalist paramilitaries were: Johnny Adair was relatively unconcerned with the wider political context within which he directed the activities of the UDA's Lower Shankill C Company. He often seems to have been exasperated with the internal political compromises required in a relatively loose organisational structure such as the one utilised by the UDA and, in discussions with 'brigadiers' from other areas in the province, Adair showed little patience or desire to contemplate pressures that were not central to the experience of the Shankill loyalist community. Indeed, he was eventually ousted from the UDA in late 2002, partly at least as a result of his alleged flouting of the UDA's Inner Council, which had sought to end a damaging feud with the UVF over the previous year.[49] Adair had formed close relations with some of the LVF leaders, and this effort to construct a new alliance and power base had angered both the UVF in Belfast, and the UDA's other brigadiers. In the preface to his memoir, Adair claimed that 'despite being forced from my home, and being betrayed by people I would have died for, I have not sought to settle scores in these pages.'[50] In fact, much of the latter part of his book is devoted to his view of the feud, and his bitterness at being forced into 'exile' by the UDA leadership. Adair seemed uninterested and even bored by broader political discussion and rarely intervened in meetings, such as the one held with Secretary of State, Mo Mowlam in the Maze in January 1998 (soon after the killing of LVF leader Billy Wright); according to Wood, Adair 'was out of his depth in any political dialogue', and in any event was already in contact with the LVF outside the jail.[51] Predictably, Adair's own version is somewhat different: he does not report the meeting in any detail, but he does record that 'Dr Mowlam asked me directly what would happen if the Provos killed someone close to me. I answered by saying I hoped that day wouldn't come.'[52] He was streetwise enough to understand that after the renewal of the IRA ceasefire in 1997, resuming the simplistic, but powerful, militaristic campaign of the early 1990s was not a realistic option for loyalists; but, building a genuine non-violent *political* career was not something that appealed to Adair in the new dispensation. Indeed, his 'interest in political analysis, from the UDA or any other source, was minimal'.[53]

Unlike some of those who had served lengthy jail terms for UVF activities, and who had come under the influence of Gusty Spence (for example, David Ervine, Martin Snodden[54] and Billy Hutchinson[55] of the PUP), Adair's spurious claim to be keen on constructing such a political route, based around his close relationship to John White[56], was proved groundless by the subsequent ignominious collapse of the C Company 'empire'. He simply did not have the skills or aptitude for such a transformation. Whilst Adair was a charismatic leader of his immediate 'team' within the UDA, he was never wholly trusted outside his confined, claustrophobic geographical area and he could not articulate a mobilising political vision along the lines of some other leading figures from the organisation's recent past, such as John McMichael[57] or Ray Smallwoods.[58] Other than 'fighting fire with fire' and 'taking the war' to the republican movement and the community from which it drew its support and sympathy, Adair's political strategy was almost entirely undeveloped. In some ways, as a microcosm of the brutalisation visited by the Troubles upon the Shankill, and the political-cultural vacuum at the centre of loyalist West Belfast by the 1990s, Adair and C Company could be said to authentically represent or symbolise the impoverished *political culture* of this area.

Yet, for other loyalists, sometimes of a different political generation, similar objective social circumstances could certainly produce highly divergent political trajectories; this is most obvious in the highly localistic sectarian patchwork of Belfast.[59] The position of loyalist paramilitaries in South or East Belfast, where David Ervine and Michael Stone became active, was rather different from that of loyalists in the west or north of the city and different again from the Portadown experience of Billy Wright or the Lurgan experience of Alistair Little. Crudely put, loyalists were in the overwhelming majority in East Belfast, and their position was relatively secure, whereas in West and North Belfast the perception that hostile enemy forces were just around the corner (on occasion, literally) produced a highly unstable and fearful mentality, both the fabled 'siege mentality', but also, as has been argued, a 'self-besieging' posture.[60] The socio-economic deprivation endured in working-class loyalist districts of the city in the earlier years of the twentieth century is vividly recalled in the testimony of Gusty Spence. For Johnny Adair and Michael Stone, social conditions were somewhat less deprived by the 1960s, but the labourist ideological impulses (exemplified in the mid-century evolution of the Northern Ireland Labour Party) of the earlier generation were in steep decline by the mid-1970s.[61] Ervine and others in the PUP would try to reinvigorate this tradition as progressive loyalism in the 1990s, but with little obvious electoral success and to the scorn of loyalists like Adair. The latter's early ideological influences had come from a very different source: the neo-fascism and violent rhetoric of the late 1970s and early 1980s skinhead movement. Adair was heavily involved in the National Front in Belfast at this time, and travelled to London to follow gigs by skinhead bands; he was 'infatuated with the whole movement', and was arrested after fighting with anti-fascists in Camberwell.[62]

Loyalists, Life-Writing and Motivation: Exploitation or Reconciliation?

The most astonishing example of the same social circumstances producing very different political beliefs is illustrated by Spence who, together with his brother, Ned/Eddie, was raised in the hard conditions of the Hammer district of the

Lower Shankill during the 1930s. Ned broke with Orangeism, became a socialist and trade unionist, then a member of the Communist Party and in the late 1960s joined the Northern Ireland Civil Rights Association. Meanwhile, Gusty served in the British Army in Cyprus and on his return to Belfast joined the reborn UVF and was convicted of the 1966 murder of a Catholic barman, Peter Ward. He served almost nineteen years for the crime, before his release in 1984. Spence wrote privately to his brother:

> As you know I have very much changed – not because of what prison has done to me, but because of what I have done for myself. If I had to serve a lifetime in dungeons like these, I wanted to know for what reason, and I searched for the truth […] I feel deeply embarrassed when I think of my former 'truths' which when investigated did not stand up to scrutiny or fact.[63]

The localism of Spence's experience was extreme and it is clear that his remarkable approach to his long years in prison and the autodidactic education he gained there helped him to transcend his enclosed world and draw broader lessons for his own ideological beliefs, the future of the UVF and loyalist politics generally.

Spence's influence on the approach of, particularly, young UVF prisoners who were jailed in large numbers during the early and mid-1970s, is often evident in these memoirs. David Ervine recalled that Spence challenged loyalists to think about what sort of constitutional and political settlement might be feasible, to consider the merits of power-sharing with nationalists, and to think *politically* about their personal and collective futures, rather than simply in terms of 'returning the serve' (i.e. responding with equal ferocity to the IRA's violence). Ervine argued that Spence 'was way ahead of the game, and was almost a devil's advocate. He was constantly facing us with theories that were weird.'[64] Spence had been the main instigator of a Camp Council in Long Kesh bringing together all of the paramilitary factions, republican and loyalist. Ostensibly, the function of this council was to pressurise the prison authorities to improve conditions, but in fact Spence saw the desirability of dialogue across the sectarian divide for its own sake, which would lead to a better mutual understanding of what was motivating the diverse groups, and ultimately, he hoped to export this model to the outside. Spence was viewed as a 'provocateur', constantly asking simple, but fundamental, questions about the loyalist cause; his influence upon a generation of key UVF personnel ('the class of '75') helped to develop the UVF (and later the PUP) into a 'more sophisticated and settled' organisation. The clear implication of Ervine's comment is that, by comparison, the UDA tradition was less politically astute.[65]

Other loyalist prisoners appeared to make much less of their prison experiences.

There are a number of tensions, if not downright contradictions, in Michael Stone's account of his motivation for publishing his memoir. In the foreword he offered an apology to the families of those he killed, but immediately nullified this by stating: 'I regret that I had to kill [...]. I committed crimes as an Ulsterman and a British citizen and that was regrettable but unavoidable.'[66] Stone's confused position with respect to his violent past is also captured in an earlier interview for the UDA magazine, *Ulster*, in which he argued: 'as for remorse with regard to the deaths of the three people killed at the terrorist funeral in Milltown cemetery, remorse to an active loyalist volunteer is a luxury which one regrettably has to forego.'[67] The sincerity of these expressions of regret was further undermined by the decision (it was unclear whether this was Stone's or the publisher's) to include in the book the celebratory 'Ballad of Michael Stone', which refers to those killed at Milltown as 'rebel scum'.[68] The tone of Stone's writing was that of a veteran, though he was only fifty at the time of publication. He suggested that he had matured sufficiently to understand what had motivated his enemies, but his subsequent attack at Stormont in 2006 (which he attempted to pass off as 'performance art') appeared to give the lie to this claim.[69] In an illustration of the dangers of taking ex-paramilitaries' apologies at face value, after his release Stone was involved in 2006 in a controversial BBC programme, *Facing the Truth*, in which Archbishop Desmond Tutu brought together ex-perpetrators of violence in Northern Ireland and relatives of victims.

But what was most instructive about Stone's reflection on his prison experiences is how little he appears to have connected with the political developments that were taking place during the 1990s. This stands in stark contrast to many of the ex-UVF memoirists whose emphasis upon the political lessons to be drawn from their experiences was uppermost in their thoughts. The emphasis upon self-discipline and self-improvement in the prison regime set up by Gusty Spence for UVF inmates in the 1970s and 1980s provides a very different picture from that painted by Adair and Stone for a later period. Dillon has argued that the solitariness of loyalist paramilitary prisoners' experience could lead some individuals to embrace religion and adopt born-again fundamentalist Christian tenets, and Billy Wright arguably provided one example of this phenomenon.[70] For Adair, his periods behind bars from 1995 until 1999 (and subsequently) seemed to provide the opportunity to plot and embark on personalised rivalries and vendettas (not least with his erstwhile 'hero', Stone). This dispute was not political in origin or content, but is better understood as emanating from internecine power struggles, petty jealousies and a competitive urge to be viewed as the most 'notorious' of the loyalist icons.[71] Both Stone and Adair often appeared more willing in their reminiscences to discuss failed 'spectaculars', or 'operations' that were planned against high-profile targets (such as Irish PM Charles Haughey or RUC Chief Constable John Hermon), but did not come to fruition, rather than the mundane but indiscriminate and brutal sectarian killing campaign against ordinary Catholic civilians.

There is also a recurring theme in these loyalist memoirs, by those belonging to the UVF and UDA traditions, which seeks to place the individual's previous commitment to paramilitarism and the use of violence in a broader societal context. This might be understood as an effort to evade personal responsibility for violent actions in some cases, but it can also represent a genuine attempt to understand the social and political pressures that helped shape the choices made by these protagonists. Alistair Little, writing from the contemporary perspective of his strong commitment to non-violence, was nonetheless at pains to point out that his purpose in writing his memoir was not to help the reader understand the conflict in greater depth, but instead to 'shed light on what turns an ordinary boy, growing up in a loving family anywhere, into a man of violence, and then what helps him turn his back on bloodshed'.[72] Little's argument was that no individual is born as a 'terrorist', but they are shaped by particular, extreme circumstances:

> unless we recognise the humanity in the one we have labelled as inhumane, we'll never address our own capacity for inhumanity. My own story shows how people are deluding themselves if they think their own lack of violent action, or indeed of any action, in a time of conflict exempts them from the responsibility for the violence within their community and beyond.[73]

Whilst there may be some strength in this argument, there is a clear danger that it could be utilised to pretend that all within a conflict-ridden society bear the *same* degree of moral or political responsibility for violence, which surely is unsustainable. The corollary is that it could also be used by some protagonists to argue that everyone in the society has also shared in an *equality of victimhood*, which is also a dangerous notion, although it has obvious appeal to ex-paramilitaries. Martin Snodden argued that 'my story began even before I was born. I inherited the conflict that had been erupting periodically in N. Ireland ever since 1922. It was in the sixties when I was a teenage boy that the conflict was visited on me in the area where I lived.'[74] In this respect, UDA figures like Adair put forward very similar self-exculpatory reasoning:

> my family had no history of involvement with paramilitaries and there was certainly nothing there that hinted at the path I would later take. I firmly believe that if I had grown up anywhere but west Belfast I wouldn't have got drawn into the Troubles and spent so many years behind bars, let alone become the leader of the UDA [...] It was what I was born into and what I had to accept.[75]

There is perhaps something of a contrast in the family backgrounds of these loyalist memoirists, who appear rarely to have grown up in highly politicised or committed loyalist households, and the experience of many republicans, such as Gerry Adams, Gerry Bradley or Brendan Hughes (see Chapter 2). Alistair Little expressly argued that there was no explanation for his subsequent embrace of violence in a dysfunctional upbringing. Indeed, 'blaming the family can be a way of protecting ourselves from the real truth about what can propel a person into violence.'[76] Johnny Adair was also keen to defend his parents from any responsibility for his involvement: 'I tried to keep my parents from knowing more than they needed to. The fact that I'd ended up in prison was nothing to do with them at all.'[77] It is interesting that Little is anxious, in his memoir, to avoid causing further pain to his family, or putting them in harm's way, and this appeared to be of greater import to him than the pain carried by his victim's family. Although both Little and Adair grew up in the sectarian cockpits of Lurgan and west Belfast, both rarely met with Catholics of their own age, except in street confrontations. Early teenage experience of rioting soon became translated into more meaningful contact with loyalist organisations. At that stage, it was probably more a matter of geographical accident, rather than political ideas, that determined which of the various groups an individual joined.

The memoirs suggest that, in these formative years, these future paramilitaries often held contradictory attitudes towards the police and the British Army. On one hand, there was an inherent sympathy for the British soldiers, at least at the start of the conflict, who loyalists understood were primarily on the streets to uphold the constitution, and save Northern Ireland from republican subversion. Both Adair and Little reported that they were keen to join the state's security forces, reflecting their willingness to contemplate a lawful reaction to the republican threat.[78] On the other hand, increasing anger was directed at both the RUC and the army, particularly when there were raids and searches in loyalist districts: 'when any RUC or UDR men were shot dead, my friends and I mourned and promised revenge. Such men were our neighbours and sometimes our friends, but they were also the upholders of the law which we were increasingly breaking.'[79] Little's hatred for the *British* Army only intensified after his arrest, and rough physical treatment during questioning, and from this point on he was firmly set upon the path to joining the Mid-Ulster Battalion of the UVF. However, the tone of Little's reflections became very different from either Adair's or Stone's when he considered with hindsight his role in the use of violence. He argued that it took him several years 'before I'd fully own the tragedy of it all', and the 'legacy of darkness for me from which I think I will never be free'.[80] It is difficult to imagine a similar sentiment being expressed by Stone or Adair.

Conclusion

Ultimately, this survey of recent loyalist memoir-writing tends to confirm an emerging academic consensus with regard to some core distinctions to be drawn between the trajectory of many leading figures in the UVF/PUP, on one hand, and those within the UDA/UDP tradition on the other. Whether these works are characterised by a politically conscious and, at least partial, self-criticism (as in the cases of Spence, Little and Ervine), or whether they are apparently motivated primarily by commercial and parochial interests (as in the cases of Stone and Adair), all of them can shed light upon the multiple loyalist narratives of the Northern Ireland conflict, even where it is the 'gaps' in the stories that appear most telling. Of course, researchers (especially from outside Northern Ireland itself) may be expected to take a more detached attitude towards these works than those who have lived day-to-day with some of the consequences of paramilitary violence, particularly the direct victims/survivors of some of the protagonists considered here. Still, this chapter has argued that political memoir by prominent or (in)famous actors in the Troubles can provide a symbolic and collective aspect to a necessary process of addressing, if not 'coming to terms', with the past in Northern Ireland. However complex or even contradictory some of the results, a fuller, more rounded understanding of what motivated these actors is only one necessary condition for edging towards a public consensus concerning the rights and wrongs inflicted and suffered by all parties to the civil strife. It will almost certainly be impossible to find agreement about the essential *character* of the Northern Ireland conflict, its causes and even its outcome. For all their many problematic elements, these works can be used to contribute to this very necessary debate about the past.

Chapter 5

Memoir-Writing and Moderation?
Ulster Unionists Face the Troubles

Introduction

Much of the memoir-writing devoted to political lives to emerge from Northern Ireland over the course of the last forty years has been undertaken by paramilitaries, or those previously affiliated to such organisations. There have been contributions written by unionist and nationalist politicians, but these have often been overshadowed somewhat, in terms of their popular reception and impact, by the more sensational accounts of the violent conflict. This chapter concentrates in particular upon the memoir-writing of mainstream, 'constitutional' politicians, largely from the Ulster Unionist Party (UUP). It may be noteworthy that few memoirs have, to date, been published by leading members of the Democratic Unionist Party (DUP), and the same may be said for other, smaller parties operating in Northern Irish political life.[1]

Of course, a key distinction between these political memoirs and those published in, for example, Great Britain in the same period, is that between the prorogation of the Stormont parliament in 1972 and the restoration of devolved power-sharing government in the wake of the inter-party agreement of 1998, locally elected politicians in Northern Ireland only very rarely held ministerial office. As a direct consequence, although there have been several conventional ministerial memoirs associated with the Stormont era (such as those of former UUP Prime Ministers, Terence O'Neill and Brian Faulkner), the scant opportunities for Northern Irish politicians to exercise authentic legislative or Executive policy functions after 1972 meant that the scope for publishing the 'usual' form of political memoir was curtailed. The staple features of British political memoirs, concerning the process of making and implementing decisions in government, are largely absent from the Northern Irish memoirs of the Troubles era. There were, of course, periodic elections to a range of assemblies (including the Constitutional Convention of 1975 and the Northern Ireland Assembly from 1982 to 1986), which provided some of these memoirists with material. Some politicians from the UUP and SDLP were also elected as MPs in Westminster, but their influence was generally limited. The exception to this rule came during the short-lived power-sharing Executive from January until May 1974, and Chapter 7 will devote considerable attention to a case-study of memoir-writing by some of the crucial protagonists during this highly significant interlude. Generally, therefore, most of the memoirs studied in this chapter are characterised by the frustrations attendant on this twilight world, in which individuals may have had bright ideas and ambitious proposals, but were left in a political limbo, not in government, and not even in opposition (in John Hume's famous quip).

However, there were also frustrations of a more telling kind: the persistence of violent conflict, and the depressing cycle of regular atrocity followed by retaliation by one or other of the armed groups, induced a note of pathos into many of these reminiscences. Joseph O'Neill has described Ireland in an earlier era as a country 'saturated from top to bottom with deadly narratives' and Northern Ireland during the Troubles may be understood in similar terms.[2] Challenging the widespread belief in such narratives was dangerous work, and many of these memoirists incurred threats, intimidation and worse for their stance in opposing those who offered only violent solutions to Northern Ireland's apparently intractable problems. 'Moderate' or 'constitutional' politicians who eschewed the certainties and superficial attractions of paramilitary 'solutions' to the Northern Ireland problem, but were nonetheless confronted by ongoing brutal violence emanating from both communities, found their influence limited and their voices often ignored. In some senses, the stalemate for much of this period granted these memoirists the freedom to concentrate upon 'what might have been' rather than the minutiae of 'who said what, to whom, and when'. The absence of socio-economic policy debate and parliamentary events to rationalise, explain and order into a coherent narrative often left something of a lacuna. This gap could be filled with the author's own imaginative schemes for overcoming conflict, but could also be borne out in a sense of futility or inadequacy. Those who have published memoirs tend to be haunted by their inability to overcome or curtail the violence (at least until the ceasefires of the mid-1990s). This can produce a valedictory tone, but also some interesting self-criticism, the authors asking difficult questions of themselves and other 'moderates' who were, for so long, unable to agree a more peaceful way forward.

During the period of 'direct rule', the British government placed a great deal of emphasis upon locating and broadening the fabled 'middle ground' of moderates in Northern Ireland. To put it mildly, this search proved elusive. One of the hard questions which a study of memoir-writing by these moderate forces can attempt to answer is why many of those who could appreciate that violence was, literally, a dead-end, and who could sketch the fundamental elements of a power-sharing settlement, nevertheless were unable to construct the anti-sectarian politics and trust necessary to forge a lasting cross-community agreement. Ultimately, then, these memoirs are stories of failure, at least from the 1960s until the 1990s, and yet they offer tantalising glimpses of 'what might have been', had progress towards power-sharing devolved government not been stymied so regularly. The chapter examines unionist memoir-writing, focused upon the 1960s and 1970s, with particular emphasis upon Terence O'Neill and Brian Faulkner, two of the critical figures of this era. The next chapter analyses the memoirs of leading SDLP politicians, such as Austin Currie and Paddy Devlin. Finally, the highly significant experience of the power-sharing Executive of 1974, its negotiation and rapid collapse, will provide a focused case-study of the way in which memoirs can be utilised to study a very specific set of events.

Unionists and Reform: O'Neill and Narratives of Frustration

Terence O'Neill, who had been elevated to the House of Lords (as Lord O'Neill of the Maine) after his resignation as Prime Minister of Northern Ireland in April 1969, published his autobiography in 1972. It dealt largely with his time in office as PM, and the tone of his reflections can be gauged in a comment he made in the introduction: his 'overwhelming sentiment is one of regret', that as UUP leader and PM he had not been capable of 'breaking the bonds of ancient hatreds', as he memorably put it.[3] At the outset of the memoir, O'Neill bemoaned the failure of his administration to successfully carry through the much-needed and long-overdue reforms to the Stormont system of government, as well as the system of local government, which had also been the cause of much disquiet due to allegations of gerrymandering and discrimination against the Catholic nationalist minority population, particularly in terms of housing and employment. He argued that he had decided to wait some time to publish his memoirs (or his 'small scribble' as he self-deprecatingly referred to it), in order to write from a 'more detached angle'. However, by the standards of some memoirists of the Troubles, O'Neill's three-year hiatus after he stepped down, before publication of his autobiography, was hardly a case of prevarication. Also in the introduction, he established the core of the difficulties that faced him and which he subsequently explored in depth in the rest of the book. Essentially, the fundamental problem, in his estimation, was that in seriously trying to tackle the 'attendant evils' that had been bred by one-party rule under the Stormont system, it was almost inevitable that his administration would face concerted resistance from other unionists, in a political environment where any reform could be characterised by some as treachery. O'Neill's narrative, therefore, is driven by a powerful sense of a failed mission.

O'Neill's patrician background, and his education at Eton, placed him in a position from the outset which meant many unionists feared that he was not as implacably committed to the visceral defence of the Union as they were. Indeed, he stated that he felt little affinity for the rhetoric of the first PM of Northern Ireland (James Craig, later Lord Craigavon, PM 1921–40); this was an oratory that was 'alien to all my progressive policies'.[4] When O'Neill won the UUP nomination for the Bannside seat at Stormont in 1946, it seemed a natural progression; he took up a seat as a family duty, reprising the role played by both his father and uncle. His election was unopposed, and this was the norm over the course of the next twenty years. A number of other unionist memoirs make similar points with regard to the 'amateurism' associated with the process of UUP nomination for the Stormont parliament.[5] In such circumstances, it was hardly surprising, therefore, that the Stormont parliament was not characterised by a great deal of dynamism, on either the government or opposition (Nationalist Party) benches. As O'Neill's Private Secretary and chief speechwriter during his tenure as PM (1963–9) put it: 'the Unionist benches were too largely made up of small men, whose small talents and small experience exactly matched their narrow sympathies.'[6] O'Neill won rapid promotion to the Cabinet, and served as Home Affairs Minister, and then Finance Minister for seven years, before his elevation to PM after the eventual resignation of Lord Brookeborough. He 'seemed the natural successor', although O'Neill himself noted that the lack of real consultation within the UUP stored up future problems.[7] O'Neill stressed in his memoir the critical necessity, as he saw it when he became PM and continued to see it over the coming decade, of the Stormont government and wider political system in Northern Ireland maintaining good, co-operative relationships with the Westminster administration. An imperative of policy should be not to alienate British opinion, whether at the elite or popular level. This was a lesson that subsequent unionist leaders did not always take to heart. O'Neill bemoaned the prevailing attitude of many unionists towards Great Britain later on: '"Keep out of our [Northern Ireland's] affairs and give us some more money!"' On the other hand, it was not always an easy task to explain the mentality of Ulster unionism to the English political elite: O'Neill recounted a discussion with British PM, Alec Douglas-Home, and his attempt to elucidate the attraction of 'No Surrender!' unionism to many of his co-religionists. The resulting incomprehension perfectly illustrated the 'gulf between the average British person and the average [Protestant] Ulsterman'.[8]

A further instance of the rueful register of much of O'Neill's reminiscence turned upon his argument that Brookeborough, with his much deeper roots in Orangeism than O'Neill himself, had missed the myriad opportunities to persuade his fellow unionists of the necessity of reform. Instead, O'Neill felt that the attempt to maintain an 'impossible position of Protestant ascendancy' set back the prospects for real change even after 1964, when he was committed to bold policy initiatives (such as inviting the Irish Taoiseach, Sean Lemass to

Belfast in 1965).[9] At the Stormont election in 1965, it appeared as if O'Neill's comfortable victory augured well, based as it was on a manifesto with, for the first time, 'no sectarian overtones or undertones'. However, another familiar theme was developed by O'Neill, with respect to his pessimistic prognosis for the fiftieth anniversary commemorations of the Battle of the Somme and the Easter Rising, crucial to unionists and republicans respectively. As Bloomfield described the government's position,

> they could see in all of this great potential for mischief and disorder. At best, efforts to encourage the communities to turn away from a divisive past and face a shared future could be damaged or delayed; at worst, ancient animosities would resurface and the hands of the extremists and ultras would be greatly reinforced.[10]

O'Neill had hoped some prominent Catholics in Northern Ireland might renounce the Easter Rising commemoration, but he was to be disappointed. Over the next two years, O'Neill's room for manoeuvre gradually narrowed as the expectations and demands of the Catholic nationalist minority grew, and at the same time the unionist and loyalist critics of the government were further emboldened. The reforms in socio-economic policy and local government reorganisation were viewed as too little, too late by the incipient civil rights movement, but equally for unionists like Harry West (Minister for Agriculture) they went too far, and too fast.

From almost the first manifestation of public disorder on the streets in October 1968 (although critics cited police over-reaction as the key cause of disorder), O'Neill's pessimism was to the fore. Even though his goal to improve inter-community relations was 'lying in pieces in the gutter', and he felt tempted to resign, he nevertheless committed himself to soldier on, in a spirit of *noblesse oblige*.[11] As his private secretary noted, O'Neill was in the habit of writing him an end-of-year missive which invariably predicted dire fortunes for the coming year. In 1968, the roof did come crashing in; as Bloomfield reflected in his own memoir, written with the benefit of twenty-five years' hindsight,

> in retrospect, too few of the changes implied in O'Neill's rhetoric (for much of which I shared responsibility) had been carried out in practice. The cabinet was not a collection of convinced reformers, and the metropolitan manners of O'Neill better commended him to leader writers in *The Times* than to the party faithful in Portadown or Enniskillen.[12]

Ultimately, although O'Neill's 'five-point plan' to usher in meaningful reform was greeted with considerable support from liberal unionists in November 1968, unfortunately more malevolent forces had been unleashed in both communities, and the 'sectarian genie' was clearly out of the bottle. Both O'Neill and Bloomfield share the appraisal in their memoirs, that had such measures as fair housing allocation and an end to gerrymandering in local government (especially in Derry) occurred at an earlier juncture, then it might have been feasible to avoid the ever-growing communal polarisation. The five points would have 'made a major impact if proffered at an earlier stage as an act of generosity rather than as an apparent response to irresistible pressure [from London]'.[13] Once again, with a fatalistic air, O'Neill speculated in his memoir whether those within his own party (such as Minister of Home Affairs, Bill Craig) who had so strenuously opposed the 'timid reforms' of the five-point plan, would have reacted with such scorn if they had realised the extent of Westminster's subsequent 'interference' during the next year, and beyond.[14]

As O'Neill's position became more and more attenuated, his memoir made clear his deep-rooted sense of vulnerability. He felt himself under concerted attack from two prominent Cabinet Ministers, and aspiring PMs: Bill Craig (described by O'Neill as a 'narrow-minded sectarian') and Brian Faulkner (who was, by contrast, 'able and dedicated'). In December 1968, squeezed both from within the UUP and from without (as pressure grew from both the civil rights movement and the London government), O'Neill made perhaps his most celebrated appeal, known as the 'crossroads' speech, broadcast live on television.[15] He attempted to appeal directly to the Northern Irish populace, arguing that the majority of law-abiding citizens needed to raise their voices in favour of his reform programme. He also directly addressed the civil rights movement, appealing for time to permit the reforms to bed in, and for a reduction in tension through a moratorium on street protest and demonstrations. And, finally, he also sought to tackle his internal, UUP audience, as well as other non-aligned unionists, many of whom were hostile to his line of march. According to Mulholland, 'this speech is remembered as a statesmanlike appeal to warring communities, indeed as virtually the final appeal to sanity before the descent into chaos. Looked at in context, however, it was apparent that the broadcast was a much more party political, indeed factional, tactic.'[16] Whatever the nuances of O'Neill's intentions, there was a positive response from many in what might be termed the *Belfast Telegraph*-reading public (or, broadly speaking, 'middle unionism', with a consciously small 'u'). But, crucially, there were also signs that the civil rights movement was willing to react to O'Neill's entreaty, by calling an effective truce on further marches for at least a month. Emboldened, O'Neill proceeded to sack Craig, who he accused of supporting moves towards independence for a Protestant-dominated Northern Ireland, and the UUP parliamentary party gave its leader a clear vote of confidence. In his memoir, O'Neill did not recall this incident as a moment of triumph; instead, there was again the ever-present air of regret. He stated that he was unwilling to settle personal scores in his memoir-writing: 'it would be pointless to rake over these ashes today.' However, he did damn Craig with faint praise: he was 'a man of great charm with a fatal fluency of speech.'[17] In a tone at once self-critical but also defensive, O'Neill made it plain that he wished he had called a snap election for Stormont at this juncture, but he argued that it was easy to be wise after the event. In fact, it was to be another two months before O'Neill did decide to go to the electorate, and by then the mood had shifted.

Reflections on Unionist Political Division: O'Neill and Faulkner

If Bill Craig was an irritant, O'Neill's real *bête noire* in the UUP hierarchy was Faulkner, an energetic Minister of Commerce. Faulkner had been effectively brought into parliamentary politics, as Stormont MP for East Down in 1949, through O'Neill's good offices, but nonetheless the relationship between the two was strained, particularly after O'Neill became PM.[18] Faulkner recollected that he was aware of O'Neill's sensitivity to his younger, ambitious colleague from the start of his period in office: 'Conscious as I was of O'Neill's concern for his political position I did my best several times to assure him that I wanted to work with him rather than undermine his position.'[19] Although Faulkner stated that O'Neill always said he accepted his *bona fides*, it was Faulkner's view that the favourable publicity he received at the Ministry of Commerce seemed to worry O'Neill. Ken Bloomfield, who worked closely with both men, was of the opinion that, due to their different social backgrounds (Faulkner was 'a home-made Ulsterman of the thriving middle-class') and political skills, their strengths were 'potentially complementary [...] In partnership, the two would have provided a formidably cohesive collective leadership for party, government and state'.[20] Whilst O'Neill was typically rather circumspect in his retrospective judgment of Faulkner, it is clear from a contextual reading that he did not trust the latter's intentions. Indeed, O'Neill intimated that Faulkner (along with Harry West) had been plotting to undermine his leadership as early as 1966; in Faulkner's account, he was approached by some UUP backbenchers, who asked him to resign from the Cabinet, in order to spearhead a heave against O'Neill. He refused, but when asked whether he would take on the leadership, he produced a rather ambiguous response: 'my reply was, "Only if that is the wish of a majority of the Parliamentary Party"'.[21] Academic judgment on this question is nuanced: although Faulkner did not align himself with the backbench rebellion openly, 'nor did he do anything positive to back his Prime Minister. He was, in effect, signalling the availability of his services should the rebels succeed in toppling O'Neill.'[22] Another contemporary observer of these events, and a strong supporter of O'Neill, was the editor of the *Belfast Telegraph*, Jack Sayers, who disparaged

Faulkner's near-treachery: 'Brian F hardly played the game – he ought to have backed his leader and he didn't. I pray that it is not too late for him and Terence to come to terms. Together they are invincible.'[23]

Interestingly, although the poor relations between O'Neill and Faulkner have sometimes been understood in terms of the former's more enthusiastic embrace of thoroughgoing reform, and the latter's cautious, arguably more defensive rationalisation of one-party dominance, Bloomfield argued that, in fact, policy differences were marginal to the core dispute. This turned around personality, ambition and O'Neill's sense that Faulkner was essentially disloyal. Bloomfield went on to bemoan their inability to forge a *modus vivendi*:

> What should have happened, I thought at the time and think more emphatically now, was that O'Neill should have sent for Faulkner at a very early stage to say: 'Look Brian, you are still quite a young man, and I do not intend to serve more than *x* years as prime minister. Let us work together for that time, since there is much to be done, and you can be assured of my total backing. In the meantime, I intend to accord you very clearly the position of second man in my government.'[24]

Perhaps it is instructive to note that Faulkner, in his posthumously published memoir, stated that O'Neill did make some sort of overture to him, at the end of the damaging episode of 1966: Faulkner had left Belfast for a ministerial trip to the US at the height of the furore, and when he returned, O'Neill confronted him with his disapproval of his half-hearted support. According to Faulkner, he 'also said that he did not intend to stay on as Prime Minister indefinitely but only for a few years.'[25] For O'Neill's part, he did declare in his autobiography that he had intended to stand down at the forthcoming election (expected by September 1969), but there is no recollection of a commitment, unspoken or otherwise, to Faulkner. Andrew Gailey, in his biographical study of Jack Sayers, argued that 'O'Neill did attempt a reconciliation of sorts with Faulkner', and the co-operation between them was 'wonderful' for six months.[26] However, Sayers himself was more sceptical: 'I have been doing my best to make Terence and Brian Faulkner see eye to eye, but I doubt if there has been any great improvement.' Sayers, writing in the immediate wake of the leadership challenge of 1966, was anxious that if the relationship continued to deteriorate, 'the Unionist party will not be able to do the things it simply has to do. History will have much to say about the disparate personalities of these two men in particular.'[27] This proved a perspicacious fear.

The hope engendered by the 'crossroads' speech dissipated quickly in early 1969, as O'Neill appeared to expect. He had written to Bloomfield at the end of 1968: 'What a year! I fear 1969 will be worse – or that portion of which we may survive [...] In such an atmosphere of hatred would one in fact wish to continue this job – I doubt it.'[28] In the wake of renewed marches by civil rights demonstrators in early 1969 (notably what came to be known as the Burntollet march, organised by People's Democracy, which met with loyalist violence outside Derry), O'Neill had proposed a commission to investigate the causes of the disturbances since October 1968.[29] Faulkner argued that this was an abdication of responsibilities which should properly be borne by the government, and he argued in his memoir that as the Commission was expected to recommend the abolition of the ratepayers' franchise in local elections (in other words, the introduction of one person, one vote), and the government was already reconciled to introducing this legislation, to set up a supposedly independent commission was 'not only dishonest, [but] it was a disastrous political tactic which could only damage trust between people and government.'[30] Faulkner offered his resignation: 'it was a very personal decision, and it was a heart-breaking one.'[31] However, as a close reading of the two men's memoirs makes clear, this dispute was much more personal than it appeared. Indeed, O'Neill specifically questioned the rationale for Faulkner's resignation, and also his commitment to one person, one vote in local government elections. A number of academic commentators have sided with O'Neill in this dispute, describing the issue of the Commission as Faulkner's 'excuse' to make a move that would undermine the government, and arguing that 'O'Neill's anger at his colleague's [Faulkner's] late conversion [to one person, one vote] was understandable.'[32]

The strength of O'Neill's reaction to Faulkner's resignation illustrated the depth of the animosity between the men, and the bitterness that had been stored up since at least 1966. Bloomfield recalled that, although he was professionally in the O'Neill camp at this stage,

> it has to be admitted that a rereading of the subsequent exchange of correspondence shows Faulkner as the more dignified and restrained party in these exchanges. By this time, the prime minister had convinced himself that the hand of Faulkner had been behind all the conspiracies to unseat him since 1966.[33]

Bloomfield made it plain that he saw a certain degree of paranoia in O'Neill's reaction. In his autobiography, O'Neill was more restrained, but between the lines it is evident that he remained deeply hurt by the perceived disloyalty displayed. On the other hand, Faulkner himself was very keen to use his memoir to plead his case, and to argue that *he* had been the injured party:

> It seemed that the full weight of the government publicity machine was utilized to fix on me, quite unjustly, the image of a scheming, disloyal and

ambitious colleague for whom this resignation was merely another stage in a devious political game. Terence was presented as the 'beleaguered moderate' and I as the leader of a 'black reactionary group' (so described by Harold Wilson in his memoirs) who were trying to unseat him.[34]

Ultimately, what these distinct versions of the O'Neill/Faulkner relationship illustrate is the extent to which personal relations at the highest echelons are often critical for the smooth functioning of an administration. Ministers may not always need to work in harmony, but a dysfunctional absence of trust between key figures is likely to be debilitating, and not just for the individuals involved, but for the government as a whole.

Equally, in terms of what this case can reveal about the utility of studying memoir-writing, it may be that external observers cannot reach a simple judgment of 'right' and 'wrong' from a close reading of the respective protagonists' memoirs, but they do reveal the sensitivities and retrospective rationalisations of these key players. They can highlight the complex interaction of personal animosities, policy divergences and the subsequent effort to shape the historical narrative such that a particular version of events becomes widely accepted. In this case, Faulkner was writing his memoir with the advantage of having available to him O'Neill's considered public account (which was published in 1972, five years before Faulkner was writing). He was able to construct his 'defence' of the resignation in direct response to O'Neill, attempting to rebut his argument forthrightly: 'So successful were Terence's personal attacks on me at this time that for many years it was widely believed that I had been spending most of the previous six years plotting against him.'[35] Why did Faulkner believe that these accusations against him had gained such currency? His explanation was based upon the policy implications of the action he took: 'The fact that my resignation was exploited by those opposed to O'Neill's policies lent credibility to these accusations.'[36] Faulkner had been championed by some of those very same opponents of O'Neill as a potential successor, but according to Mulholland, 'Faulkner's position on the franchise had confused the right of the party who heretofore saw him as the most widely acceptable party leader.'[37] It was certainly true that when O'Neill did resign as PM three months after Faulkner's alleged betrayal, the latter was unsuccessful in the leadership contest with James Chichester-Clark, perhaps at least in part because there were those in the UUP Parliamentary party at Stormont who distrusted Faulkner with regard to his willingness to resist the 'reform agenda'.[38] Bloomfield, although he was firmly in the anti-Faulkner camp at this point, believed, on reflection, 'that it would have been much better for Northern Ireland if Faulkner had won the premiership at that time rather than two years later.'[39]

The final word may be left to the two protagonists: for O'Neill, the loss of office came as something of a relief, given the strain he had been under; he remained committed to thoroughgoing reform of the Stormont system, but he was wistful about the fact that the bulk of his party thought the 'good old days' could rumble on forever. Some eventually changed their minds, but too late to avoid both the collapse of the system, and the descent into violence. Faulkner served once more under the Premiership of Chichester-Clark, before eventually becoming PM in March 1971. He proved himself to be both a loyal minister and a PM committed to furthering the reform agenda. However, in 1969 'the ship of State had taken some heavy hits on its superstructure but it was not yet taking in water or failing to respond to steering'; by the time Faulkner became PM two years later, he was forced to 'hoist his broad pennant on the mast of a sinking vessel'.[40] The timing of Faulkner's memoir-writing may be significant here: because he was writing in the wake of his own failed attempts (as both the last Stormont PM, and as the Chief Executive of the short-lived power-sharing Executive in 1974) to preside over a definitive shift in the character of government in Northern Ireland, perhaps it can be speculated that he could finally understand the deep-seated frustrations that beset O'Neill. In the end, Faulkner used the pages of his memoir to plead:

> I can truthfully say that neither in 1969, 1966, nor at any other time during O'Neill's Premiership did I initiate or was I involved in any plots to oust or replace him [...] Terence's fertile imagination sometimes created plots where none existed, and commentators were too ready to attribute cynical motives when criticisms of naivety might have been more appropriate.[41]

There is, however, a final paragraph in this section that began by paying a back-handed compliment to O'Neill ('a hard-working Prime Minister who had much to contribute to Northern Ireland'), before arguing strongly that although O'Neill could say the 'right things' with regard to reform, 'his personal remoteness made it difficult for him to lead his party along new and difficult paths at a very crucial period in the Province's history. And in so far as some of the mud he threw in my direction stuck he made it more difficult for his successors to carry through further political changes.'[42] What is clear here, aside from the more or less subtle point-scoring between these two former UUP leaders and PMs, is the struggle to inherit and don the mantle of reform within unionist politics. That neither succeeded in embedding the necessity of this 'reform agenda' securely within the Protestant community only adds to the pathos of their subsequent memoir-writing. It inevitably raises the question of whether the results might have been different if these two leaders could have found a way to work together.

Another flavour of the period is provided by one of O'Neill's staunchest supporters in the UUP, Basil McIvor. He had been elected in the newly-created Larkfield seat on the outskirts of Belfast in February 1969 in the snap general election called by O'Neill in a vain effort to bolster his leadership. McIvor was a successful lawyer, but was induced to stand from a range of motives: 'ambition, restlessness, the pressing call by Terence O'Neill for the Unionist Party to support him in creating a more acceptable Northern Ireland, together with an intrinsic sense of public duty which has plagued me all my life, all played their part in my decision'.[43] At this juncture, McIvor was unusual in his outspoken support both for liberalism in Northern Irish political life, and his insistence that the minority Catholic population had a wholly legitimate right to a role in government. His memoir is, once again, suffused with regret for the failed enterprise over the course of the early to mid-1970s to bring these values and objectives to the fore. In his introduction, he stated that 'these memoirs have allowed me to purge a lingering bitterness fuelled by frustration and sometimes fear.'[44] Once again, geographical differences are significant in explaining some of the political diversity that existed in Northern Ireland, even within ostensibly unified parties. McIvor reflected on his Methodist roots in Co. Fermanagh where, in his account the two communities, of almost equal size, lived in 'reasonable harmony', even if 'underlying bitterness' was never too far below the surface.[45] In his childhood, the Irish Free State was not viewed by local Protestants as a 'foreign country', and for McIvor the raw sectarianism of Belfast was outside his early experience. Nonetheless, after his election, he came to appreciate that liberalism among Ulster's Protestants had always been a minority trend, and that it was often associated with counter-productive results, destabilising the political system through the upsurge of Orange reaction that was provoked. Still, it is hard to imagine alternative liberal strategies that could have avoided such destabilisation.

O'Neill's victory in the February 1969 election had been 'confused and Pyrrhic' and the legacy was a divided and unmanageable governing party.[46] Indeed, Bloomfield was one of those who, while he laid particular stress upon the personal differences between leading figures in the UUP, still felt that observers could

> attribute too much importance to the character and behaviour of individuals rather than the nature of the party they struggled to lead. Ill-disciplined, ill-organised, in reality more of a series of local 'cells' rather than a centralised party, and heavily influenced by the presbyterian priority of individual conscience over centralised direction, the UUP proved over many years almost impossible to lead.[47]

Brian Faulkner also expressed his frustrations with trying to master this notoriously fissiparous party: 'I think there must be few Prime Ministers or party leaders in western democracies who found their parties as difficult to handle as Unionist Prime Ministers did, nor was this only due to the crisis situation in the Province.'[48] Another of the factors that made the UUP unreceptive to moderation, in McIvor's estimation, was the culture of aloofness of the Protestant middle-class. Many Protestants from the professional sector were unwilling to dirty their hands in the politics of the province, 'preferring to be seen as apolitical and neutral'. Nonetheless, although McIvor noted that this was a natural reaction during the worst of the Troubles, he was critical of their willingness to turn a blind eye, and 'coast' along during the 1960s, when the risks were relatively minor.[49] Whilst McIvor classified himself as a 'zealous supporter' of O'Neillism, and its 'new deal' for Northern Ireland, he was also frank about O'Neill's personality (he projected a 'patrician, somewhat languid air'), which served to undermine that zeal: 'I was impressed with the message but not the messenger.'[50] Although McIvor judged that 'history will remember him kindly as the politician who pointed Northern Ireland to higher ground and a better way', he confessed that he 'would not [...] have felt like dying in a ditch for him'.[51] A more heroic figure would have been necessary to communicate a difficult message to the fearful, disoriented unionist population. The familiar sense of regret at the missed opportunity of the mid-1960s suffuses McIvor's reminiscences. As with Bloomfield's *post hoc* judgment with respect to the UUP leadership election in April 1969, McIvor wrote of his regret at having backed Chichester-Clark, and not Faulkner. He accepted this was a mistake, but an understandable one, given that Faulkner had not embraced the cause of reform, at least not openly, at that stage. 'I saw him as a hardliner. I believe now that I misjudged him then. He was essentially a fair-minded, even-handed politician of great integrity, who would never have countenanced discrimination in any form.'[52]

As the moderate centre-ground began to give way to vicious sectarian violence, McIvor was disarmingly candid about his incapacity to affect the slide towards the abyss. McIvor was chosen by the UUP to address the Conservative Party annual conference in 1969, in the wake of the deployment of British troops in Derry and Belfast. He recounted the Tories' bewilderment at the breakdown of law and order on such a scale, and the lack of empathy for the UUP's position among the Conservatives he encountered. He had a clear sense of the dangers inherent in this combination of indifference and ignorance from a constituency that ought to have provided a bulwark of support for the unionist cause. In the end, McIvor ploughed an increasingly lonely furrow in the UUP, but refused overtures from the new, avowedly cross-community and liberal Alliance Party (APNI). He served as a Cabinet Minister for Community Relations under Faulkner, despite deep-rooted misgivings over the introduction of internment without trial in August 1971. It is instructive to compare McIvor's recollection of this period, with that of Faulkner himself. If the latter is associated with a hardline security-led policy during his time as PM, especially regarding the growing threat of the IRA, then it is internment that has largely dominated his subsequent reputation.

After Chichester-Clark's resignation, Faulkner finally became PM in March 1971, at a time when 'the Premiership of Northern Ireland was not a political prize to be coveted.'[53] One of his earliest commitments was to institutional reform, in the shape of new functional committees at Stormont in which the opposition would have a guaranteed leading role. This met with a cautiously positive response from the SDLP, in Faulkner's recollection: 'hope was in the air as July [1971] approached.' However, the fallout from the British Army killing two Catholic men in Derry soon put paid to this 'lost opportunity' (as Faulkner entitled this chapter in his memoir).[54] In the wake of these events, the SDLP demanded an official Westminster government enquiry and, when this was rejected, the party withdrew from Stormont, setting up an alternative assembly at Dungiven. Faulkner claimed to be 'astonished and saddened' by the SDLP response, and he speculated in his memoir that the SDLP leaders from Londonderry (in particular John Hume and Ivan Cooper) were 'susceptible to extremist pressure'.[55] The criticisms that Faulkner directed at the SDLP, namely that 'they no longer sought reform, they were supporting a revolutionary change, and resorting to the old dead-end Irish tactics of boycott and abstention to achieve it', illustrate the gulf in attitudes that continued to characterise relations between the two major 'moderate' forces.[56]

Faulkner's writing style in his 1977 memoir is measured, yet it is clear that he placed primary responsibility for the failure to grasp this opportunity for political progress squarely at the nationalist door. Critics of Faulkner would point to his persistence in hinting at the unreasonable character of nationalist grievances; the shortcomings of the Stormont system and UUP rule are always prefaced by the term 'alleged' in his writing. What is clear is that Faulkner displayed few signs in his memoir-writing of appreciating either the depth of nationalist alienation, or the pressures which were applied to the SDLP, both internal and external. Whether this lack of appreciation was the result of genuine misunderstanding, or alternatively a shrewd attempt to shape the historical narrative, is difficult to determine. However, a balanced account would also have to acknowledge that SDLP memoir-writing often underestimated the loyalist pressures upon Faulkner, particularly with respect to security policy, of which his government was not in full control. Perhaps the introduction of internment without trial in August 1971 marks the apogee of these mutual 'misunderstandings' in the memoir literature. Of course, a more worldly interpretation would argue that these unionist and nationalist memoirists understood each other only too well. In this view, the conscious refusal to recognise the genuine difficulties of the 'other side' serves the purpose of installing oneself as the victim of unreasonable intransigence, helping to shape a narrative based upon one's own flexibility and authenticity. The *bona fides* of one's interlocutors are thereby called into question, at least implicitly. The innocent reader is invited to judge both the memoirist, and the narrative they espouse, as essentially reasonable and mature in their retrospective judgment, while the alternative perspective is painted as cynical and manipulative.

Faulkner portrayed internment as a decision which was 'virtually forced upon us', by both the 'level of ferocity' reached by the IRA campaign of violence in the summer of 1971, and by the strength of the unionist demands for concerted action in response.[57] However, Faulkner's tone in the chapter devoted to internment was uncharacteristically defensive. He argued in his memoir that he was not 'very anxious' to introduce internment, but that 'we [Faulkner, British Army GOC, General Tuzo and RUC Chief Constable, Graham Shillington] were rapidly running out of arguments against it'. He made clear that his approach to this hugely sensitive topic 'relied entirely on the advice of the security forces'.[58] Faulkner tried to justify the one-sided implementation of internment, despite the advice received from Home Secretary Maudling to 'lift some Protestants' as well as Catholics, on the basis that 'there was no evidence of organized terrorism by "Protestants"', and 'the idea of arresting anyone as an exercise in political cosmetics was repugnant to me.'[59] Interestingly, Faulkner used his memoir to cast some doubt on the timing of the decisive point at which he, and his security advisers, became convinced that internment was required: 'because of the intense secrecy surrounding the matter and our reluctance to commit anything concerning it to paper there are few records which can be consulted, even in Cabinet documents.'[60] This appears an odd and perhaps disingenuous muddying of the waters. As Tom Hennessey has subsequently made clear, in a detailed treatment of the relevant documents, Maudling and the UK government understood the pressures on Faulkner, but their security advice was, at best, equivocal; the Home Secretary wrote to Faulkner on 4 August and stated that 'as I understand it the GOC is not in present circumstances recommending internment on military grounds.'[61] Maudling also linked the timing of any introduction of the measure to the question of banning political processions (this would predominantly affect the loyal orders, and in particular the Apprentice Boys' parade in Londonderry, which was due to take place on 12 August). Presumably, Faulkner could have acknowledged in his memoir these expressions of concern by the UK government *prior* to internment, but it suited his purposes to ignore such a letter, suggesting as it did that it was Faulkner himself who had pushed hardest for internment, and its immediate introduction.

Ultimately, Faulkner's memoir betrayed a lack of confidence regarding the outcome of internment. There was some recognition of the damage inflicted on the prospects for progress in working with the SDLP, and an even clearer understanding that critics could point to escalating violence in the months after August 1971 as evidence for the failure of the policy. Notwithstanding such views, Faulkner attempted to set out another interpretation: the fault that he was willing to acknowledge was one of presentation. The government had not done enough to prepare people for the long-term nature of the security policy: 'many people expected quick results and they were very discouraged when they did not appear. Personally, I had expected a more speedy improvement.' In order to combat the republican propaganda campaign, Faulkner recognised that the government had 'probably overstressed the advantages of the operation'.[62] This muted self-criticism did not prevent Faulkner from claiming that by the end of 1971 the overall range of security measures was beginning to show real results, and 'would, if consistently and firmly applied over succeeding months, have resulted in the virtual defeat of the IRA by the end of 1972.' The implication here is very clear: the UK government's ultimatum on security policy in March 1972, which triggered Faulkner's resignation as PM, and the end of the Stormont parliament, was not followed by such consistent and firm policies designed to eradicate the IRA's challenge to the state. Unionist leaders were forced to adjust their sights with the demise of Stormont, although this process was neither easy nor comfortable. The memoirs studied here betray a sense of grief at the failure of unionist-controlled reform, and the British government, constitutional nationalism, as well as republican violence, are all seen as having scuppered the prospects for the survival of Stormont. The end of majority rule in Northern Ireland was profoundly disorienting for unionists, but within two years Brian Faulkner was attempting to lead his party and community towards a renewed devolution settlement, based precisely on the type of proportionality in government that he had disparaged for much of the previous decade. This experiment, and the memoir-writing it helped to produce, is the subject of Chapter 7.

Chapter 6

Northern Nationalists and Memoir-Writing: The Social Democratic and Labour Party and the Troubles

This chapter analyses the memoir-writing that has emanated from the ranks of the Social Democratic and Labour Party (SDLP), for many years the leading party representing the predominantly Catholic Irish nationalist minority community in Northern Ireland. Founded in 1970, as an extension of the civil rights movement of the late 1960s, the party produced some of the key protagonists of the Troubles era, and it could be argued that many of its institutional and policy prescriptions found their way into the eventual settlement of the 1998 Agreement. This has not been borne out in increased popular support; indeed, since 2001, the SDLP has been firmly eclipsed by the growth of Sinn Féin (SF), and despite several changes of leadership since the retirement of the iconic figure of John Hume, the party remains marooned in the doldrums. If it should come as little surprise that there is a gulf in understanding and interpretation between nationalist memoirists and their unionist counterparts, then it may be noteworthy that the memoirs studied here do tend to reveal subtle distinctions *within* the SDLP. This chapter uncovers some of the complex diversity of lived experience within the Catholic nationalist political class, and specifically seeks to examine the evolving attitudes of these men towards the Stormont system (and the Northern Ireland state more generally), towards power-sharing with unionists, and towards the violent armed campaign of republican paramilitaries. The chapter concentrates upon the early period of the Troubles, paving the way for a specific case-study of the power-sharing Executive of 1974.

It should be noted that the memoirists considered here are all males. It is an important point that there exist few memoirs by women in the context of the Northern Ireland conflict; this is an accurate reflection of the dominance of men in both the 'constitutional' political sphere and also in paramilitary organisations. This chapter will make occasional reference to the memoir-writing of Bernadette Devlin (born 1947), a student leader of People's Democracy in the late 1960s, before her election as a Westminster MP for Mid-Ulster in 1969.[1] Although her politics were certainly a long way from those espoused by the SDLP (and remain so), she was a significant player in the civil rights movement, alongside many of those from the Catholic community who subsequently founded the party. Therefore, Bernadette Devlin's perspective on the period of the civil rights campaign makes for an interesting comparison with those of the SDLP figures examined here. The main memoirists considered in this chapter are Paddy Devlin (1925–1999)[2], Paddy O'Hanlon (1944–2009)[3] and Austin Currie (born 1939)[4], all of whom were founding members of the SDLP, and played important roles within the party during its early years. The significance of these individuals is made plain, if it is noted that they comprised three of the six key founding members (alongside John Hume[5], Gerry Fitt[6] and Ivan Cooper). However, whilst all three were leading figures, they all subsequently either left the SDLP to pursue other political directions (Currie), were expelled (Devlin) or dropped out of party activity (O'Hanlon).

This chapter analyses these memoirs from a number of perspectives: in generational terms, it should be noted that Paddy Devlin was significantly older than Currie and O'Hanlon, and this difference coloured his experience in several important ways. He grew up in Belfast's Falls district, and saw first-hand the economic depression of the late 1920s and 1930s. His political outlook was influenced by poverty and deprivation, even if his family circumstances were less impecunious than many others in the area. Both Currie and O'Hanlon were born in the shadow of the Second World War, and both enjoyed relatively comfortable upbringings (at least by the standards of the time, and in comparison with Devlin). However, aside from their difference in age, perhaps the most striking aspect of the early years of these three men related to the social and geographical characteristics of their childhoods: Devlin's experience was in urban Belfast, where the twin forces of working-class culture and sectarian identity were both interwoven in a Gordian knot that remained stubbornly resistant to Devlin's lifelong effort to disentangle it. As has been pointed out by Connal Parr,

> Devlin represents the injection of these class currents into the Northern Irish political discourse, charging the parties he joined and founded with this dynamic […] In the context of tribal Northern Irish politics this was – as Devlin was well aware – a largely fruitless endeavour but it was something he persisted with until his death in August 1999.[7]

An illustration of Devlin's commitment to the elusive quest for non-sectarian working-class political action was his historical study of the outdoor relief riots in Belfast during the early 1930s.[8] John Hume's family background was in the working-class Bogside district in Derry, and his father was oriented towards socialist politics, rather than the Nationalist Party.[9]

By contrast, Currie's upbringing was in rural Co. Tyrone, in the townland of

Edendork, near Coalisland. O'Hanlon was born in Drogheda, and spent his early childhood in the seaside village of Blackrock, Co. Louth. His parents were both originally from Mullaghbawn near Newry in South Armagh, and they moved back to this village when Paddy was eight. Compared with the visceral sectarian politics in Belfast, both Currie and O'Hanlon heralded from rural districts, where relations between the Protestant unionists and Catholic nationalists were conducted in a different register, even if conflict was never too far from the surface. For example, Currie related a story of his father's unproductive visit to the chairman of the local rural district council, dominated by the Unionist Party; attempting to convince the chairman of his growing young family's need for a council house, Currie senior handed over the customary small bribe, only to be informed that he would only be considered for a house when 'a suitable one [was] vacated by one of your own kind'.[10] Bernadette Devlin, from Cookstown in Co. Tyrone (only ten miles or so from Currie's family) presented a somewhat harsher version of community relations, but one inflected with class, as well as sectarian, prejudice: from a poor background, the family's circumstances were difficult, even before her father died when she was only nine. Although 'our poverty wasn't extreme', the family only had 'the minimum necessary to support life in decency'.[11] The relationship of the Devlin family to the town was strained: 'We had lived independently of the entire town – not in isolation, exactly […] we were brought up to ignore Cookstown, on the principle that it didn't care about us and we didn't care about it.'[12] However, the depth of sectarian animosity was illustrated when a Protestant neighbour, who had helped the family out in times of hardship, and was 'one of the most genuine friends we ever had', turned on Bernadette when she was fighting the by-election in Mid-Ulster in 1969: 'she stood in the streets of Cookstown and howled at me, "You fenian scum!" All because of the Reverend Ian Paisley, and civil rights, and unemployment. Since then she has never spoken to me, but slams the door when she sees me coming.'[13]

Currie, O'Hanlon, Hume and Bernadette Devlin were among the generation of northern Catholics for whom third-level education was the route to a broader political outlook, one which looked beyond the constrictions of traditional nationalist politics in Northern Ireland. It needs to be acknowledged, though, that those, like Paddy Devlin, who had not enjoyed access to higher education, could also take a broader political perspective. On arrival at Queen's University, Belfast, Currie found the experience unsettling for several reasons: he had never been to Queen's before he registered there and he confessed to finding the atmosphere 'alien to someone from my background, with the Union Jack flying from the roof […] I found the company of those wearing Pioneer pins more congenial than those wearing poppies.'[14] The fact of the matter was that, apart from his immediate neighbours, Currie had never had any dealings with Protestants, 'and certainly never had any discussions with them about religion or politics'. Throughout his time at Queen's, Currie stated that 'although I made a number of friends from a unionist background, some of them still friends to this day, the segregation that was such a hallmark of Northern society was only slightly dented for the majority of students.'[15] Currie said that the thought of attending university further afield, perhaps in England or the Republic of Ireland, never entered his head; on the other hand, for Paddy O'Hanlon, 'Students at Queen's University needed special skills. There was a need to know the safe drinking places or you ended up with your head in your hands. Belfast was a sectarian city and I did not need the hassle so I went off to UCD [University College Dublin].'[16] Hume begins his book with the anecdote that his father, who was unemployed for long spells and who had left school at twelve, was nonetheless convinced that public education was critical to the Catholic community: '"Stick to the books, son, it's the only way forward."'[17] Having passed the eleven-plus exam, Hume received a government scholarship to attend St Columb's College in Derry, and then studied French and History at Maynooth in Co. Kildare, but decided not to pursue a vocation in the priesthood.

These varied upbringings may also be interpreted from the perspective of broader currents in the nationalist community's attitude to the Northern Irish state and the Stormont political system. For many northern Catholics, abstention from participation in political life and a refusal to confer legitimacy upon institutions that were regarded as alien impositions, were touchstones of political identity. The Nationalist Party under Joe Devlin did decide to take up its seats in the Stormont parliament after 1925, but there was no realistic prospect of either forming an alternative administration, or having any real influence on the Unionist government. This effort to work within the system was short-lived, with Devlin complaining that the unionists had rebuffed all attempts to co-operate. During most of the 1930s and 1940s, nationalists remained semi-detached from parliament. Their representatives 'sank into an already well-worn rut of sulkiness and whinging. For this they were to be criticised by northern nationalists in the 1960s and 1970s.'[18] Currie and O'Hanlon could both be counted among such critics, even though the former was elected (at the young age of twenty-four) as a Nationalist Party Stormont MP for East Tyrone in 1964. Any attempt to engage with unionists, in a system that they dominated, was a recipe for deadlock. Currie understood the deep sense of frustration and impotence that nationalist representatives felt, and he underlined his respect for men like Eddie McAteer (leader of the Nationalist Party at Stormont from 1964–9): 'his misfortune was to have spent a career in nationalist politics at a time when there was no mobility, no chance of change, a period of frustration and hopelessness.'[19] For the bulk, if not all, of its existence, the Nationalist Party could be characterised as a largely middle-class and conservative institution, with a strong clerical influence.[20] The labourist and on occasion socialist politics of some Catholics in Belfast and

Derry stood in clear contradistinction to such sentiment, and helps to explain to some degree the later currents of opinion within the civil rights movement and the SDLP.

Rejecting Republicanism?

Of course, as well as the Nationalist Party, ineffective as it was, there was a radical political alternative available to Catholics in Northern Ireland: the republican movement. Paddy O'Hanlon's family, hailing from the disputed border region of North Louth/South Armagh, were stalwarts of the 'old' IRA, but many of his family had also supported the anti-Treaty side in the civil war, and had continued to pledge allegiance to the IRA and SF into the second half of the twentieth century. His father had had part of a leg amputated after a skirmish with Free State soldiers during the civil war; his uncle Mick had been involved in the IRA ambush of British intelligence officers in Dublin in November 1920 (the killing of the 'Cairo gang'), took the anti-Treaty side and was interned by the Free State at the Curragh camp in Tintown One, from where, as Officer Commanding, he took part in the mass escape in April 1923. An aunt had been a member of the republican women's organisation Cumann na mBan, and O'Hanlon recognised that the family had been 'lucky', in the sense that the civil war had divided many families irreparably, and the O'Hanlon clan had avoided that fate. Paddy was keen to establish these credentials in his memoir; the family's republican heritage is set out in detail in the opening chapter. It is clear that he retained a certain pride in this heritage, even though he followed a different political path: 'The family did not do bigotry or sectarianism. They were stubborn to the point of public despair and over-loyal to organisations and individuals at times but they refused to hate on the grounds of race, colour or creed. I hope that I inhabit the same world.'[21] O'Hanlon was evidently inculcated in this republican mindset from an early age; he made speeches at the republican plot in the Mullaghbawn graveyard in the early 1960s. However, he also began to question the efficacy of the republican challenge to the Northern Irish state, and he was scathing in his assessment of the South's rhetorical commitment to unity: 'The North was an interest-free zone where Dublin was concerned. It disappeared off the map after the election, out of sight and out of favour [...] The harsh truth was that partition worked for everybody except northern Nationalists.'[22]

Interestingly, O'Hanlon was not very explicit in his memoir in outlining the rationale for his rejection of this historical attachment to traditional republicanism. The impression is given that O'Hanlon's political education was rather unfocused during his student days in Dublin (except for discovering the writing of Thomas Davis), but it was 1968, and the worldwide convulsions of the Prague Spring and anti-Vietnam war protest, that seemed to galvanise local civil rights demonstrators. O'Hanlon did not explain in any depth why and how he came to throw in his lot with the Northern Ireland Civil Rights Association (NICRA), but he made clear that 'the substantial Sinn Féin influence in the local community did not support the aims and objectives of the CRA. They looked upon the CRA marches as a recognition of the [Northern Irish] state, a campaign for internal reform and a betrayal of traditional Republicanism.'[23] Clearly, in this rural heartland, the fashionable ideas of socialist republicanism had made little serious impact. However, O'Hanlon's politics had moved definitively away from those of his upbringing and the local community, even though he believed his father supported his efforts: 'The link with family tradition was broken when I joined the Civil Rights movement and it came at a personal cost. Many people in South Armagh took it badly that I forsook the old ways. They viewed it as a form of desertion but I toughed it out.'[24]

For Austin Currie, a number of events in the early 1950s stirred his youthful political interest: the election of ex-IRA man Liam Kelly for Clann Uladh as Stormont MP in Mid-Tyrone, and his subsequent six-month imprisonment for a seditious victory speech, was one such event. At nine years of age, 'Dan Breen's *My Fight for Irish Freedom* was my favourite book'; this vignette illustrates the significance of earlier republican memoir-writing in maintaining and transmitting the rudiments of republican political culture from one generation to the next.[25] Currie reflected that he responded emotionally to these events, including the deaths of Seán South and Fergal O'Hanlon during the Brookeborough arms raid in 1956. Although he was keen to acknowledge in his memoir that the 'real courage' had been displayed by the Royal Ulster Constabulary (RUC) men in the barracks, nonetheless Currie was willing to recognise that as a teenager he felt satisfied to see 'someone putting the boot into the arrogant and dominating unionists.'[26] It is interesting to compare the school experiences of Currie and Bernadette Devlin, who both attended St Patrick's Academy, Dungannon, although they were eight years apart. Although Currie did report that his education led to him being 'engrossed in Irish history and seduced by stirring nationalism', he does not have much to say directly about the political ethos of the school. On the other hand, the role of segregated schooling in exacerbating these youthful idealistic political views (which also contained a fair measure of sectarian animosity) was made plain in Devlin's case: 'I went to a very militantly Republican grammar school and, under its influence, began to revolt against the Establishment, on the simple rule of thumb, highly satisfying to a ten-year-old, that Irish equals good, and English bad.'[27] The vice-principal, Mother Benignus, who had a very strong influence upon Bernadette, '*hated* the English – and with good reason: her entire family had suffered at the hands of the British forces [...] She didn't hate Protestants, but her view was that you couldn't very well put up with them, they weren't Irish, and that clinched the argument.'[28] Although Devlin argued that she 'outgrew' this crude anti-British political education, and even called Mother Benignus a 'bigot' whilst she was Head Girl, nonetheless she remained deeply marked by this upbringing. There is no evidence that the paths of Currie and Bernadette Devlin crossed during their school years, but they certainly did so in the late 1960s, when 'wee Bernie' (as Currie rather patronisingly described her) won the nomination for the Mid-Ulster Westminster by-election as a 'Unity' candidate, after Currie and the republican, Kevin Agnew, had withdrawn their respective candidacies. Writing in 1975 (after Devlin had been defeated in the February 1974 election, largely due to the decision of the SDLP to stand against her), in a newspaper article that he reprinted in his memoir, Currie praised Devlin's courage, both physical and moral, but this was merely a preface for a highly critical appraisal:

> The 22-year-old girl could easily have become the articulate voice of a frustrated and angry people; this phenomenon of Ulster [...] could have been a bridge-builder in a community where such bridges were nearly non-existent. The tragedy of Bernadette Devlin is that she threw all these chances away. She polarised rather than united and became the equivalent of Paisley on the other side. She played for Celtic, he for Rangers.[29]

As he reflected upon this judgment, almost thirty years later, Currie maintained that this view had been amply justified: 'her total irrelevancy over this long period in a number of changing political scenarios suggests strongly that a considerable talent had been misused.'[30]

Perhaps as a result of his parents' influence, Currie's youthful infatuation with republican history was not allowed to develop into a fully-fledged political commitment: his mother was a 'strong nationalist, but her family background was Hibernian and trade union', whilst his father 'had a more down-to-earth approach despite, or maybe because of, a cousin's involvement with the IRA'. Although the republican movement, and a broader republican sensibility, were clearly powerful factors in their younger years, both Currie and O'Hanlon consciously avoided the temptation to join the 'struggle for freedom', and committed themselves to a different form of activism. However, it is important to note that, even for many nationalists who eschewed the IRA and SF, the republican movement was not experienced as an alien force which existed outside the community, but rather it was viewed as an organic outgrowth of the circumstances of partition, even if it could not realistically overturn the injustice by physical force. This is not to suggest or imply that the bulk of northern nationalists were necessarily likely to be 'sneaking regarders' for the republican movement (although this was certainly a real phenomenon amongst some). But, it does illustrate the degree of complexity within non-violent nationalism, particularly during the 1950s and 1960s, when the republicans could still be indulged by some as one more element on the spectrum of possible responses to an unjust system that confronted northern Catholics and nationalists. For Hume, who was brought up in a family environment where politics 'were never discussed', nonetheless he learned at an early age to distrust the 'emotionalism of Republican mythology – patriotism was about dying for Ireland'.[31]

For Paddy Devlin, this question of his political relationship to the republican movement was both more urgent and more personal. According to Devlin's own account, he inherited both labourist and nationalist politics from his parents (the former more from his father, and the latter from his mother), who squabbled about who to support during elections on the Falls Road. However, Devlin joined Na Fianna Éireann (the youth organisation of the republican movement) as an eleven-year-old, although 'there was no great political passion or patriotic zeal behind this move.'[32] His motivation was the status that attached to those boys who were members, and soon enough Devlin had been promoted to leader of his *sluagh*. As with Currie, the young man became 'emotionally and romantically attached to what I saw then as the just and uncomplicated cause of freeing Ireland from British exploitation'.[33] By 1940, in the wake of the IRA's reorganisation, and the bombing campaign in England during 1939 (the S-Plan), Devlin had joined the adult republican movement, much to the chagrin of his mother. Nonetheless, Devlin included several anecdotes in his memoir that indicate the paucity of support for the IRA in Catholic nationalist districts of Belfast at this time; when, as a callow seventeen-year-old, he attempted to commandeer a car for an IRA operation from one of the few men on the Falls who owned one, he met with a dusty response; 'he swept me scornfully aside and said: "Fuck off, you wee bastard, or I'll give you a toe up the arse!"'[34] Of course, it should be taken into account that the older Devlin, in composing his memoir, had long-since renounced his youthful infatuation with the violent republican movement, and a significant part of his political purpose in *Straight Left* was to convince his readers of the political and moral folly of believing the republicans' dangerously simplistic analysis.

One recent sympathetic portrait of Devlin argued that his memoir-writing was the 'logical conclusion' of his political trajectory away from violent republicanism, which involved 'expunging elements of his republican past he had come to regard as incongruous and cementing the way he most wished to be seen [as a radical socialist and trade unionist] in the eyes of friend and opponent alike'.[35] However, it could be argued that, in fact, Devlin did not so much want to hide or 'dispel' the 'republican trace [that] never left him', but that he did understand where that important current in Northern Irish Catholic nationalist politics came from, and he was determined to *expose* its more recent violent manifestation, in the shape of the Provisionals, to a hard, unforgiving scrutiny. Parr concludes that 'in its desired over-simplification of Devlin's politics and encasement of a final resting place, his autobiography succeeds in obfuscating a republican past.'[36] Whilst it can be agreed wholeheartedly that 'Devlin objected deeply to the monopolisation of the republican aspiration and nomenclature by the Provisionals and later Sinn Féin, whom he unequivocally regarded as profoundly conservative Catholic militarists', his discussion of his past commitment to the republican movement is by no means obfuscated.[37] Indeed, Devlin was precisely committed to *utilising* this discussion of his past in the service of his contemporary goal of undermining the Provisional movement, if at all possible. Whether, when he was writing in 1993, this was motivated by anti-republicanism *tout court*, or rather Devlin's perception that authentic republican aspirations had been usurped by the Provisionals is, perhaps, a moot point. Yet, Devlin's primary desire at the time of the publication of *Straight Left* is surely not in doubt; he wished to deny powerfully the claim of legitimacy advanced by the Provisionals, which had been used in an effort to justify a sectarian murder campaign over more than two decades. It would be surprising if the mark of his republican past had been entirely erased from Devlin's later politics, and it can be doubted whether his 'autobiographical recollection of events is principally symptomatic of his desire to distance himself from his own republican past.'[38] In the same article, Parr cites the Northern Ireland Labour Party's Chairman, Brian Garrett, who believed that Devlin was always 'up front' about his IRA past, and that this transparency was more of a strength rather than a weakness: 'it meant he could look into that tradition and see its warts.' This relationship of Devlin to his personal memory of the past, and the related, but distinct, question of the primary purpose of his memoir-writing, is complex and hard to disentangle. Ultimately, in the maelstrom of events after August 1969, Devlin's commitment to a non-violent and cross-communal politics was placed under heavy strain, as we shall discuss below.

Devlin's arrest and internment in 1942 heralded what he acknowledged as the most formative years of his life. During his period of internment (which ended in 1945 at the end of the Second World War), Devlin reappraised his political thinking in a profound fashion. He suggested that 'the real political purposes of the IRA were something I only vaguely understood, but I clearly recall beginning to feel a sense of Irishness.' Devlin was deeply disappointed by the disillusionment and low morale amongst republican internees, but nevertheless he threw himself into self-education, Irish language classes, Gaelic football and reading classical literature, both fiction and politics. He came into contact with left-wing republicans, who helped him to realise the type of political principles he really wished to advance: 'although I was highly streetwise when I was first locked up, I was hopelessly idealistic, naïve and immature. Prison broadened me and matured me in all sorts of ways.'[39] The political lessons that Devlin drew were twofold: first, he contemplated the nature of majoritarian politics in a divided society, and the democratic obligations that a majority unionist government had (or should have) towards the rights and needs of the minority. Second, the debates in the jail regarding the moral foundations for the republican movement's armed campaign helped cause Devlin to 'question, and finally reject, the violent republican ethos'. Ultimately, in a classic example of the memoir-writer's trial by ordeal, followed by conversion, Devlin stated in retrospect:

> I realise that this period of my life forged attitudes and a personal style that governed my entire approach for years to come. I became competitive, confident and articulate to a high degree. It was as if I emerged from a tunnel of darkness [...] I had gone into the Crumlin Road jail a boy and come out a man.[40]

Devlin finally made his break with the republican movement in 1950, and initially joined the Irish Labour Party in Belfast. He won his first electoral contest (against Gerry Fitt, ironically) at the age of 30, when he won a by-election for the Falls ward on Belfast Corporation in 1956. After losing the seat two years later, a result he blamed upon the mobilisation of Catholic anti-communists from the Clonard confraternity, Devlin left the Irish Labour Party to join the NILP. He was subsequently elected to Stormont for the NILP in February 1969.

A Paradigm Shift? Civil Rights and the Attitude to Unionism

Unlike Paddy Devlin, the other memoirists studied here cut their political teeth in the diverse conditions of the 1960s. Currie, O'Hanlon, Hume and Bernadette Devlin all owed their burgeoning political interest to their experience as students. Austin Currie saw at an early stage that the Nationalist Party required profession-alising, particularly in terms of engaging with the pressing social and economic needs of the Catholic working-class, but also the new constituency of young Catholic graduates, whose ambitions had been thwarted up to that time by the dead hand of Stormont inaction, discrimination and hidebound conservatism within the clerically-dominated Catholic community. He was an early supporter of the Campaign for Social Justice (CSJ), the pressure group founded by Conn and Patricia McCluskey,[41] and from his election in 1964, the parliamentary and extra-parliamentary strands of Currie's activities formed a complementary approach to political reform. However, almost right from the start, the complexity of sectarian and intra-communal political and electoral calculation in Tyrone and Fermanagh was evident: the Nationalist Party announced its intention to stand candidates for the 1964 Westminster election in Mid-Ulster and Fermanagh-South Tyrone (the Stormont seat Currie won was East Tyrone, which was divided between the two Westminster constituencies). If the Catholic vote was split between abstentionist SF candidates, and Nationalist Party representatives, then unionists were likely to prevail. Republicans threatened to undermine Currie's campaign in retaliation, and he was forced into an ambivalent position, neither stating clearly that he would refrain from supporting nationalist candidates for the Westminster contests (as SF wanted him to do), nor able to openly express his preference for a candidate who would attend (rather than the traditional abstentionist).[42] Currie's relationship with the Nationalist Parliamentary Party was soured from the beginning.

Currie's early experience as a Stormont MP mirrored to some extent the unease he had felt at Queen's. Even if many of the unionist MPs were 'friendly and welcoming', there was no disguising the fact that Stormont 'truly was an alien place for a nationalist'.[43] The symbols and surrounding ambience were unabashedly unionist, and Paddy O'Hanlon (after his election as an independent for South Armagh in 1969) experienced a similar sense that the Stormont parliament was intended to be a 'Fenian free zone [...] It looked like a gig where the minority was barely tolerated.'[44] O'Hanlon admitted that his 'mind was full of prejudice' when he arrived at the parliament for the first time; as he prepared himself for combat with the serried ranks of UUP MPs (a 'squad of captains [...] a sniff of aristocrats and back benches crammed with frozen city burgers'), O'Hanlon 'climbed the stairs after I was sworn in, the archdukes of discrimination tracked me down the corridor, glowering at me from the panelled walls in the Strangers Dining Room so I glowered back'.[45] He drew upon his education in the roughhouse world of County Gaelic football, and readied himself for the parliamentary game. Stormont could certainly be intimidating for new MPs, of whatever affiliation, but it also required that the small band of non-unionists stuck together. The man to show Austin Currie the ropes was Gerry Fitt, even though the latter was not in the Nationalist Party, but had been elected for Republican Labour. Paddy Devlin, also elected to Stormont in 1969 (for the NILP), characteristically framed a very similar initiation in terms of *class* prejudice: a fellow MP offered him advice on how to act when meeting the governor at Hillsborough Castle, and offered that his wife would teach Theresa (Devlin's wife) to curtsey! Needless to say, Devlin brusquely rejected the offer.

In terms of the tumultuous years of 1968–9, the memoirists threw themselves into working for the civil rights movement, both inside and outside Stormont. As well as the focus upon challenging O'Neill's UUP government to broaden and deepen a meaningful reform programme, the civil rights movement consciously sought to pressurise the Westminster Parliament to turn its attention to the problems of Northern Ireland, chief among them UUP domination. The views expressed regarding O'Neill's government tend to be disparaging, but once again there are some subtle distinctions to be drawn from a careful reading of these memoirs. For Austin Currie, who had the experience of seeing O'Neill's *modus operandi* at close quarters in parliament from 1964 to 1969, the meetings of the PMs of Northern Ireland and the Republic in 1965 created the hope for change. He was favourable to the idea that the Nationalist Party should accept the symbolically problematic title of "Her Majesty's loyal opposition": 'my own view was that the sneering references had to be tolerated for the greater good. If we were to demand our full rights as citizens, we could not be diverted by such emotive sloganising.'[46] Currie stated that his attitude to O'Neill had been to accept his *bona fides* as a genuine advocate of a fairer Northern Ireland. However, this interpretation was undermined in May 1967, when the PM read out in parliament a letter purporting to come from a Falls Road Catholic, containing allegations that the local Catholic clergy had instructed parishioners to boycott Protestant-owned shops, and refuse to employ Protestants. During an exchange of letters with O'Neill, Currie received an acknowledgement that this letter had not been authenticated, and that the PM accepted that the Catholic Church had unequivocally denied the allegation. However, the damage had been done as far as Currie was concerned; the very fact that O'Neill appeared to believe the letter's contents suggested his liberalism 'was only skin-deep, and that the commendable sentiments in favour of reconciliation were more likely to be the product of his speech writers, Jim Mallie and Ken Bloomfield, than of the Prime Minister himself.'[47]

Paddy Devlin did not directly question O'Neill's sincerity during this period, and when the PM announced the five-point reform programme in November 1968, he recognised that 'there was an overwhelming groundswell of support', which seemed to herald the stabilisation of relations between the unionist government and the Catholic population. On the other hand, Devlin argued in *Straight Left* that he was not persuaded by the call from some in NICRA to suspend marches and demonstrations in the wake of O'Neill's broadcast:

> I was uneasy that they [the five-point programme] still did not go far enough to rectify the years of unionist abuse and misrule, and I favoured keeping up the pressure that had been created to achieve the fundamental and lasting changes in society that I knew in my bones were necessary.[48]

Currie also reacted to the 'minimal concessions' of the five-point plan by arguing that whilst they represented a 'step in the right direction, many of us attacked it as being "too little, too late"'.[49] What precisely 'keeping up the pressure' meant was unclear at the time, and is not clarified in these memoirs. Devlin appeared most concerned that the gerrymandering of electoral boundaries was not directly addressed, while for Currie the reform plan did not promise 'one man, one vote' for local elections. The following month the NICRA executive took a decision that there would be a moratorium on civil rights marches and demonstrations until mid-January (as O'Neill had requested). Currie argued in the wake of O'Neill's 'crossroads' speech, that the 'great majority of those involved in civil rights, myself included, were prepared, warily, to give him [O'Neill] a breathing space'.[50]

The 'small minority' refused to go along with this cautious approach, and some students at Queen's organised the so-called 'long march', or Burntollet march, from Belfast to Derry in early January 1969. For Currie, 'it was dangerous and irresponsible. It was also a two-fingered gesture to NICRA and the rest of the civil rights movement.'[51] Paddy Devlin, conversely, supported the march, even though he recognised that there was a good chance of potentially violent confrontation as the march passed through loyalist districts.[52] Unsurprisingly, Bernadette Devlin (a supporter of PD) was instrumental in 'keeping up the pressure' on the O'Neill administration. Her memoir, written and published within a year of the events it described, gives an authentic flavour of the hectic pace of change; she disarmingly recognised that PD 'started off without any political affiliation, with very little political awareness even'.[53] The movement gradually tacked to the left, but it is telling that Devlin (along with some other young republicans/nationalists) acknowledged the unease this created in the ranks: 'we were at the stage where if the move [to the left] became overt in any way, it frightened people off. We still had the attitude, "My God, we might be socialists!" and we scurried back to the middle.'[54] Within a couple of months, Devlin had 'moved from traditional, mad, emotional Republicanism to socialism in the context of Ulster; now I was joining my new-found socialism to my old belief in a united Ireland.'[55] It is easy to imagine the fervour and excitement of this period for young civil rights agitators; whether it made the development of a rational and sensible political strategy any easier is a moot point. But Bernadette Devlin's testimony, delivered without the benefit of significant retrospection, provides the interested reader with an authentic understanding of the lived experience of the radical fringe of the civil rights movement. The marchers limped into Derry after a concerted attack by loyalists which left eighty-seven hospitalised. But, sectarian tension was once more at fever pitch, and any lingering hope for O'Neill's approach was fatally undermined. The prevailing judgment upon O'Neill can be gauged from Paddy Devlin's words:

> in spite of claims to the contrary, O'Neill had never had any heart for the reforms forced upon him by the Labour government [...] In my view he should have stood up to the extremists on his own side and hammered them. This was, in reality, O'Neill's big weakness and because of his lack of guts he made it virtually impossible for those coming after him to lead the [UUP] party.[56]

It is worth pointing out that the attitude towards the police during this period of increasing tension can also represent an important gauge of these politicians' interpretation of the state. In Newry, a week after the Burntollet march, civil rights demonstrators were involved in fomenting violence for the first time. O'Hanlon recognised that the march was a 'shambles', and he (along with the rest of the Citizen Action committee in the town) tendered his resignation in the aftermath, although the committee was re-elected by acclamation.[57] However, in an indication that provincial, or even parochial, prerogatives are never far from the heart of political activity in Northern Ireland, O'Hanlon reported that the committee decided to resign *en bloc* from PD: the students from Belfast, he implied, did not understand the intricacies of political life in Newry, and the local group jealously guarded their autonomy. Currie, one of the speakers at the march, bemoaned the actions of extremist elements in fomenting the violence, but he also attempted to lay some blame with the RUC, who apparently sat back and allowed the destruction of a number of police vehicles.[58] Given that civil rights demonstrators had been castigating the RUC for its heavy-handed approach to policing demonstrations over the course of the previous year, this criticism seems disingenuous.

As the tension mounted during 1969, the resolution of the civil rights movement (whose unity was increasingly under strain) to maintain its non-violent stance was questioned, both from within and without. With the serious rioting and burning out of Catholics in Belfast in August, some future SDLP politicians flirted dangerously with the notion of arming the Catholic nationalist community for self-defence. Paddy Devlin and Paddy O'Hanlon were both involved in a trip to Dublin in order to impress upon the Fianna Fáil government the necessity to help those who had been forced to flee their homes. At a 'spontaneous meeting' outside the iconic GPO in O'Connell Street, Devlin made remarks that subsequently became notorious. He related it thus in his memoir:

> In response to a prompt from someone I said that we needed guns to protect our community, that the security forces were not carrying out their duty towards Catholics. These words were to haunt me and to be used against me for years to come, but I have to say again that they were uttered in the heat of an emotional moment. I had long ago rejected the use of violence and severed my connections with the IRA.[59]

It is instructive that Devlin remained keen to distance himself from these comments, and felt it necessary to address this subject, even after twenty-five years, recognising their continuing power to harm his carefully nurtured non-violent credentials. It is also significant that even for an avowed socialist, who explicitly rejected the sectarian logic of political realities in Northern

Ireland, in the maelstrom of inter-communal violence in August 1969, Devlin reverted to the discourse of 'our community'. He did not appear to appreciate the tension this language implied for his broader political project, given that he used it unproblematically in his memoir. Devlin went on to meet representatives of the Irish government, and returned to Belfast with the promise of help and temporary lodgings for displaced families.

It is noteworthy that O'Hanlon dealt with the same trip to Dublin in a quite distinct fashion. According to O'Hanlon, he accompanied Devlin and Paddy Kennedy (a Republican Labour Stormont MP for Belfast Central) 'to ask the Taoiseach Jack Lynch for guns. Lynch did not meet us and we got no guns but the demand concentrated minds on the gravity of the situation'.[60] This seems to suggest a more explicit embrace of the purpose of the visit than Devlin is willing to acknowledge. Indeed, O'Hanlon betrayed few qualms about the nature of his response:

> there is a major question that arises out of that visit to Dublin and I will address it. I supported the civil rights movement but I am not Mahatma Gandhi. I defended myself on a number of occasions from physical attacks by my political enemies [...] there is a very thin line between defence and attack, between participants and civilians, and it is too easy to cross it.[61]

What is clear from this discussion are the dilemmas that faced Catholic nationalist politicians in this fraught period. Whilst O'Hanlon did not shrink away from his commitment to the necessity for communal self-defence in his memoir, Paddy Devlin's tone is much more equivocal. Ultimately, he attributed his lapse in judgment to the frustrations that he had met in the previous months:

> I had strained every muscle trying to achieve reform and justice through the democratic parliamentary process in the teeth of deep-seated unionist intransigence and violence. My remarks at the GPO did not accurately represent the thrust of my approach to the ongoing problem and I did not, of course, get any guns or take any steps to do so.[62]

The SDLP and the Troubles

Austin Currie introduced the chapters of his memoir dealing with the early years of the Troubles with a somewhat paradoxical reflection: despite the intensifying violence, and ultimately the huge disappointment of the failure of Sunningdale (see Chapter 7), nevertheless 'the period between Caledon in June 1968 and the fall of the power-sharing Executive in May 1974 was the most satisfying and fulfilling in my whole political career. Things were happening and I was helping to make them happen.'[63] However, at the same time 'these were also stressful and dangerous years when, on a number of occasions, I was lucky to survive.'[64] Shots were fired at Currie's house, and many of the other founding members of the SDLP found themselves confronted with similar personal trials. In retrospect, given the diversity of the political backgrounds represented by the core group of founding members, not to mention the all too evident personality clashes that were to come to the fore almost immediately, it should not be a surprise that the formation of the SDLP was no straightforward task. There were four different efforts made to form a new non-unionist political alignment between March 1969 and August 1970.[65] The new party was very clearly a parliamentary construct, with the key figures united by some broad political principles (such as non-violence), but particularly by the perceived necessity to counter both intransigent unionism and resurgent physical force republicanism. The coalition that had been created in the broad front of NICRA had come apart, partly as a natural consequence of its key demands being met, and partly as more extreme voices and demands came to prominence. For Currie, the key problem in policy terms was the classic dilemma of nationalist politics since 1921: 'the need for strong representation to fight discrimination versus the fear of buttressing Partition by active participation in its institutions.'[66]

From the beginning, the six founding MPs also met regularly in Donegal for the purposes of policy discussion, but these gatherings were also social affairs. However, tensions between some of these individuals were never too far from the surface. One example will suffice here: Paddy Devlin included brief portraits of his fellow SDLP founders in his memoir, and his distrust of John Hume was plain. Whilst he recognised Hume's intellectual ability, Devlin felt that 'from the outset of our relationship I had misgivings about his motives and doubted the strength of his loyalty to us as a group.'[67] One of the issues which tended to divide the ex-NILP man from the ex-Nationalist was the political tactic of boycott or abstention. According to Devlin's interpretation, Hume pressed the SDLP away from the Stormont chamber on several occasions: 'I allowed myself to be dragged into these boycotts and walk-outs, sometimes reluctantly, for reasons of unity, but deep down I harboured doubts because I believed that outside parliament is no place for a democrat.'[68] Devlin feared that this stance could provide a vacuum which would be filled by the paramilitary organisations, which needed no encouragement to argue that 'constitutional politics' was a busted flush in Northern Ireland. This 'dangerous posture', argued Devlin, proved that, 'despite his apparent radicalism, Hume was cast from the stuff that old nationalists were made of.'[69]

Moreover, Devlin went further in *Straight Left*, and alleged that he had received word from an unidentified 'friendly Catholic lawyer' that Hume had been in parallel discussions, with the objective of forming a 'Catholic political party', which could only undermine the prospects for a genuinely non-sectarian and cross-communal party. Currie, in a direct response to Devlin's charge, made the point that Devlin had not raised any such concerns at the time: 'I did not have then, nor have I seen since, any evidence of John Hume attempting to establish a Catholic political party and, frankly, I don't believe it [...] For John to have been involved as alleged would have been the basest of hypocrisy and double-dealing.'[70] Without Hume's direct testimony or Devlin's source it is difficult to provide a definitive answer to this dispute, but on the face of it, the evidence is not there to support such an accusation. However, what it does illustrate powerfully is the degree to which Devlin distrusted Hume's intentions and political instincts. O'Hanlon's view of the creation of the SDLP was that the key differences between the new formation and the Nationalist Party were threefold: first, the SDLP were genuinely interested in exercising power, whilst the older party was primarily concerned with protesting from the sidelines; second, the new party would be properly and efficiently organised, with a branch structure and central direction; third, 'we were non-sectarian in motivation and social democratic in outlook. Our ambition was to attract the descendants of Roddy McCorley and William Orr to our ranks in spite of the emerging storm.'[71] However, O'Hanlon was realistic enough to see that the hope that radical Presbyterians would support the SDLP, in the spirit of the United Irish rebellion of 1798, was a 'big ask'.

One of the instances of boycott that illustrated the tensions between what might be termed the 'participationist' wing of the SDLP, and those more attuned to abstentionist politics, came in the summer of 1971. As we have discussed in the previous chapter, the UUP government and Westminster were contemplating the policy of internment, but the SDLP withdrew from Stormont *before* its implementation. The immediate catalyst was the killing on 8 July of two Catholic men in Derry by the British Army.[72] The SDLP leaders in Derry reacted to the outrage in nationalist areas of the city and delivered an ultimatum: unless an independent public enquiry was forthcoming, the SDLP MPs would withdraw from Stormont. According to Paddy Devlin and Currie, this unilateral demand had been taken without prior agreement of all the party's MPs. Devlin argued that he and Fitt were 'livid with anger'.[73] Politically, the Faulkner administration had just offered a new committee structure at Stormont, with the opposition guaranteed an enhanced role (a reform which Devlin believed was of real significance, whilst Currie remained more sceptical).[74] The proposals had wrong-footed the SDLP, which although it had suggested the policy, had had no advance notice that Faulkner was contemplating its introduction. Devlin was adamant that the party should not paint itself into a corner: 'just at a time when there were signs we might be getting somewhere the old nationalist knee-jerk of abstention was brought into play.'[75] In order to ward off suggestions that the

SDLP manoeuvre might play into the hands of the Provisionals, an alternative Assembly was put forward in the event of withdrawal from Stormont. Fitt hoped he would be able to agree a face-saving formula with Home Secretary Reginald Maudling, obviating the threat of withdrawal, but the best he could get was a promise that the inquests on Cusack and Beattie could be brought forward; Devlin and Currie both described this position of the British government as: 'Our boys [the soldiers] – right or wrong'. In the end, the SDLP united around the threat of withdrawal, but much to Devlin's chagrin: 'Gerry [Fitt] and I were unwillingly sucked along with the majority feeling, which was emotional rather than practical. Unable to maintain our opposition, we agreed to withdraw from parliament, but for all the wrong reasons.'[76] In an effort to deny the republican movement a propaganda victory, an alternative, oppositional assembly was created, but it met only twice in Dungiven.

On one level, this episode can be interpreted as shedding important light upon the internal dynamics of the early SDLP. Especially in terms of the nuances of the debate surrounding participation versus abstention, and the attitude to adopt towards the UUP government, the judgments of the protagonists, both contemporaneously and retrospectively, were complex and difficult ones. Currie's memoir is subtle in attempting to justify the party's stance; he recognised that 'abstentionism had always come easier to West of the Bann nationalists than to Belfast representatives.'[77] However, even though he was clearly anxious that withdrawal from Stormont increased the possibility of handing the initiative to the republican movement, Currie did acknowledge that the SDLP's policy had hardened, partly as the relationship with the Conservative government proved more fractious than that established with Labour. Ultimately, Currie supported the decision to withdraw, and perhaps understood the position of the Derry SDLP leaders better than either Devlin or Fitt. On the other hand, he also understood the dangers involved in undermining Stormont to the extent that direct rule from Westminster became the only realistic option. After all, it was Westminster that had political responsibility for the deployment of the army, and for the deaths of Cusack and Beattie, and it would be illogical to effectively hasten the takeover of Northern Irish politics by that government. With the benefit of hindsight, Currie argued that it was 'possible to see that our withdrawal from Stormont […] was a mistake. It had one consequence to which we had not given sufficient consideration: it removed from Faulkner one concern which might have prevented him from introducing internment.'[78] Reading Paddy Devlin's memoir, it is clear that he regretted the SDLP's brinkmanship: he stated that both he and Fitt believed the party had 'fallen for a Provo trap'.[79] By the same token, Devlin was also highly critical of the British government's high-handed response, which only intensified the damage done by the army's cavalier approach.

In summary, a close analysis of the memoir-writing of some of the key protagonists demonstrates that there are at least two different ways to interpret the SDLP's decision: first, as a short-term and highly localised response to the killings in Derry; in this view, Hume had either calculated that the SDLP required a hardline reaction if it was not to lose considerable support to the Provisionals, or it was a response that reflected the emotional turmoil and sense of genuine outrage of Catholic nationalists, particularly in Derry. Second, it could be understood as a strategic response to both increasing pressure from the republican movement, and a perception that Stormont (and perhaps Westminster) was either unable or unwilling to push reform at the necessary pace or magnitude. What might have appeared significant change at an earlier juncture (the committee proposals of Faulkner), was no longer viewed as sufficient, or even relevant to the situation on the streets, by the majority of SDLP leaders. Whilst it is idle to speculate about the possible trajectory for Northern Ireland had the SDLP not withdrawn from Stormont, it is nonetheless clear that once internment without trial was introduced a matter of weeks later, then any hope for a reformist agenda under the auspices of Stormont, and with cross-community support, was doomed.

In Currie's view, 'by introducing internment, Faulkner had thrown down the gauntlet, not only to the SDLP but to the whole Catholic community.'[80] However, he immediately qualified this opposition, by recognising that the UUP government had to 'try to stop the escalating Provo campaign' and that, had internment been introduced in a more even-handed fashion, 'it might have been tacitly accepted as a *fait accompli* if it had been successful in reducing the level of violence.'[81] The decision to target only suspected republicans, and the allegations of brutal treatment meted out to internees, meant that 'no compromise was possible. I was determined this was the issue on which the whole Stormont system would be brought down.' Paddy O'Hanlon used his memoir to reproduce some of the communication between Faulkner and the UK government in this crucial period; these intelligence documents (the G bundles) were made available to the Saville enquiry into Bloody Sunday. O'Hanlon's interpretation is that the Stormont tail was allowed to wag the Westminster dog, and that Faulkner was allowed to introduce a measure that 'was a political and military disaster and was certain to fail', despite the misgivings of both the British Army and the Heath government.[82] The alienation of almost the entire Catholic population was guaranteed; a campaign of civil disobedience and a rent and rates strike followed, and Faulkner became a political figure despised by many in the SDLP. Even Devlin, who had been more impressed by Faulkner's reformist credentials than most of his colleagues, argued that the one-sided implementation of internment was the PM's 'most fundamental mistake [...] there was no excuse, other than bigotry, for directing the swoops against only one side'.[83]

Arguably, however, despite the SDLP's best efforts to channel 'the anger and resentment at internment, [and] the hatred of Faulkner for introducing it' in a non-violent direction, the political life of Northern Ireland became dominated by those wedded to violence during the next two years.[84] Of course, the Stormont parliament would be suspended within the year, and some in the SDLP saw nothing to lament in its passing. However, as we shall see in the following chapter, progress towards a more equal society and polity in Northern Ireland remained painfully slow for the SDLP, even despite their participation in the power-sharing Executive during 1974. The tone of these memoirs is often suffused with regret, particularly that extremists on either side of the communal divide were able to dominate the policy agenda. These memoirists often display a genuine ambivalence with regard to the potential of reform during the period 1965–72, but there is little doubt that this period came to be understood as an opportunity lost, even if it paved the way for the concept of power-sharing devolution, with an 'Irish dimension', which was to define SDLP policy for the next three decades.

Chapter 7

A Case-Study of Memoir-Writing and the Elusive Search for a Political Settlement: The 1974 Power-Sharing Executive and Sunningdale

Introduction

It is a measure of the great significance attached to the experience of the power-sharing Executive (and the closely-related Sunningdale agreement) of autumn 1973 to spring 1974, that this short period has loomed so large in the published memoirs of many of the core protagonists. There are at least two important reasons for the concentration upon this era: first, for many of the Northern Irish politicians involved, this was their last (and sometimes only) experience of holding ministerial office, and therefore the failure of the short-lived Executive affected them deeply, in terms of their personal political lives; second, and perhaps of broader societal significance, after the collapse of Sunningdale, and the restoration of direct rule from Westminster, it took the best part of quarter of a century for British, Irish and Northern Irish policy-makers to re-engineer the conditions for a renewal of power-sharing devolved government in the guise of the 1998 Belfast Agreement. Many of the memoirists analysed here share a lasting sense of regret at the failure of the experiment, and if it is considered that approximately 2,500 deaths attributable to the political violence occurred between the end of May 1974 and the 1998 Agreement, then it is not too difficult to imagine the extent of this remorse. However, if there is deep-rooted frustration articulated in these memoirs, it is also the case that there are diverse explanations for the demise of power-sharing, and the lessons that ought to have been drawn. The intention in this case study is to compare the reflections of some of the unionist and nationalist political figures who were direct actors in this drama, either as ministers in the devolved administration (Brian Faulkner, Paddy Devlin, Basil McIvor, Austin Currie), as civil servants who worked for the administration (Kenneth Bloomfield, Maurice Hayes, Robert Ramsay), or as British ministers who were engaged with the Northern Ireland government (William Whitelaw, Merlyn Rees). On occasion, the reflections of other interested parties may form a counterpoint for the analysis. The political and personal relationships that evolved during this experience, and the level of trust (or continuing *distrust*) that characterised these interactions, are critical factors in any explanation of the failure of power-sharing at this juncture. Analysing the memoir-writing of key protagonists is one method of understanding these complex inter-relationships, both in terms of inter-party and intra-party developments.

There is not space here to look in detail at the period of direct rule from March 1972 up until the Sunningdale conference of December 1973. Suffice to state here that the introduction of direct rule ushered in a period of difficult adjustment for the Northern Irish parties. This was particularly true for the Ulster Unionist Party (UUP), which had to acknowledge the loss of the Stormont parliament and government, which they had dominated exclusively since 1921. Brian Faulkner, the UUP PM at Stormont from March 1971 until March 1972, recorded his sense of shock when the Heath government in London proposed the removal of law and order powers from the Stormont government, a move which precipitated the resignation of his government: 'I was shaken and horrified, and felt completely betrayed.'[1] For the Social Democratic and Labour Party (SDLP), the demise of Stormont was greeted with celebration, but there remained trepidation concerning the UK government's future policy under direct rule. In addition, the SDLP remained pledged to a policy of refusing to engage in talks until internment without trial (introduced by Faulkner's government in August 1971) was ended. Of course, the republican movement had also claimed the 'credit' for bringing down Stormont, and were determined to maintain the pressure of the IRA's campaign, believing that the suspension of the parliament was merely a prelude to total British withdrawal.

An indication of the substantial distance between the UUP and SDLP during the early months of direct rule is provided by a close reading of the respective party memoirs. Before the advent of direct rule, Faulkner was persuaded in talks with the British that there must be an 'active, permanent and guaranteed' role for the minority population in any future political dispensation, but he was also of the view that it was not possible 'to provide statutorily entrenched positions for the anti-partitionist (as distinct from the religious) minority, as this would lead inevitably to PR government, which we regarded as intrinsically unworkable'.[2] For one of the SDLP's founding members, Paddy O'Hanlon, this stance of Faulkner's in late 1971 and early 1972 provoked the observation that, 'Mr Faulkner is bluntly stating that he will not share power with Catholics [...] he] cloaks extremism and inhumanity in the jargon of democracy.'[3] When talks involving the SDLP and the UUP, as well as Alliance, began in October 1973, in the wake of elections to a Northern Ireland Assembly in June, Austin Currie confessed that he 'didn't quite believe' that the result might be a successful negotiation, and ministerial posts for him and his colleagues, 'particularly as that outcome would have meant we had reached agreement with the architect of internment, Brian Faulkner.'[4] For his part, Faulkner had his own reservations about some of the individuals he faced across the table in the SDLP: Currie was viewed as having articulated a 'crude and angry response' when then Home Secretary, Reginald Maudling, had invited the parties to talk together in the autumn of 1971 (before the advent of direct rule). According to Faulkner, Currie had argued, '"Why the hell should we talk to you?" he had said. "We are winning and you are not."'[5] Currie reflected in his memoir that Faulkner might well have had good reasons for being sceptical about his intentions; after all, 'he had been the recipient of my jibes [...] Recently, with the publication of documents under the thirty year rule, it was confirmed that Faulkner's reservations about me were as great as mine about him.'[6] Faulkner recognised in his memoir that 'because I had been the Prime Minister responsible for internment I had personally suffered uniquely from the bitter opposition to that measure, and some of that feeling remained [at the start of inter-party talks].'[7] It was clear that there was substantial distrust, and some rancour, between these key individuals, as Secretary of State for Northern Ireland (SOSNI), William Whitelaw determined to bring the parties together in the autumn of 1973.

However, not all of those within the SDLP negotiating team were as vehement in their characterisation of Faulkner as Currie and O'Hanlon. Paddy Devlin had words of praise for the last Stormont PM, even though he had seen the internment policy as a disastrous error: 'I had long regarded Brian Faulkner as the most able individual among the overwhelmingly dour unionists and, looking back, I feel that the real tragedy was that he got his chance to solve our problems too late, when the sands of time had almost run out.'[8] In some respects, therefore, the personal relationships across the sectarian divide were not always quite as entrenched as the public discourse might lead one to imagine. On the other hand, even though many of the SDLP negotiators had been elected to Stormont in the previous decade, their relations with unionist ministers and MPs were often perfunctory, and sometimes hostile. In March 1973, a Border Poll (boycotted by the SDLP) produced a strong signal from unionists; overall, on a 59% turnout, 98% voted for Northern Ireland to remain in the United Kingdom. Fortified by this result, which he interpreted as a 'settling of unionist nerves' in the wake of the suspension of Stormont, Faulkner proceeded to give a cautious welcome to the British White Paper on Constitutional Proposals for Northern Ireland. According to one academic judgment, Faulkner stored up many of the future difficulties he encountered, due to his 'unduly optimistic' reading of unionist willingness to contemplate compromise, given his view that the Border Poll had cemented Northern Ireland's fundamental constitutional position.[9]

From the perspective of a senior civil servant, Kenneth Bloomfield, who had worked as an adviser and speech-writer to successive UUP PMs since the early 1960s, the parties needed to avoid making the necessary flexibility and compromise harder to achieve, through a public discourse that encouraged fear and mistrust within their respective constituencies: 'too often, Northern Ireland politicians have built for themselves walls of commitment behind which, in changed circumstances, they have found it frustrating to be confined.'[10] Of course, those 'moderates' who would be absolutely central to any eventual negotiated power-sharing settlement, were also under constant pressure from 'outflanking' extremists, whether in the republican movement or among intransigent loyalists. Bloomfield made the important point in his memoir that civil servants in conflict zones, perhaps particularly in a relatively small polity like Northern Ireland, are not immune from the everyday experience of violence; indeed, 'we who sat at Stormont Castle were both players and spectators, for it was our city – our shops, our buses, our restaurants, our public offices, our fellow citizens – which were coming under daily attack. The shadow of violence never left us.'[11]

In terms of Faulkner's motivation, and the vexed question of internment, Bloomfield pleaded for a more rounded judgment: he recognised that there was a picture of Faulkner as 'a dyed-in-the-wool law and order man, lusting throughout the Chichester-Clark interregnum to get his hands on the levers of power so that he could implement methods of ferocious repression.'[12] However, the truth was more complex, according to Bloomfield, and not all those who attacked internment *after* its introduction were so hostile beforehand. Clearly, Bloomfield had worked closely with Faulkner, and it should not be too surprising that he was willing to reflect on his policy intentions with a certain degree of sympathy.

For another memoirist and civil servant, Maurice Hayes, internment represented a 'profound mistake whose repercussions were likely to be dire [...] Of all the stupid things that government could do this was probably the worst.'[13] Hayes recalled meeting with Faulkner after the introduction of internment, and suggesting with a sense of *realpolitik*, 'of which I am now a little ashamed', that if the policy was to have any chance of success then some suspected loyalist paramilitaries would need to be picked up and detained.[14]

Evidently, therefore, the lead up to the negotiation of the power-sharing Executive involved both the UUP and SDLP in a process of fine judgments. Both parties, and their respective leaderships, needed to calibrate the extent of their members' and supporters' willingness to accept the kind of compromises which would be required to reach a comprehensive agreement. However, they also had to distinguish their rivals' negotiating rhetoric from the reality or substance of their position. The extent to which personal relationships and understandings affected this complicated process should not be underestimated, and is revealed to an important degree in the memoir-writing. Basil McIvor represented an unusually liberal unionism, and indeed was courted by the fledgling Alliance Party as a potential defector. McIvor resisted these entreaties, on the grounds that it would have been treacherous to absent himself from the fight for the soul of the UUP, and that the fight was winnable for the moderate wing. Moreover, 'I felt that to walk away would be to walk out into the wilderness, as I did not believe that a nonsectarian party in Northern Ireland would get anywhere.'[15] Brian Faulkner might have seemed an unlikely champion for McIvor's form of liberal unionism, but, 'although he had long been regarded by us [liberal unionists] as something of a hardliner, I am satisfied that in the end he was a genuine convert to substantial reform in the mould established by O'Neill.'[16] Ultimately, in McIvor's estimation, it was *precisely* Faulkner's credentials as a 'mainstream unionist' and an 'irreproachable Orangeman' that enabled him to carry an unenthusiastic party to the negotiating table with the SDLP, and over the threshold into a power-sharing administration. Such a subtle reading of Faulkner's political positioning might not always have been appreciated by his counterparts in the SDLP.

In the aftermath of Stormont's suspension, McIvor indicated his willingness to work with the incoming British government machinery, something that he knew would be deeply unpopular among many Protestants, who viewed such a stance as 'collaboration'. However, 'to walk away in a huff from the new administration would in my view have been irresponsible and have exacerbated a desperate situation.'[17] McIvor captured well the sense among many unionists that a violent attempt to overthrow the state had been rewarded with the decision to prorogue the parliament. In such circumstances, he acknowledged that his efforts to strike out for the moral high ground, and keep alive the dream of cross-community rapprochement, were bound to be met with irritation by many unionists and outright hostility by loyalists. As far as McIvor was concerned, even though the UUP had always been a broad church, those members who flirted with the idea of independence for Ulster (in particular, former Home Affairs Minister, William Craig's Vanguard pressure group) ran the real risk of alienating British political and popular opinion, and driving the key policy-makers into the arms of Catholic nationalism.

When the talks got under way, Faulkner continued to face problems of party management, with a party bitterly divided between pro- and anti-White Paper unionists. For members and leaders of the UUP, these divisions between 'pledged' or 'Official' unionists and unpledged unionists, were something of a culture shock. During negotiations, individuals from both the UUP and SDLP began to think about the larger picture of what form of compromise might be acceptable and deliverable. But, given the enticing prospect of ministerial office in the event of a successful deal, these politicians were also keenly interested in their personal standing, and some are honest enough to admit that they engaged in efforts to manoeuvre themselves into favourable positions. The SDLP's decision to leave Paddy O'Hanlon out of the negotiating team (in favour of Eddie McGrady) meant he was the only one of the party's key founders not to be directly involved. He did attend the Sunningdale talks, but he acknowledged in his memoir that the leader Gerry Fitt was correct to exclude him from the SDLP's ministerial team; he was struggling badly with a drink problem at this time, and subsequently reflected that Fitt had made the right decision.[18]

Hope and Hesitation

For Faulkner, the talks with the SDLP held out hope, but this was tempered by the knowledge that 'so much still seemed to divide us and our supporters, and the bitter memories were no longer deep in history but in the recent past.'[19] As far as unionists were concerned, they entered the negotiation with several conditions for sharing power, and it was by no means certain that the SDLP would be able or willing to meet them. Faulkner gave an indication of the depth of distrust:

> to many Unionists the SDLP were the party whose leaders had started off the violence with irresponsible demonstrations on the streets, who had criticised and undermined the security forces ever since, and who had encouraged their supporters to opt out of the system by a rent and rates strike [...] There was still some doubt as to their attitude on the very right of the state to exist.'[20]

According to Faulkner, any coalition government with the SDLP required an unambiguous commitment to the majority consent principle (or the right of self-determination for the people of Northern Ireland); a firm support for the security forces (including the RUC); an end to the rent and rates strike; an acceptance that there would be a unionist majority on the Executive (reflecting the majority sentiment of the population); and, by no means least, there would need to be safeguards and limitations upon the role of any putative Council of Ireland. The latter idea was of great significance for Irish nationalists in Northern Ireland, as it would embody both symbolic and practical aspects of the 'Irish dimension' of their identity. McIvor, one of the unionist negotiators, remarked to his party leader that, 'someone had to do what we were about to do, but that it could be the end of a political career for all of us.'[21]

As far as the SDLP was concerned, they had established a range of sub-committees to deal with specific policy areas, so that by the time inter-party talks began the party had reasonably well-organised priorities. The party felt confident, reflected in Paddy Devlin's argument that 'Whitelaw needed the co-operation of the SDLP more than any other party to get his show on the road.'[22] The most controversial areas in the talks concerned internment (or detention) without trial, policing, and the cross-border or 'Irish' dimension (specifically, the function of the mooted Council of Ireland). It is perhaps instructive that socio-economic policy was not an area of deep-seated dispute; Faulkner stated that the UUP and SDLP had only 'differences of emphasis' with respect to these questions.[23] As so often in Northern Ireland, it was communal status, intra-bloc manoeuvring and the symbolism attached to 'constitutional' questions that really motivated the parties. Whitelaw's strategy for dealing with the most difficult subjects, particularly policing and internment, was to stress that these were matters under the jurisdiction of Westminster at that juncture, and therefore it would not make sense for the parties to become stalemated in those areas where they were not directly responsible. In the memoirs of both unionists and nationalists there is an uncommon unanimity regarding the skill with which Whitelaw oversaw the negotiations. Currie referred admiringly to his 'deliberately bumbling' way of addressing some of the core problems, whilst Faulkner stated that his 'sensitive and skilful handling of the talks' had proved invaluable.[24] It is a measure of Whitelaw's influence that his threatened removal from the SOSNI post was met with genuine consternation.[25] Gradually, personal relationships improved, and the negotiators saw that their counterparts were professional, serious and committed to an authentic search for progress. As Currie eloquently described it, they were learning to control their 'tendency to partisanship'.[26]

With the talks dragging on over two months, and opponents among both republicans and loyalists able to fill the void created by the formula that 'nothing was agreed until everything was agreed', the memoirs record the intense pressure to overcome divisions and sign up for a deal by late November 1973. Basil McIvor recorded that 'complete breakdown was never far away', especially over the vexed question of the 'numbers game', or the parties' respective ministerial portfolios.[27] In the end, after the number of ministers was increased to accommodate the demands of the UUP and SDLP, agreement on the Executive was finally reached. The mood amongst the delegates is captured well by Faulkner: 'we were united as people who had come through an ordeal together, pushed closer together by the attacks made on us from outside by politicians and terrorists who shared the common objective of wishing to see us fail, if not a common rationale for their hopes.'[28] This short period between the successful agreement to form the power-sharing Executive and the tripartite Sunningdale conference (involving the Westminster and Dublin governments, as well as the Executive-designate), has been called the 'high water mark of genuine consensus'.[29]

'A Government of All the Talents'[30]

With the untimely removal of Whitelaw, whom all of the participants had grown to trust, some of the obstacles that had been steered around in the preceding months came once more to block progress. Chief among these was the north-south dimension, and the proposal for the Council of Ireland. There is a lively academic debate surrounding the significance of the Council to the eventual unionist rejection of Sunningdale and the power-sharing Executive. In particular, Gillespie has argued that the London government permitted the Irish and the SDLP to pressurise the unionists 'into signing an unsellable deal'.[31] It has also been argued that had Whitelaw still been at the helm of British policy, rather than PM Edward Heath, the difficulties of Faulkner's position would have been better appreciated, and the damaging effects of Sunningdale might have been averted. Patterson alleges that the conference was an 'unmitigated disaster for Faulkner's standing in the unionist community'.[32] Faulkner's memoir made it plain that he had not objected in principle to the Council of Ireland (indeed, he claimed that the idea had been put forward by the UUP in autumn 1972), provided that the unionist minority that would exist on any North-South Council had its interests protected through the application of decision-making by unanimity, for example. For Faulkner, 'the essential thing was for the Council to be seen to have a practical role; if it was seen as purely political it would not be politically saleable.'[33] It is instructive that Faulkner looked back on this episode, and recognised that his ability to 'sell' the Council was clearly in doubt from the beginning. At the time, he appeared to have few such doubts in his ability to convince a sufficient number of unionists to support this departure.

Even before the Executive had been agreed, Faulkner's position in the UUP was precarious; he had survived a proposal to reject power-sharing at the Ulster Unionist Council by only ten votes (out of almost 750). On the other hand, Faulkner still appeared remarkably sanguine regarding the prospects of persuading a majority of unionists (both inside and outside the UUP) that the Council was nothing more than a 'fig-leaf' for the SDLP. He was ready to concede on some of the nationalists' demands (for instance, the idea of a second parliamentary tier for the Council), but was unhappy at any notion that the Council would have independent executive power: 'there seemed to be a lot of mystical nonsense surrounding the SDLP approach to the Council of Ireland [...] but if this nonsense was necessary to bring their supporters along I did not see why we should be difficult, provided we could ensure that it meant nothing in practice.'[34] In his retrospective justification for this position, one which arguably concluded with his political demise, Faulkner 'felt confident that Unionists, being basically practical people, would judge our final agreement on a practical rather than symbolic level. Later events were to throw considerable doubt on the traditional view that Ulster Unionists were less interested in symbols than their Nationalist fellow-countrymen.'[35] Ultimately, this political (or, perhaps, psychological) misjudgment was to prove hugely costly, not just for Faulkner himself, but more broadly for the prospects of the power-sharing Executive. Faulkner argued that the safeguards he had secured from the Irish government regarding Northern Ireland's constitutional status (specifically, what he felt was an unequivocal recognition of the 'majority consent' principle within Northern Ireland), far outweighed the concessions on the Irish dimension, but this could be interpreted as a post-facto rationalisation.

Basil McIvor, a self-professed liberal unionist (who happily embraced an Irish cultural identity), declared himself much more pessimistic than Faulkner: even during the Castle talks at Stormont,

> Protestant opposition was growing. [The Council of Ireland] worried us most, as around it was coalescing a formidable loyalist opposition. A Council of Ireland, an institution regarded by many Protestants as an external threat and as specifically designed ultimately to bring about a united Ireland, was something we could not sell.[36]

McIvor remained a supporter of Faulkner's efforts, and he reserved his ire at the outcome for John Hume (and Garret FitzGerald, the Republic's foreign minister): 'Either deliberately ignoring or being unaware of Unionist fears to the point of arrogance, Hume's was to be a fatal misjudgement.'[37] Of course, McIvor was writing with the benefit of hindsight, and with Faulkner's posthumously published memoirs available, but it is hard not to agree with his view that 'powersharing and a Council of Ireland were to prove a fatal mixture. Throughout the course of the conference [Sunningdale] I felt it was all a pretty hopeless exercise.'[38] Faulkner, at least initially, believed that Sunningdale had been nothing short of a triumph for the UUP; he recorded that 'that Sunday evening [at the conclusion of the Sunningdale conference] all of us in the Unionist deputation were convinced that we had come off best [...] we felt elated and expected our success to be recognized. One member of our delegation remarked that Sunningdale would go down in history as a Unionist victory.'[39] Clearly, what this example illustrates is the extent to which memoirists are likely to engage in attempts at retrospective self-justification, and the way in which the same political event may be recollected through an entirely different contemporary lens.

From the SDLP perspective, the usual differences of emphasis are apparent in the memoirs. Paddy Devlin, whose admiration for Faulkner's courage and leadership were clearly and regularly expressed in his memoir, stated that, 'given the vulnerability of his position, it was also imperative that the conference should ensure the durability of Faulkner's political powerbase in the Unionist Party and community.'[40] The clear implication is that this did not happen. Indeed, as the SDLP digested the outcome, which had gone 'beyond our wildest dreams in moving towards a realisation of Wolfe Tone's objective of uniting Protestant, Catholic and Dissenter', Devlin reinforced his anxiety: 'our one nagging worry was whether Faulkner would be able to sell the package to the unionist electorate, in view of the rising tide of hostility to him back home [in Northern Ireland].'[41] Austin Currie put forward a more nuanced interpretation, which recognised the 'squeeze' that was being put upon Faulkner, but also refused to accept that the SDLP and Irish government had been 'too successful' at Sunningdale. In Currie's judgment, although it has become 'almost a universally accepted truth' that the nationalist side 'imposed on Brian Faulkner, through the Council of Ireland, a task he was incapable of fulfilling. I did not accept that then, and I do not accept that now'.[42] The reason Currie refused to accept this verdict was that Faulkner himself did not view the outcome in this light; in a brief conversation with Faulkner at the conclusion of the conference, 'he did not give the slightest indication [...] that he had been given an impossible task to deliver.'[43] As we have established, Faulkner believed he had secured a good deal at the time, and he remained determined to propagate this version in his later memoir-writing. In *Memoirs of a Statesman*, Faulkner was still characteristically unwilling to acknowledge that he might have been out-negotiated, or that his powers of persuasion had been exposed as ineffectual. His explanation for the subsequent weakness of his position rested on the lack of clarity with regard to the Dublin government's commitment to self-determination for the people of Northern Ireland (this issue became mired in the Irish judicial process, known as the Boland case[44]), and the ambiguity of the Sunningdale formula with respect to the Council of Ireland. For McIvor, however, Hume's 'extraordinary insensitivity' to the genuine fears of unionists meant that he was 'the man who, at Sunningdale, blew out the light at the end of the tunnel.'[45] The leader of the Alliance Party, Oliver Napier, also blamed Hume and Garret FitzGerald; although both were 'superb' at Sunningdale, 'they were going out to negotiate the best possible deal they could get from Faulkner for the nationalist tradition and to hell with everything else, and they did it very well.'[46] What these exchanges in memoir-writing display is the way in which differing perspectives, both personal and ideological, can come to play a critical role in the hermeneutic understanding of a contested series of historical events. Despite Faulkner's valiant effort to defend his record at Sunningdale, which received some support from Currie, the historical narrative which suggests that Faulkner badly misjudged the mood of the unionist population is now firmly in the ascendancy.

The power-sharing Executive which took office on 1 January 1974 had several important strengths, according to Bloomfield, who acted as permanent secretary for the Executive: it enjoyed a clear majority in the Assembly; 'its members included some of the most articulate and persuasive people in Northern Ireland politics'; it ought to have had the full support of the Westminster government; and, 'for the first time, an administration in Northern Ireland truly crossed the community divide.'[47] However, this rosy picture rapidly gave way to a much bleaker outlook. Faulkner's leadership of the UUP had been dealt a crushing blow in the immediate aftermath of Sunningdale, and he lost what was effectively a vote of confidence in the UUC only three days after taking office as Chief Executive. Whilst he bemoaned the lack of clarity in the Sunningdale communiqué's wording on the Council of Ireland, and the 'archaic' character of the UUP's internal decision-making machinery (which, for instance, permitted members of other parties to vote as members of the Orange Order), nonetheless Faulkner felt he had no option other than resignation as leader of the UUP. He remained as Chief Executive, and continued to defend the consensual relations which were developing between the UUP and SDLP. However, for Gillespie, Faulkner's resignation 'ended the moral legitimacy of the Sunningdale deal', thereby killing it as an 'effective political package'.[48] Neither Faulkner nor any of the Executive members were willing, either at the time or subsequently, to see the writing on the wall.

Notwithstanding this broader picture, the incoming ministers record their enthusiasm at getting their hands on the levers of power; in the case of SDLP ministers like Currie (Head of Department of Housing, Local Government and Planning) and Devlin (Head of Department of Health and Social Services), this represented an historic opportunity, and one they were determined to seize. For unionists like McIvor (Head of Department of Education), the shock to the system may not have been as great, but he admitted that his sense of personal pride and ambition meant he was primarily interested in his own performance. The wider fate of the Executive took something of a back seat, at least initially. Currie admitted to a sense of trepidation on becoming a minister, in part at least due to what Bloomfield described as the 'feeling of unease experienced by those of his tradition about Stormont. The signs of a very British tradition were, after all, everywhere'.[49] However, the feeling was probably mutual; Bloomfield noted that 'quite a lot of civil servants from the Protestant and unionist tradition probably approached their new SDLP minsters with a guarded wariness.'[50] Currie quickly built a good rapport with the permanent secretary in his department, John Oliver, despite the concerns that both harboured about each other: Currie reported that 'there had been whisperings about him, which had been brought to my attention. He was so well-connected with the ancient regime that in the aftermath of Bloody Sunday he had been sent to the Washington Congressional Hearings to hold a watching brief.'[51] For Oliver, 'there had been some open questioning in Social Democratic and Labour Party circles of the readiness of the civil service to give their full allegiance to a power-sharing cabinet and some agitation for the replacement of protestants by Roman Catholics in the higher ranks.'[52] Ultimately, these fears appeared unfounded, although Currie did comment that 'I had expected to find that fifty years of one-party rule would have had an effect on the civil service in terms of conditioning, and I was right. There were two civil servants in the Department [...] who I felt had difficulty accepting me.'[53] For his part, Paddy Devlin recalled receiving, on his first day as minister, a list of candidates for the post of private secretary, which included only males and Catholics; he sent it back asking for some qualified Protestants and women to be included. Devlin interpreted this as a process of testing the new minister, but he also argued,

> given that we were the first non-unionist party to hold office in Northern Ireland, I knew from the first day that we would be treated with suspicion [...] The mandarins in the key areas [...] had seen off O'Neill, Chichester-Clark, Faulkner and Whitelaw and some of them, whose unionist views they did not even bother to conceal, made no secret of their scorn for us and doubts about our capacity to do the job.[54]

Whilst the machinery of government gradually adjusted to the new regime, and progress on policy-making at least began to take shape, greater events were to supervene. The untimely decision by PM Heath to call a Westminster election for February 1974 was made with scant regard for the likely effects on the stability of the Executive in Northern Ireland, despite the best efforts of both unionists and nationalists to warn him of the dangers. There is an unusual degree of consensus in the memoirs concerning the election, which was 'more disastrous than any of us had feared'.[55] With the anti-power-sharing United Ulster Unionist Coalition winning 51% of the total poll, 'the claim that the Executive was "widely accepted" was now clearly farcical.'[56] Faulkner was evidently aware of his increasingly precarious position, but he insisted that the result was 'a serious but not necessarily fatal blow to the Executive.'[57] Amongst SDLP ministers there was also a similar degree of wishful thinking: Currie argued that although the results were a 'serious setback', the Executive could continue to soldier on: 'all we could do was to reiterate that Assembly elections were not due for another three years and press on doggedly [...] I did not have great fears for the future of Sunningdale.'[58] Paddy Devlin rated the election campaign 'the most divisive and bitter I had ever experienced', with IRA attacks upon SDLP candidates and election workers after the party had decided to contest all twelve seats.[59]

The memoirs reveal that ministers from both unionist and nationalist sides were committed to maintaining the Executive, but the lessons drawn for the post-election period were, as usual, quite different. For Faulkner, whose position was now very obviously threatened, the realisation was dawning that the

Sunningdale settlement required urgent amendment, particularly with regard to the cross-border dimension. Faulkner argued that amongst the SDLP leadership there were differences of emphasis between the Belfast representatives (like Fitt and Devlin), and the 'countrymen', who were more Dublin-oriented.[60] There is some evidence to support this view, perhaps especially in the case of Fitt, but his biographer laments that

> there was no one in the party [SDLP] who would advise it to lower its sights when the future of the Executive lay in the balance – primarily over the ambiguity of the Council of Ireland. That role should surely have been played by its leader [...] But Fitt did not have the status or authority to change the direction of the party.[61]

In retrospect, what had looked like one of the strengths of Sunningdale, its open-ended and ambivalent quality, had both permitted the loyalist scare-tactics to succeed, and also allowed a significant gap to grow between the parties of the Executive. By mid-March, formal efforts to (re-)negotiate the Council of Ireland had started, with Faulkner proposing a two-stage plan for its implementation, involving a consultative role in the first phase, and the creation of executive functions and a permanent secretariat only *after* the next Assembly elections. Implicit in this stance was the unionist perception that the Boland case had materially altered the landscape, with Faulkner now pressing for a firm commitment that Articles 2 and 3 would be the subject of a serious proposal for repeal. Whilst the Executive attempted to deal with this critical obstacle, the Assembly was debating a motion (proposed by an 'unpledged' unionist, John Laird) that called for a complete re-negotiation of the whole constitutional settlement. Devlin described this as the start of 'the direct course of events that led to the fall of the Executive', and he recalled that the debate was 'viciously bruising'.[62]

In his evaluation of the process which led to the settlement's unravelling, Devlin looked back and acknowledged that the SDLP had 'paid little heed to his [Faulkner's] fears at first, for we judged he had enough support to carry the day inside and outside the Assembly'.[63] However, Devlin also recognised later on that Faulkner's fears were justified, given the further splintering of his support base. In the meantime, violence from both republicans and loyalists was intensifying (seventy-four people were killed between January and April 1974), and it is easy, in retrospect, to overlook the debilitating effects of regular news reports of murders and bombings. Many of these memoirists recall their despair at this time, both in terms of the personal effects of the violence, which often touched elected representatives directly, and with regard to its capacity to undermine the Executive's *raison d'être*.[64] As well as the Assembly debate, the deteriorating security position, and the problem of the stalled negotiation on the Council of Ireland, the British Labour government was accused by all the Northern Irish politicians of failing to take concerted action. As far as the SDLP was concerned, the UK government was 'clearly not in control of the situation, neither providing security, nor moving to end internment'.[65] The unionist camp within the Executive had been deeply concerned at 'another of the early Labour gaffes': Defence Secretary Roy Mason had intervened in Northern Ireland policy by offering the view that there was a widespread public desire in Great Britain for troops to be withdrawn.[66]

There may well have been some truth in this view, but to state it publicly could only inflame unionist sentiment. The UK Secretary of State, Merlyn Rees, was subject to criticism for his tendency to prevaricate; he was accused of sitting on the fence and ducking difficult decisions. On the other hand, it is difficult to see how firm decisions (particularly in terms of security policy and internment) could have done anything other than drive a more pronounced wedge between Faulkner and the SDLP. Indeed, the continuation of the phased release of some detainees allied to the deproscription of Sinn Féin and the Ulster Volunteer Force antagonised many in both communities, though for very different reasons. In truth, the new Westminster government found itself in a difficult position right from its inception; as Bloomfield interpreted things, the government and Rees were sincere in their commitment to support the Executive, but it was understandably preoccupied with trying to shore up its own fragile position, and Northern Ireland was not the policy field uppermost in the British Labour Party's considerations. Ultimately, 'a Labour government did not feel for the Sunningdale Agreement and the Executive system that almost proprietorial solidarity that a Conservative government, with Whitelaw in high office, would feel.'[67]

The Ulster Workers' Council Strike:
'A Nightmarish, Surreal Experience'[68]

The denouement for the Executive came in the shape of the loyalist Ulster Workers' Council (UWC) strike over the last two weeks in May 1974.[69] The strike (more akin to a 'putsch' in the view of Faulkner), began on the day the Assembly finally agreed to an Executive amendment to Laird's motion; this effectively closed down the parliamentary route for loyalist protest over Sunningdale. The memoirists considered here maintain divergent views regarding whether this challenge could have been met and, if so, how. Therefore, whilst the prevailing emotion at the time was one of bitter frustration, and the passage of time has not lightened the sense of gloom and sorrow for the demise of power-sharing, there is no easy consensus concerning the fate of the Executive, and where primary responsibility lies for its historical failure. Most of the political memoirs studied were written largely from a self-justifying stance, although it is instructive that several make a sincere effort to portray other views sympathetically. In the cases of many of these ministers, the UWC delivered the *coup de grâce* to their careers, at least as office-holders in a government administration. Some, like McIvor, effectively walked away from frontline political activity. Thus, they had deeply personal reasons for regretting the ending of this experiment, but it is also clear that their reflections are infused with a broader sense of having failed in their societal responsibility.

Who exactly should shoulder the bulk of the blame for the failures of this era remained a moot point: as one might expect, the paramilitary groups on both sides come in for vehement criticism. However, for Faulkner and his supporters, the refusal of the Irish government to do more on the recognition of the constitutional status of Northern Ireland, as well as the SDLP dragging its feet concerning the re-negotiation of the Council of Ireland, were key issues. Yet, it was the *laissez-faire* attitude of the British government that perturbed Faulkner most. He argued that Westminster, having refused to transfer responsibility for law and order policy to the Executive, was 'now well and truly hoist with its own petard'.[70] According to Faulkner, the ambivalence concerning the strike from Rees (Labour NIO ministers 'were more accustomed to viewing strikers sympathetically than taking action against them') was compounded by the fact that he 'seemed to have gone into a flap. I was never sure later if his failure to give any leadership from the beginning was due to his hope that the strike would peter out, or to warnings from the Army that it should not get involved in a second front by taking on the para-military Protestants. I believe it to have been the latter.'[71] Predictably, Rees himself took a different stance. In his memoir, he cited Faulkner's own admission that the UWC had been underestimated, but he nonetheless acknowledged that his security advisers had also failed to spot the danger approaching: 'in retrospect, it was a threat that should have been taken more seriously.'[72] Others, from both unionist and nationalist backgrounds, have concurred with this judgment: Austin Currie reported 'no great concern [in the Stormont bar] that the strike, scheduled to begin at 6.00pm, posed any major threat to the Executive.'[73]

At the time, the reaction of many nationalists was that robust security force action could have nipped the UWC strike in the bud. In his memoir written almost twenty years later, Paddy Devlin continued to profess astonishment at the lack of action by 'a combined security force of over 30,000 soldiers and policemen, who did not lift a finger to stop it'.[74] In Currie's opinion, 'had there been effective action, in the early days of the strike, to stop intimidation and to keep roads open, it would have fizzled out.'[75] This 'acquiescence' to the strike by Rees and the British Army simply encouraged loyalists to believe they could intimidate with impunity: 'in all the years since I have never been given a believable explanation of why the strikers were allowed to gain such an initial grip.'[76] An Irish government minister, Garret FitzGerald, took a similar line in his recollections when he argued that Rees had 'spectacularly failed to tackle the extreme loyalists who organised the Ulster workers' strike'.[77] Civil servants such as Ken Bloomfield and Maurice Hayes also reported their sense of frustration at the inaction of the police, who seemed willing to allow the UWC to set up roadblocks with impunity. For both ministers and civil servants during this fortnight, the daily commute to Stormont became more than the usual wearisome chore, and instead a hair-raising drama, with the streets apparently under the total control of the strikers. Hayes recalled that 'nobody who was involved at the time believes that the strike could not have been halted by a couple of jeeps taking effective action patrolling up and down the Newtownards Road [in East Belfast] on those first couple of days.'[78]

However, there are also more nuanced accounts of this period, which cast considerable doubt on the implication that the prospects for the Executive would have been relatively bright, if only the UWC strike had been successfully challenged. This alternative view takes into consideration the degree to which the power-sharing Executive was already deeply damaged, and particularly recognises the strength of popular support among Protestants for the overthrow of the Sunningdale settlement. As McIvor understood, this was 'an extraordinary rebellion by the vast majority of one million Protestants, which brought down a government with hardly a shot being fired'.[79] Merlyn Rees also reflected that the UWC enjoyed 'massive support from the [unionist] community'.[80] Such sentiment applied across the class divide within unionism; as Bloomfield pointed out dejectedly, many business people and members of the respectable middle-class were ultimately pragmatic in their approach to political authority. Once it became clear to them that the strike was not going to be dealt with robustly, they effectively transferred their allegiance, or at least withheld their support, from the Executive.[81] Gordon Gillespie argued convincingly that

> those who attribute the success of the strike only to weak government and bully-boy tactics are misreading the situation. Given the background against which the strike took place, even if the strike had failed, the most likely outcomes were either a continued leaking of support from Faulkner and his eventual resignation, or a head-on confrontation between loyalists and the security forces leading to casualties.[82]

In a revealing passage, Currie appeared to endorse this view at least to some extent, even if he subsequently used it to reinforce a wider argument concerning unionist intransigence: 'for a significant section of the Protestant population, it was "payback time". Some of them felt that it had been one-way traffic since

1968, with the erosion of the Protestant and Unionist position and one defeat after another for them and one victory after another for the "other side."'[83] Rees also gave an insight into the thinking of the NIO in the aftermath of the UWC strike: 'there was a feeling of tit for tat: the republicans had toppled Stormont, the loyalists had now brought down the Executive. It was one victory each.'[84]

In a final ironic twist, the parties of the Executive eventually agreed a deal on the Council of Ireland, which reflected in large measure Faulkner's proposed phased implementation, but only after the SDLP had voted to reject the compromise once. In the end, such movement came too late to make a substantive difference; if anything, although the re-negotiation had taken several months, it was greeted as an emergency response to the strike, and effectively as a concession to the UWC. Faulkner, in a last throw of the dice, put a proposal to the Executive to approach Rees with a view to appointing an intermediary to contact the UWC; the SDLP rejected the move. Rees was also unwilling to negotiate with the strikers, and Faulkner resigned. There was, unusually in Northern Irish political life, little recrimination amongst the politicians who had invested so much in the Executive. Indeed, what these memoirs make plain is the overwhelming sentiment of profound regret at the failure, and the firm belief that if Northern Ireland was to have any hope for a peaceful future, the constitutional parties would have 'to come back to this point again'.[85] Faulkner composed his memoirs only three years after these events, but he was to be proved correct, eventually, though only after a great deal more blood had been shed. Other memoirs were written with greater distance from the events, but the emotions expressed remained raw; if anything, given the intervening years of violent conflict, the loss felt at the failure of power-sharing was even more intense for these later memoirists.

The psychological toll imposed during these months, and the genuine feeling of despair in the aftermath, is reflected in McIvor's admission that 'the strain of the last hours of the Executive became almost unbearable. For the first time, I experienced real, stomach-gripping fear [...] The last chance had gone, and I did not believe there would be another in my lifetime.'[86] In the SDLP, the emotions were similarly suffused with a valedictory melancholia. Currie, who had proven himself an energetic minister, described the period following the fall of the Executive as one of 'depression and frustration, personally and politically'; he found himself in the political wilderness, and he came close to turning his back on his political career.[87] Ultimately, Currie chose to concentrate his energies on political life in the Republic, where he was elected as a Fine Gael TD in 1989 (and stood unsuccessfully as the party's candidate in the Presidential election the following year). Paddy Devlin chose to stress the significance of this experience (regarding his time in office as the 'defining episodes of my private and political life'[88]), but he also introduced a strong sense of pathos into his conclusion: 'I don't really know how much I achieved in my career […] I have a great feeling of disappointment that a labour movement did not emerge to break the cycle of sectarian conflict.'[89] For the civil servants who had been intimately involved with the operation of power-sharing, the sense of loss was barely any less acute. Bloomfield recounted his tearful reaction to the fall of the Executive:

> I wept for the triumph of narrow-mindedness and deeply entrenched prejudice […] I wept for the success of the hard men with the dark glasses, balaclava helmets and pickaxe handles; I wept for the inevitability of a sweeping British judgement that we were all hopeless cases, doomed to endless conflict in an inferno of our own creation; I wept for the eclipse of local democracy.[90]

Maurice Hayes, writing in the mid-1990s, could still lament the demise of the Executive and Sunningdale with the words 'I believe it was the nearest we came to a resolution of the problem of governing Northern Ireland, and possibly the nearest in my lifetime. Any foreseeable outcome of the present peace process is not likely to differ markedly from Sunningdale.'[91] This judgment was arguably borne out after the negotiation of the Belfast Agreement.

The memoirists studied here tend to take a generous approach to the political legacy of Faulkner, partly due to a genuine belief that the Chief Executive had displayed a 'decent and honest willingness to take real risks for political progress',[92] but also perhaps due to the opprobrium he endured. His untimely death due to a horse riding accident may also have played a role. Still, it is instructive that Faulkner, who had clearly misjudged the prevailing mood within unionism during this period, is rarely criticised directly in these memoirs. Instead, he tends to be praised for his efforts, and blame for the breakdown of the Executive is more often laid at the door of those who are viewed as having pushed him too far. Bloomfield characterised the matter thus: '[Faulkner] allowed himself to be pushed into a politically unsustainable position.'[93] Here, Bloomfield was writing in a sober reassessment of the governance of Northern Ireland over the course of the Troubles. Perhaps a better flavour of his feelings about Faulkner may be found in his memoir: 'I had formed, in those traumatic months, a profound admiration for Brian Faulkner, for his unfailing courage, endurance and generosity of understanding. The bogeyman of the sixties had become the man of principle of the seventies […] He deserves to be remembered with respect.'[94] Basil McIvor 'came to like and admire him [Faulkner] as a man whose buoyancy, optimism and capacity to face the most difficult challenges did much for my morale […] I would have followed him almost anywhere, and did.'[95]

If it comes as little surprise that those who worked closely with Faulkner, and to a large extent shared his political outlook, should be highly supportive of his record, and solicitous of his memory, then it should be noted that even for a political opponent like Devlin, Faulkner revealed himself as the 'lasting surprise' of this period; he emerged not as 'a dour, scheming sabbatarian, but [as a] courageous visionary who relaxed with us, shared our jokes, and even accompanied us to the Members' Bar and bought his round. There is no doubt that he was by far the most effective politician ever to walk the corridors of Stormont.'[96] Devlin was unusual amongst SDLP memoirists in that he believed at the time that Faulkner, 'whose political support was already haemorrhaging dangerously, had been asked to swallow too much in one gulp at Sunningdale'.[97] Others were not quite so effusive, but Whitelaw was also willing to recognise that 'I did not give enough thought to helping Brian Faulkner [...] Under the circumstances I am convinced that [he] handled his party bravely and skilfully.'[98] Robert Ramsay, another senior Northern Irish civil servant, who was based in Brussels during the Sunningdale negotiation, was also slightly more circumspect in his judgment on Faulkner: whilst he recognised that the forces ranged against the UUP leader were formidable, nevertheless, 'despite these disadvantages, Faulkner might have achieved a better deal had he played harder to get.'[99] Both the British and Irish governments knew they required Faulkner to make any deal stick, and this was his 'only strong card', but he failed to play it, according to Ramsay, because he was determined to get Stormont up and running again, almost to the exclusion of all other considerations, even his own prospects.

In the final analysis, while there may be room for disagreement concerning the precise mix of factors that contributed to the demise of power-sharing, there is remarkable consensus in these memoirs that 'the fate of the Executive was to be like that of a frail new boat of radical and untested design sent out for its trials into the middle of a typhoon.'[100] Whether one places more weight upon the strength of loyalist intransigence (Rees), or upon the Council of Ireland and SDLP unwillingness to modify earlier the pyrrhic victory they had won at Sunningdale (Bloomfield, Devlin), upon the Westminster general election of February 1974 (Whitelaw, Hayes), or upon the UK government's pusillanimous response to the UWC strike (Currie), ultimately the people of Northern Ireland paid a heavy price for the fall of the experiment. Reading these memoirs from many of the key protagonists can help us construct a fuller interpretation of these critical few months, when 'if the Executive failed, the men who served in it did not fail.'[101]

Chapter 8

British Ministers and the Politics of Northern Ireland: Reading the Political Memoirs of Secretaries of State

Introduction

This chapter will analyse the politics of memoir-writing by British government ministers during the 1970s and up to the present, in particular examining the ways in which British Secretaries of State for Northern Ireland (SOSNI) have used their published memoirs to interpret and reflect upon their period in office, and their perceptions of the Troubles. The chapter will argue that for the majority of SOSNI incumbents, Northern Ireland and its politico-military problems tended not to be central to their political identities, and for many of them the experience of being responsible for the governance of, and policy-making in, Northern Ireland was deeply unsatisfactory. At times, a sense of regret and futility pervades these accounts; many admit to a sense of uncertainty or even bewilderment at the outset, with most SOSNI being largely unschooled in the complexities of political life in Northern Ireland before taking up their posts. The memoirs reflect a steep 'learning curve', but very often accompanied by a strong desire to make progress with regard to the constitutional reform process, and the search for stable power-sharing devolution, the consistent though elusive goal of UK government policy.

In the absence of significant progress on the core constitutional dispute, many SOSNI express feelings of weariness and frustration at the end of their period in office. Analysis of the memoirs reveals that there was often a gulf between the perceptions of the incumbents, and both the local Northern Ireland politicians and the members of the Westminster cabinet. The chapter will concentrate upon the memoirs of the following SOSNI from the period of the Troubles: William Whitelaw (1972–3); Merlyn Rees (1974–6); Roy Mason (1976–9); James Prior (1981–3); Douglas Hurd (1983–5). In partial contrast, the memoirs of SOSNI from the period of the 'peace process' will also be investigated, in order to compare the significant differences between these periods: Mo Mowlam

(1997–9), Peter Mandelson (1999–2001) and Peter Hain (2005–7) have also published accounts of their time in Northern Ireland. In addition, this chapter will include some analysis and discussion of other British politicians who, whilst not serving as SOSNI, nonetheless played important roles in the UK government's response to the conflict, and who have published memoirs that deal explicitly with their contribution: James Callaghan (as Labour Home Secretary in 1969 at the outbreak of communal disorder and rioting) published *A House Divided: The Dilemma of Northern Ireland* in 1973, and was one of the first politicians based at Westminster to have some responsibility for the governance of Northern Ireland, although not to the same degree as the later 'direct rulers'.[1] Equally, Richard Needham was the longest-serving UK minister under direct rule, spending seven years (1985–92) in the Northern Ireland Office (NIO) during the Thatcher and Major governments. He published his memoir in 1998, as the negotiation of the Belfast (or Good Friday) Agreement was ushering in a period where the promise of devolution of power to a Northern Ireland Executive would potentially change the engagement of London-based politicians dramatically.[2] The chapter concludes with some reflections on the utility of studying these ministerial memoirs and the light they can shed upon the role and position of SOSNI in the historical interpretation of the Troubles.

To a certain degree, these memoirs may be interpreted as a sub-genre of Westminster ministerial memoirs, and as such they are often used to attempt to seal a minister's reputation, perhaps to settle old scores, and to promote the individual's place in the political history of the times. As Andrew Gamble has argued, the ministerial memoir has 'become an expected rite of passage for political celebrity, and also a highly profitable one'.[3] Of course, as with most political memoirs, the extent to which the author reveals merely their 'political self', rather than unveiling important dimensions of their personal, emotional lives, is a key feature of such publications. It may be that the monetary value of such publications is somewhat overstated, but certainly even if ex-ministers are more likely to feather their nests through company directorships and the like, many remain keen to write their memoirs, and make an effort to shape the historical agenda to some extent. In the context of the bloody conflict in Northern Ireland, British ministers may also believe that they have some insight into the problems afflicting the region, and they may also hope that their experiences, for good or ill, can be utilised by future policy-makers.[4] Moreover, at least as far as those SOSNI involved in the, ultimately successful, 'peace process' of the 1990s–2000s were concerned, they have a 'good news' story to tell. So, whether the primary motivation is self-exculpatory (if events have gone badly during their time in office), or self-celebratory, many ministers have been keen to explain themselves, to relate the lived experience of their involvement with Northern Ireland, and to seek to preserve or augment their place in posterity. Also, lest we be too cynical regarding the motivations of ministers, there is at least some evidence that some SOSNI have been genuine and sincere in their commitment to Northern Ireland and its people, and have maintained their desire to improve their lot, even when no longer in office. On the other hand, there are those for whom Northern Ireland was an unwelcome posting, and one they were only too happy to move on from. In these memoirs, therefore, can be seen a wide variety of approaches, but also a number of significant continuities in the fashion in which British government ministers have reflected upon their time in the province.

There are a number of important differences from other Cabinet posts, not the least of which is that, during the Troubles at any rate, lives were directly at stake in Northern Ireland, in a fashion that wasn't very often the case in other departments. Arguably, it might be logically expected that this would result in a sensitive appointments process for SOSNI, but there is only scant evidence to suggest that this was, in fact, taken into consideration by Prime ministers. Secondly, the SOSNI was not elected by the people of Northern Ireland and the perception of both nationalists and unionists was that these individuals had been 'parachuted' into Belfast, often with little prior knowledge or understanding of the complex issues to be dealt with. By the same token, SOSNI could also be removed or reshuffled out of Belfast, often at a time which may have suited the purposes of the Prime Minister and government in London, but which could also destabilise the precarious politics of the province. This added to a perception, shared by both the general public and civil servants in the Northern Ireland administration, that many British ministers saw their time in Belfast as an exotic interlude.[5] Undoubtedly, many SOSNI recognised that the local population felt they had been 'foisted' upon the province, and this was often a difficult starting point from which to build new relationships. As Bloomfield and Lankford argue, 'the fortunate Secretary will simply be treated with general suspicion from all sides on arrival [...] A less fortunate one may find him or herself rejected in advance by one side in particular.'[6] The upshot of this often contested arrival is that the problems associated with a difficult post are likely to be exacerbated: if many in both communities are suspicious, and view the new SOSNI in a negative light, this very fact *in itself* increases the difficulties.

On the other hand, many incumbents recognise that although Northern Ireland might not represent one of the 'great offices' in government, nonetheless under direct rule from Westminster, SOSNI enjoyed a degree of power (and responsibility) that was not always available to other Cabinet ministers based in London. The Secretary has 'effectively the full range of Cabinet powers in one'[7]; as Peter Hain remarked, the SOSNI was 'quite literally in charge of everything there [in Northern Ireland ...] I rather enjoyed the opportunity to run the place myself. There was no other job in Cabinet, aside from being Prime Minister, where you effectively governed a whole country, in charge of everything from agriculture to security.'[8] The breadth of the SOSNI's role, and the existence of a stark democratic deficit, led some incumbents and observers to refer to the post as somewhat akin to a Governor-General: 'within Northern Ireland, no-one elects them. Within Northern Ireland, no-one even appoints them [... they are] answerable in the first place not to those they govern but to those by whom they were appointed.'[9] James Prior argued that the SOSNI fulfilled a dual role, acting as the representative of the Crown on one hand, and as a 'boxing referee' between the two antagonistic communities on the other; the best he or she might hope for was to be 'equally resented' by both sides. Unsurprisingly, given this rather downbeat assessment, Prior felt himself 'a foreigner in another land'.[10]

The SOSNI had overall responsibility for political and constitutional matters, for the broad policy outlines of the Northern Ireland Office, and specifically for security. In certain policy areas, SOSNI would delegate to junior ministers, but for better or worse, it was the Secretary of State who tended to have the high public profile, whether during the violent conflict, or during the search for peace. Whilst this public profile (in Northern Ireland, at least) meant that SOSNI had a greater degree of media interest than comparable ministerial jobs, this was not always appreciated by the incumbents: Douglas Hurd confessed that he felt 'like a doomed French aristocrat facing a bloodthirsty mob', during his first Stormont press conference.[11] Echoing the themes of innocence (and ignorance) of Northern Irish affairs upon his appointment as SOSNI, Hurd continued,

> I knew little more about the Province than any other conscientious follower of public events. Suddenly, dressed in a little authority which might or might not be brief, I had to assume the manner of a proconsul, and a proconsul exposed to constant public examination by journalists longing for him to stumble.[12]

For William Whitelaw, the chosen metaphor was of a 'lamb to the slaughter'. What these impressions divulge is the extent to which many SOSNI viewed themselves as neophytes in the maelstrom of Northern Irish politics. They may have been self-confident and assured in the corridors of Westminster and Whitehall, but in the unfamiliar surroundings of Stormont, this could be a lonely and bewildering environment. From a different perspective, the public profile of SOSNI could be understood as diminished by a posting to Belfast; Mo Mowlam recognised that the 'vast majority [of the British general public] did not want to know what was going on [in Northern Ireland]. They were aware of the violence but it was not their problem.'[13]

The Experience of Northern Ireland: Marginal or Central?

For many of the memoirists considered here, their time spent as SOSNI was a minor interlude in a ministerial career whose main achievements lay elsewhere. For Douglas Hurd, the Northern Ireland post represented a first rung on the Cabinet ladder, which would lead on to stints as both Home Secretary and Foreign Secretary. Understandably, his time in Belfast merited only a relatively brief chapter in his memoirs. Similarly, Peter Mandelson and William Whitelaw's experience in Northern Ireland was relatively short-lived, and their period as SOSNI did not define their careers. By contrast, for a smaller number of SOSNI, this role proved to be *the* central aspect of their ministerial experience, and perhaps their political lives *tout court*. The memoir-writing of Mo Mowlam, for instance, is devoted to her period in Northern Ireland, although she did subsequently occupy another ministerial role at the Cabinet Office. It is probably not incidental that both Mowlam, and one of her predecessors, Merlyn Rees (who also devoted his memoir to his views of and experience in Northern Ireland), had served lengthy periods as Shadow SOSNI before they took up the post in government. Both knew a good deal about the political situation prevailing in Northern Ireland at the time of their appointment, in contrast to the position of Hurd, for instance. They were schooled in the nuances of political life in Belfast, and had met and (at least to some degree) understood the political views of the main parties and protagonists that they would be dealing with. Clearly, foreknowledge of the major personalities, and in addition a sound grounding in the historical evolution of the conflict, were important advantages, which were unavailable to those SOSNI who found themselves thrust into the job with little or no warning. Those with a background of interest and knowledge had at least two advantages over the others: first, they had the opportunity to build up contacts in Northern Ireland, amongst both politicians and civil society; second, they had some time to develop their thinking about potential approaches to policy development.

Mowlam had served as a junior shadow minister in Labour's team in 1989–90, and then as Shadow SOSNI from 1994 until the party's election victory in 1997. After 1990, she had maintained her interest in political developments, partly because these were the fledgling days of the peace process, but also 'because once you have engaged in the problems of N. Ireland it is very difficult to let go.'[14] After Tony Blair became leader in 1994, she oversaw a period of policy change in the Labour Party, moving away from the 'unhappy position' of unity by consent (the policy that had been adopted in 1981, as a compromise with the growing demands at that time of a faction in favour of British withdrawal from Northern Ireland), and towards a more balanced constitutional outlook.[15] Merlyn Rees had spent two years as Labour Party spokesperson before he became SOSNI, and he had also been interested in the issues during his time at the Home Office, when

James Callaghan had been engaged with the breakdown of law and order in 1969: 'the province and all its problems entered my bloodstream.'[16] Even James Prior, who was neither as well-prepared nor as keen on his appointment as SOSNI, recognised that 'once Northern Ireland gets into your system, I doubt if you can ever be free of it.'[17] This formulation appears rather less fulsome than either Mowlam or Rees', and it suggests that Prior reflected on his experiences with a degree of ambivalence.

Whether thrown in at the deep end, or taking over with a certain degree of confidence, most of these memoirists are willing to recognise their feelings of trepidation upon their arrival at the NIO. However, this also tends to be mixed with excitement; the SOSNI post appeals to the ego of British ministers, according to Prior. There is the prospect of succeeding where others have failed, although the scope for policy innovation and what might constitute 'success' could be dependent upon factors outside the control of the office-holder. For example, Prior arrived in Belfast whilst the 1981 republican hunger strike was still underway, and he was immediately struck by how deeply polarised the communities were. Although the hunger strike came to an end in October 1981, Prior does not seek to present this outcome as his own success, given his appointment only the previous month. Interestingly, in his memoir of working within the civil service in Belfast, Maurice Hayes argued that 'Prior and Gowrie [a junior minister at the NIO] between them had done much to lance the boil of the hunger strikes.'[18] Of course, the scramble by ministers to take credit for policy success, and evade responsibility for perceived failure, is not unique to the Northern Ireland experience, but it might be argued that the stakes are often higher when decisions are viewed, fairly or unfairly, in the light of the intensity of conflict, and the risks of death and violence accompanying the political process. Another SOSNI memoir captures well the idea that a term in Belfast need not be the graveyard of political reputation: 'I wasn't so puffed up as to imagine I could solve the problems of centuries. But perhaps I could make a start.'[19]

Welcome to Belfast, Minister! Appointing the Secretary of State

The process of appointing and removing ministers is usually opaque and shrouded in political calculation. Prime ministers have a large number of variables to take into consideration when making these appointments, and it is fair to say that Northern Ireland is very rarely, if ever, the number one priority during the complex manoeuvring involved in piecing together a workable Cabinet. When, in late 1978 in the dying days of the Callaghan administration, Maurice Hayes, a senior civil servant, was concerned that an incoming Westminster government would have no clear strategy for dealing with an expected upsurge in republican paramilitary activity, he arranged a meeting with Lord Donoughue in order to voice his anxieties. The response was brusque: the government only had 'time to deal with the first three items on the national news on any day. Furthermore, he said, if he were to draw up a list of the thirty issues causing most concern to government, Northern Ireland would not figure on it.'[20] As Bloomfield and Lankford argue, 'either way, as reward or punishment, the manipulation of appointments to the position of Secretary, particularly in recent years, has been interpreted in Northern Ireland as indicative of the relative unimportance of the region on the British domestic political agenda.'[21] Ultimately, therefore, despite the obvious significance of the post for political life in Northern Ireland, the appointments process for SOSNI was very likely to be governed by all manner of extraneous concerns. On some occasions, the decision might be determined largely by factors that also applied to other Cabinet posts: for instance, for the traditional motivation of rewarding loyalty; or as a testing ground for relatively inexperienced, but promising, politicians; or for reasons to do with the intra-party balance in the governing party. In certain cases, the PM's decision might also take into account that the individual concerned had a particular interest and policy expertise in Northern Ireland (as we have already seen in the case of Mowlam or Rees). More often than not, however, the appointment of SOSNI was unlikely to be based upon any perception or expectation that the new incumbent would have specific expertise or even any new policy ideas for the task.

More specifically, SOSNI have been selected (and removed) in order to send a particular message to the political parties (and, by extension, the general public) in Northern Ireland. Perhaps the clearest example of such an appointment is the decision by Blair to send Peter Mandelson to Belfast in 1999, as a replacement for Mowlam, during a highly sensitive period in which the Good Friday Agreement was the subject of acrimonious dispute. Relations between the Ulster Unionist Party (UUP) and Mowlam, which had never been warm, were at breaking point, and Mandelson was thought to be much more amenable to working closely with the Unionist leadership, thereby shoring up the position of David Trimble. This removal of Mowlam in favour of Mandelson revealed a clear rift within the Labour Party, which had both policy and personal dimensions. These have been played out in uncompromising fashion in their respective memoirs. According to Mowlam, her appointment was unusual in the sense that not only was she well-versed in the problems of Northern Ireland before taking up the SOSNI post, but she was the first woman to undertake the role. In her estimation, this fact, in addition to her determinedly informal style, shook up the complacent (and almost entirely male) world of the civil servants and politicians (and, later on, the paramilitaries) she had to deal with. Her warm reception from the ordinary people of Belfast, during an impromptu walkabout on her first day in the job, convinced Mowlam that her approach could yield dividends:

the overwhelming view [of the people she met] was: please help to stop the violence; the Brits have never sent us a woman before – perhaps you can help. I took strength from the fact that men and women on the streets regarded the fact that I was a woman as a good thing. It continued to give me strength as the months went by and I was abused as a politician and because I was a woman.[22]

Even at a relatively early stage, however, Mowlam's relations both with the mainstream unionists of the UUP and with the government at Westminster showed some signs of strain. Mowlam puts the latter down to her burgeoning public profile, and her successes, and the former is interpreted by her as essentially a product of old-fashioned prejudice, based upon her gender and her informal approach.

Two very different versions of a breakfast at the Savoy hotel may serve as an illustration both of the often self-serving character of political memoir-writing and of the harsh reality of realpolitik, individual manoeuvring for power, and brutal egotism that may be found around the Cabinet table. In Mowlam's version, she and Mandelson had been genuine friends while Labour was in opposition, even sharing a holiday together in Spain. After Mandelson had been forced to resign as Secretary of State for Trade and Industry in December 1998 (due to a scandal related to a home loan), Mowlam took him to breakfast in 'an attempt to cheer him up. He was his usual mixture of charm and arrogance. Every sentence began with "I". He did not ask me one question [...] By the end of the breakfast I regretted having asked him.'[23] Of course, Mowlam was writing retrospectively, and her bitterness at her ousting by No. 10, and what she alleged was an orchestrated campaign to remove her, is clearly present. By contrast, Mandelson, whose memoir was published in 2010 (fully eight years after Mowlam's, and also after her early death from cancer in 2005) recounted the events leading to his eventual appointment as SOSNI quite differently. The breakfast at the Savoy was a 'huge tonic. She offered sympathy and support, and said that it was not just her expectation but her wish that I would be back in the Cabinet. Neither of us, however, could have anticipated the circumstances, difficult for both of us, in which that was to happen.'[24]

In Mowlam's account, her position was progressively undermined in several ways: on one hand by the PM, who increasingly bypassed his SOSNI in favour of trusting the delicate negotiations involving the Northern Ireland parties to his close personal adviser, Jonathan Powell. On the other hand, Mandelson is accused of planting stories in the press, to the effect that Mowlam's position had been fatally weakened, and that she was likely to be moved to the Cabinet Office:

It was clear to me that Peter was up to his old tricks [...] I was angry at what Peter was doing, but I knew I would make matters worse if I said so in public. In my opinion, Peter cared first for himself and only second for the government and what it was trying to do in Northern Ireland.[25]

Perhaps unsurprisingly, Mandelson does not engage directly with these accusations in his memoir, but he effectively acknowledges that, by the summer of 1999, No. 10 had become 'convinced that Mo's role had reached a natural endpoint'. The UUP had never been very keen on Mowlam's 'forthright style and salty language', although SF leaders had initially found her style refreshing, suggesting an openness not often associated with SOSNI. However, in Mandelson's view, 'even Sinn Féin seemed to have concluded that she was past her sell-by date, and Adams and McGuinness increasingly insisted on dealing directly with Tony and Jonathan Powell.'[26] However, Mandelson makes an explicit denial that he knew he was to be offered the SOSNI role, and he recounts a conversation with Mowlam in the spring of 1999 (which does not feature in Mowlam's own memoir), in which she wanted Mandelson to tell Blair that she was only willing to leave Belfast for a 'promotion', preferably to become Foreign Secretary. Mandelson reports that he promised to pass on this message, even though he knew that Blair's reaction would be that 'this would be hard to imagine.' Mowlam was not seen as a diplomat, and there was an implicit sense that her request was not taken seriously. Mandelson's account is that the PM

> delivered his bolt from the blue: he wanted me to take Mo's place in Northern Ireland. His reasoning was that he needed someone in Belfast who would start with a clean slate, especially with the unionists, and who could understand not just the negotiating issues but the politics that often overshadowed them. Of course I was flattered, intrigued and tempted.[27]

Mowlam was furious with Mandelson and, in his account, 'she phoned me and accused me of trying to steal her job.' He suggests that he was 'shaken by the idea of finding [himself] cast as the agent of Mo's removal, even though I realised the principal target of her anger was Tony'.[28] Mandelson claims that he tried to convince Blair to delay, and leave Mowlam in post, but eventually the Cabinet reshuffle happened in October 1999, after Mowlam had resisted for several months. The denouement to this disputed episode involved Mowlam escorting Mandelson to Hillsborough Castle in Co. Down (which had been used as the SOSNI residence since the 1980s[29]), in order to facilitate his settling in, and introduce him to the staff. Mowlam recounted that she did her best to smooth the process, but her sense of hurt was made plain: 'that was the last I heard from Peter during his time in Northern Ireland. I had served my purpose for him.'[30] Mandelson, presumably having read Mowlam's disparaging description of his actions during the process of her removal, nevertheless states that she showed him around Hillsborough with 'real delight'. This seems, on the face of it, hardly likely! These conflicting reminiscences display the vagaries of personalised history, and the problems associated with determining where the 'truth' ultimately lies in competing reconstructions of past political events. Nevertheless, these competing accounts may still help to understand the role of SOSNI, the significance of the incumbent's relationship both with the parties in Northern Ireland, and with the PM. There is effectively a consensus in these memoirs with respect to the breakdown in the relationship between Mowlam and the UUP, even if her view was that this problem was not insurmountable.

Another dimension to the SOSNI appointment relates to its distance, both literally and metaphorically, from the centre of governmental affairs. In the case of Prior, it has already been noted that he was far from keen on taking the job, viewing it as a 'punishment' meted out by a vindictive prime minister, who was intent on removing from any position of influence an individual who was out of sympathy with her 'Thatcherite' recipe for the British economy and society. This example, although quite rare in the overall history of SOSNI appointments, has nevertheless played a major role in establishing a popular conception of SOSNI as a form of 'internal exile', or in Prior's more colourful language, as the equivalent of 'being sent to Siberia'. After he had been removed from his post in Belfast, Prior reflected: 'I think it is a pity that Northern Ireland is always regarded as if it were a dustbin. I went there because Mrs Thatcher was fed up with me at home.'[31] In this case, even once he was in post, Prior acknowledged in his memoir his sense of being bypassed or ignored by the PM. Policy towards Northern Ireland was influenced at least as much by Thatcher's trusted supporter, Ian Gow MP (later to be killed by the IRA), as it was by the SOSNI. Prior's plans for a 'rolling devolution' initiative were watered down, and specifically any inclusion of an 'Irish dimension' in the plans was effectively vetoed, on the basis that the Cabinet would not have supported the implementation of the plan in such circumstances. Prior's position was undermined, both within the Cabinet, but also within Northern Ireland itself, making progress even less likely.[32] As with Mowlam, although for different reasons, the knowledge that a SOSNI does not enjoy the confidence of the PM may well make the post untenable. In the case of Prior, it was not so much that he had lost the support of one side or the other in Belfast, but that he received little or no support from No. 10. Although Mowlam was loath to leave, she nonetheless came to recognise that the constant briefing against her had made the job impossible.

For those SOSNI without a prior interest or grounding in the political affairs of Northern Ireland, the problems of being thrust into an unfamiliar and testing environment, with little or no preparation, could be almost overwhelming. In the Victorian spirit of generalism and amateurism that still seemed to prevail in the

Westminster and Whitehall model of public administration, new ministers were expected to pick up the reins left dangling by their predecessor, and implement government policy, whichever post they were 'parachuted' into, and wherever it happened to take them. In a political environment as fraught and potentially dangerous as Belfast, to effectively ask ministers to learn 'on the job' appeared an odd way to conduct government. As Hurd made plain, there was no formal handover when he was promoted to become SOSNI, even though there had been speculation for some weeks that Prior was to be relieved of his responsibility. This 'foolishness of the British constitution' left Hurd feeling distinctly unready for the challenges posed.[33] Interestingly, this difficulty was also apparent to the civil servants who had to smooth the way for the new appointment. As Maurice Hayes recognised, the civil service operated according to a similar ethos; on his promotion from the DHSS to take over as Deputy Secretary at the Department of the Civil Service, Hayes found that 'there was virtually no handover briefing, and no preparation for the new post.'[34]

The removal of a SOSNI from their position is often a decision made for reasons other than the best interests of Northern Ireland, or perceptions of the competence of the incumbent. On occasion, it has undoubtedly been the case that this has had a deleterious effect, and it is no surprise, therefore, that 'both the appointment of Secretaries and their removal are viewed with a certain cynicism by the people of Northern Ireland.'[35] For instance, William Whitelaw was removed by PM Edward Heath in December 1973, in the run-up to the hastily-called snap general election in February 1974. The fact that Whitelaw was engaged in leading the highly sensitive pre-Sunningdale negotiations, which would pave the way for the establishment of the power-sharing Executive, was clearly not thought to be sufficient cause for Heath to postpone the reshuffle. In his memoir, Whitelaw admitted that the timing of the Westminster election had been disastrous for the fledgling power-sharing Executive but, ultimately, even despite the critical importance that one might expect to attach to the prospects for devolved government, Northern Ireland was not at the head of the UK government's concerns. As the first SOSNI after the proroguing of the Stormont parliament, Whitelaw described his posting as an 'unexpected chapter' in his career; and his memoir made it plain that he had no great affinity for Northern Ireland, or desire to go there, but 'it would have been cowardly to refuse.'[36] When reading Whitelaw's memoirs, it is hard to resist the sense of *noblesse oblige* that pervades his feelings on being sent to Belfast; he was close friends with UUP MP, Robin Chichester-Clark, and there was a natural affinity in terms of class outlook and political temperament between some Conservatives, and their unionist 'cousins'. This did not always survive the rigours of office, or the policy agenda pursued by successive Westminster governments. Many of the SOSNI memoirs also confess to a sense of shock at the depth of communal antagonism, which underlines the extent to which they did not fully appreciate the rhythms of political life in Northern Ireland before their appointment.

The 'Loneliness of the Northern Ireland Secretary': Reflecting on Policy-Making as SOSNI[37]

Whether facing a potentially hostile local population (nationalist, unionist or sometimes both at once), or the probable indifference of the Westminster Cabinet, SOSNI had to make difficult judgments regarding a range of policy areas: they had to judge the prospects for any new constitutional initiative, not to mention dealing with the perennial issue of security, and the ever-present problems associated with Northern Ireland's benighted social and economic environment. The list of areas requiring the urgent attention of SOSNI could be daunting. Even an individual with some prior knowledge of the province, could find themselves, as Rees did, prey to conflicting priorities and uncertain about which direction to follow: as Shadow SOSNI during the inter-party talks leading to Sunningdale, Rees admitted that his mood 'fluctuated between hope and despair', and this appears to be relatively common amongst those closely involved with policy-making.[38]

Roy Mason appeared in his memoir to be still viscerally affected by this experience. Although he was writing twenty years after he left office, Mason vividly recalled the stress of his position, and the emotional turmoil he felt in the face of paramilitary violence: he argued that the 'unhappiest job' for a SOSNI was to write the letters of condolence that were always sent to the bereaved families of those killed (of course, this applied only to the families of civilians and security force personnel). He never got used to it, and it left him with feelings of 'inadequacy, anger and sadness'.[39] Indeed, the very title of his memoir, *Paying the Price*, gives an indication of his interpretation of this experience. The fact that there was such a lengthy period between his time in Belfast, and the publication of his memoir, could be understood in terms of Mason's efforts to come to terms with what was clearly a traumatic personal engagement with Northern Ireland. Indeed, he confessed at the outset that this had been 'an ordeal that left lasting scars' and had 'cast a shadow' over his life.[40] The book begins with a preface on the security fears that continued to concern Mason even in the period of the peace process, and he was frank about his relief when he could leave Northern Ireland for a break in his Barnsley constituency. Many SOSNI use their memoirs to reflect upon the abnormality of the security protection that accompanied their every move, whether in terms of public engagements or during their private family life. Mason, who revelled in his reputation as a hardliner with regard to anti-terrorist policy, felt as though he paid the price subsequently, as his life was still considered in danger even in the late 1990s. He argued that there was no great mystery why some republicans would want him dead; he cited Martin McGuinness' contemporary judgment that 'Mason beat the shit out of us.' Interestingly, although most SOSNI agree that the constant presence of security personnel is stifling and restrictive, one of Mowlam's complaints after she had been removed from her post was that her security status was downgraded very quickly in comparison with previous ex-SOSNI. Clearly, there may be a number of factors at work in the fashion in which these memoirists interpret their relative status and the legacy of their period in office.[41]

Constitutional Policy

One of the core elements of the SOSNI's role was certainly searching for acceptable initiatives in terms of constitutional policy. During the period after the introduction of direct rule in 1972, the overall goal of British government policy was largely unchanged, even if the emphasis sometimes shifted. However, attempting to create the conditions for power-sharing devolution, which would command the support of parallel majorities within both unionist and nationalist communities, was no simple task. The memoirs considered here display the frustrations attached to these efforts, and very often SOSNI made only slow progress, if any. Much of the time, the so-called constitutional political parties in Northern Ireland remained steadfast in their preference for continued direct rule, rather than showing a genuine willingness to engage in the sort of compromises that would be necessary for real movement towards the restoration of self-government. As Prior noted, the longer-term policy goals of SOSNI and Westminster were often sidetracked by the ongoing violence, and the pressure placed upon incumbents to respond, and be seen to respond to the day-to-day politics of the 'last atrocity'. In the wake of terrorist incidents, SOSNI had an unenviable task: on one hand, they needed to project an attitude of calm so that government would appear in control of the situation, and so that the population in Northern Ireland (and Great Britain) understood that the administration would not be blown off course by the violence. On the other hand, if those people who eschewed violence did not see the SOSNI reacting with sufficient vigour to events, then there was always a risk that the incumbent would be accused of complacency, and of being willing to effectively sanction an 'acceptable level of violence'. This was clearly a difficult balancing act, and it was extremely unlikely that a SOSNI could satisfy the complex demands of diverse constituencies in this regard. Prior confessed that he found it difficult to respond to unionist calls for 'firmer measures' in the wake of republican violence, given that such measures were rarely carefully or accurately specified.[42]

Whitelaw understood the dilemma, and made a similar point in terms of the necessity to resist the 'famous and often dangerous phrase – "something must be done!'" However, notwithstanding this injunction, and even though Northern Ireland was engulfed in a maelstrom of violence in 1972, Whitelaw's attempts to bring the UUP, the SDLP and Alliance Party into a power-sharing Executive (along with negotiations with the Irish Republic's government relating to the north-south dimension of any agreement), did show he was willing to undertake constitutional policy initiatives. Moreover, this risk-taking was, eventually, rewarded with the agreement at Sunningdale, and the inception of the power-sharing Executive in January 1974. As we have noted, Whitelaw had been recalled to London in the run-up to the implementation of the agreement and, in hindsight, he made it clear that this may have undermined the prospects for a longer-term settlement. In particular, he recognised that Sunningdale had pushed the UUP leader Brian Faulkner into a very precarious position, and Whitelaw acknowledged that he had not helped sufficiently to shore up Faulkner's support in the wider unionist community.[43] One of a number of fascinating, though ultimately unanswerable, counter-factual questions with regard to the political development of power-sharing devolution concerns what might have been possible had Whitelaw been kept in post, and the February 1974 Westminster election had not intervened. More controversially, Whitelaw also presided over a secret meeting with the Provisional republican leadership, after the IRA had called a ceasefire in July 1972. Whitelaw argued in his memoirs that although he was initially opposed to such a meeting, he came under pressure from the SDLP, the Labour opposition and influential voices in the USA, and he subsequently agreed on the basis that even if the talks failed (as he expected they would), this would permit the government to pursue stronger security action against the Provisionals. After the talks ended in acrimony, and the IRA's ceasefire was abandoned, Whitelaw's position was undermined by the leaking of the talks; he offered to resign, but was persuaded to stay on.[44]

Whitelaw was mildly critical of the Labour government for not acting with sufficient strength to combat the Ulster Workers' Council strike that brought down the power-sharing Executive in May 1974. From Whitelaw's perspective, the difficult job of SOSNI could be made much easier (or at least, more bearable) with cross-party support in the House of Commons. He was critical of the Labour opposition for dividing the House in the debate held in the aftermath of 'Bloody Sunday' in Derry, which heralded the suspension of Stormont. Much has been written concerning the idea of *bipartisanship* among the leading Westminster parties, with respect to Northern Ireland policy, and the SOSNI memoirs are an interesting source for analysis of this complex question. Rees summed up the prevailing view: 'I accepted implicitly that policy in Northern Ireland was too important for normal inter-party wrangles. The wrong word at Westminster could lead to injury and death in Northern Ireland.'[45] However, the concept of bipartisanship certainly did not mean that there were no public disagreements between the UK government and the main opposition party. Indeed, Rees recounted that the Labour party had opposed the Conservatives' decision to hold a plebiscite on the question of the border in 1973, but that had not ruptured the good personal relationship that had developed with Whitelaw. With the decision to restore direct rule in 1974, Rees endured a difficult debate in the House of Commons and, although bipartisanship did not break down, there was clearly disquiet on the opposition front bench, with some Conservatives speculating that the decision was a prelude to the Labour government attempting to engineer the conditions for a withdrawal from Northern Ireland. In fact, Rees considered a civil service 'options paper' that effectively ruled out a number of apparently simple options for the constitutional future of Northern Ireland (including British withdrawal, integration, whether within the UK or an all-Ireland Republic, and independence or a redrawing of the border). Some renewed scheme for power-sharing remained the longer-term goal, but, in the immediate term, Rees felt it was necessary to be seen to be trying to fill the political vacuum left by the collapse of the Executive. In the end, elections were held for a Constitutional Convention in 1975, despite the slim chances of the results supporting any further move towards power-sharing. Rees was frank in his memoir about his low expectations for the Convention, but in the absence of any workable alternative, the initiative would have the advantage of insulating the government from international criticism, at least to some extent.

Other SOSNI have found bipartisanship to be more elusive. Mowlam claimed in her memoir that she and her predecessor, Sir Patrick Mayhew, had established a good working relationship; even though at times 'he knew I would be critical [of Conservative policy under PM John Major ...] when it got tough we would talk in private together, so we could all work towards success in the peace process.'[46] By contrast, once in government, Mowlam found her Tory shadow, Andrew MacKay, to be unhelpful, and unwilling to operate according to the 'usual' informal rules of bipartisanship: 'MacKay came across to me as the worst kind of Tory, snide and arrogant.'[47] Jonathan Powell's memoir lends support to this account: although he argued that the Labour Party in opposition had been in disagreement with important aspects of Major's policy, particularly the government's decision to re-engage with the republican movement after the Canary Wharf bomb had ended the IRA's ceasefire in February 1996, Blair had taken the view that only the governing party had all the behind the scenes information, and therefore 'we should not try to second guess Major on the basis of ignorance. The only sensible thing to do was to support him and hope he got it right.' However, after the 1997 election, 'the Tory party maintained the façade of bipartisanship but often tried to make our lives as difficult as possible by constantly harrying us at difficult moments.'[48] Nonetheless, even the appearance of bipartisanship was felt to be a significant advantage for successive SOSNI, especially when crisis was so regularly threatening to derail the government's Northern Ireland policy agenda.

Socio-Economic Policy

However considered the SOSNI's plans, events (and usually violent events) could blow the government off course. Rees recognised the inherent problems in forward planning in a political environment that could be destabilised at any moment. In May 1974, while Rees was struggling with the UWC strike, and trying to plan a route forward after the likely end to the power-sharing experiment, his ability to focus on this critical issue was compromised by the furore which accompanied a hunger strike by the Price sisters in Brixton jail.[49] All SOSNI faced similar problems in maintaining control of the policy agenda, in the face of concerted efforts to undermine their grip. This was clearly the case in terms of paramilitary attempts to disrupt the 'normality' of political life, but it was also often the case with regard to constitutional parties too.

In the regular periods when progress towards power-sharing devolution was non-existent and the main constitutional parties were refusing to engage meaningfully in inter-party talks, SOSNI were often forced to stress the significance of their socio-economic policy initiatives. In part, this was the result of a genuine conviction, held by both major parties, which argued that improving the economic prospects for Northern Ireland would both act as a palliative in reducing inter-communal tension, and reduce the potential pool of recruits to paramilitary organisations. However, in the absence of inter-party dialogue, and an unwillingness to contemplate unilateral constitutional initiatives, concentrating upon social and economic policy was also one of the few remaining options open to British ministers. However, the scope for economic growth to allow both communities to feel they were benefiting from direct rule, whilst at the same time draining the paramilitary swamp, was severely undermined in the 1970s and 1980s by the stubborn, deep-rooted structural problems associated with a peripheral regional economy, blighted by violence and very largely reliant on the public sector. Richard Needham, a junior minister with responsibility for Economic Development in the late 1980s, recalled in his memoir his struggle with the Treasury to secure monies for the salvage operation to keep Mackies engineering company afloat. Mackies was the last significant manufacturer in West Belfast, and Needham was determined that the company should be saved. He made no bones about his explicitly *political* rationale for this decision; in negotiation with the Treasury's Permanent Secretary, 'I told him that if his ministers blocked the £13 million required [...] the economic fight in west Belfast against the IRA would be lost.'[50] Interestingly, Needham highlighted the extent to which, even as monetarist economic doctrine exerted an iron grip in the Treasury, the semi-detached nature of political life in Northern Ireland, made it feasible for him to pursue a significantly more interventionist strategy for the province, so long as it remained 'under the radar' at Westminster. Ultimately, although Needham received full support from the SOSNI at the time, Peter Brooke, it is hard to argue that social and economic development were often at the top of the policy agenda: constitutional questions and security remained the constant preoccupations of most SOSNI, and this is reflected in their memoir-writing.

Security Policy

As has been noted already, for SOSNI during the period of the Troubles, security policy was probably the main criterion by which their tenure was judged. This was clearly of crucial importance with respect to public opinion concerning SOSNIs' record in office, both within Northern Ireland, but also in Great Britain. Whitelaw accepted in his memoir that the granting of Special Category Status to paramilitary prisoners during 1972 had been a mistake, and Mason formally ended the policy in 1976, after such a move had been recommended by the Gardiner Committee. When faced with the pressure to react to particular paramilitary outrages, SOSNI could easily find themselves assailed on all sides, and bipartisan attitudes were likely to be badly strained. On occasion, the opposition frontbench found it hard to resist making political capital out of the popular perception that the government's security policy was in difficulty: as Rees argued, when he shifted policy to end the detention without trial (or internment) of paramilitary suspects, some Conservatives were hostile. Still, although 'bipartisanship was not what it was when we were in Opposition', he went on to recognise that a bipartisan approach depended 'on policy agreement [and] not on some old-boy parliamentary affinity'.[51] It is tempting to conclude that bipartisanship always looks and feels very different, depending on whether one is in government or opposition. The SOSNI would inevitably be subject to pressure from unionists who demanded a tougher response from the army and the RUC, although, as we have noted above, what this might mean in practical policy terms was often unclear. However, the SDLP and Dublin, as well as Irish-America, would often sound a distinctly different note, and compel the SOSNI to respond to allegations of security force brutality, harassment, and collusion with loyalist paramilitaries. This balancing act required a sensitive understanding of the local conditions, and the rhetorical stances adopted by politicians in Belfast. It also necessitated a strong capacity to absorb criticism, often from all the major protagonists at the same time, and maintain a consistent policy in the face of regular 'crises'. However, security policy was not immutable: after the report of the Gardiner Committee in 1974, Rees proceeded to consult with interested parties, and then to guide a new Emergency Provisions Act through Parliament, which introduced what came to be known as the 'criminalisation' policy. In the chapter he devoted to this change in security policy, Rees stated that once the new legislation had completed its passage, 'I felt a satisfaction that was rare in my job.'[52]

When Mason succeeded Rees as SOSNI he made no secret of the overwhelming importance he attached to security, which involved a concomitant relegation of constitutional initiatives. Mason was insistent that there could be no compromise in the battle of wills between a democratic government and a terrorist movement. However, it is clear from his reminiscences that he learned this lesson the hard way: as the new Secretary of State for Defence in 1974, Mason had 'ruffled the dovecot' (in Rees' phrase), when he had argued that the pressure was increasing in Great Britain to set a date for British withdrawal, which would force the leaders of the 'warring factions' in Northern Ireland to hammer out a settlement. The government was forced into a restatement of its position when the PM Harold Wilson attempted to reassure both unionists and the government in Dublin that British policy on maintaining its constitutional and security policies had not altered. Mason recognised that his 'foolish comments' had complicated the incumbent SOSNI's position, and after this chastening experience, he understood the extent to which 'careless talk can be dangerous'. Rees merely confined himself to a pithy comment: 'I was left wondering why the speech had been made in the first place.'[53] Ultimately, of course, from 1997 on, although security policy remained an important element in the portfolio of SOSNI activities, the paramilitary ceasefires by the major republican and loyalist organisations did see the focus shift to inter-party dialogue, and building the peace. But, still, one key aspect of the SOSNI role remained: the necessity to construct good working relationships with the main political protagonists in Northern Ireland.

Working with the Northern Irish Parties

The SOSNI were often treated as interlopers by the political class in Belfast, distrusted by all and sometimes rejected in advance, as either ignorant of the province's problems (however defined), or compromised by their past associations. Peter Hain, who had been a founder of the 'Time to Go' campaign in the 1980s (which argued in favour of British withdrawal), was one of those Labour SOSNI whose credentials could certainly be questioned by unionists. In his memoir, Hain argued that, 'Although I had never had any truck with the IRA, my anti-colonial upbringing [in southern Africa] made me sympathetic to the political aims of Irish Republicanism.'[54] Indeed, Hain had met with the Sinn Féin leadership well before the IRA ceasefire in 1994. Still, in Hain's eyes, this was past history, and the 'whole political landscape had changed fundamentally, making my days of activism long irrelevant'. He did acknowledge, however, that 'given my pedigree, I had to be very careful to overcome unionist suspicion – strong with *any* British Secretary of State, from whom they automatically expected "betrayal", but in my case potentially greater still.'[55] It is perhaps a genuine testament to the changed political circumstances, and to Hain's powers of persuasion, that he did manage to build a close working relationship with sections of unionism, and not the most moderate either.

As was noted above, some Conservative SOSNI have enjoyed a certain affinity with the mainstream unionists, but equally there have been occasions when such expectations have been thoroughly disproved. For example, Prior attended the funeral of a fellow MP, Rev. Roy Bradford of the UUP, who had been killed by the IRA in November 1981 as he conducted a constituency surgery in South Belfast. Prior was jostled and jeered by the mourners, and was shocked by the depth of the unionist alienation he encountered.[56] For many SOSNI, the personification of this unexpected unionist rage with the London government's allegedly inadequate defence of the union, was the leader of the Democratic Unionist Party (DUP), Rev. Ian Paisley. The memoirs reflect ambivalence when it comes to evaluating Paisley. On one hand, there is a degree of admiration for his political skill; Prior even confessed to having a 'warm spot' for the man who had been prominent in the mob at Bradford's funeral. On the other hand, many SOSNI of the 1970s and 1980s also expressed a frustration with Paisley's obstructionist tactics, and his unwillingness to brook any possible compromise. Whitelaw recalled that Paisley had 'an unrivalled skill at undermining the plans of others'.[57] Mason attacked Paisley in vitriolic terms for his role in the short-lived 'constitutional stoppage' of 1977, and in particular for his alleged flirtation with loyalist paramilitaries during this period. Hurd summed up this duality during the operation of the Northern Ireland Assembly in the early 1980s: 'I learned to distinguish between Ian Paisley the demagogue, who regularly denounced me as a traitor, and Ian Paisley the farmers' representative who would chat quietly and knowledgeably for an hour on my sofa about pig prices and the green pound.'[58] According to Hurd, Paisley

> devoted himself to persuading Unionists that the United Kingdom to which they were loyal had a Government which was bent on betraying and destroying them. There could be kindness in his behaviour, but there was nothing positive in his beliefs [...] he was never a man with whom a senior British government minister could do serious business.[59]

Later on, however, Labour SOSNI made determined efforts to court Paisley, particularly once it became apparent both that the DUP had outdistanced the UUP as the main representative of the unionist population, and that Paisley appeared to be mellowing somewhat in his old age. During the late 1990s, when the DUP had withdrawn from the negotiations leading to the Belfast Agreement, Mowlam continued to find Paisley a contradiction: 'he used to drive me mad, because when he was not making a speech he could be more than polite, even pleasant.'[60] By the time Peter Hain was SOSNI, however, Paisley and the DUP were now central protagonists in the search for a stable form of power-sharing devolution, and Hain, partly at Blair's prompting, resolved to get closer to Paisley, with a view to understanding him much better than his predecessors had. An unlikely relationship seems to have developed, between, as Hain put it, 'the high [*sic*] Presbyterian and inveterate agnostic, [the] right-wing veteran and left-wing upstart'. He found Paisley to be 'a real gentleman with old-fashioned manners [...] Like Adams and McGuinness he had moved on, and appeared to have mellowed from the ranting bigotry of his past. With a sense of humour I warmed to, he was extremely shrewd, hugely popular.'[61] This remarkable turnaround for both men culminated in Hain inviting the Paisley family to an official dinner at Hillsborough to celebrate the latter's eightieth birthday: it is safe to say that no previous SOSNI could have contemplated such a relationship!

In the experience of earlier SOSNI, as recounted in their memoirs, the focus tended to be upon the politicians of the Social Democratic and Labour Party (SDLP) and the UUP, as the perceived voices of moderation in an environment where such individuals were hard to find. Although some Conservative SOSNI shared a certain socio-economic political outlook with UUP leaders, they were nonetheless surprised to find that leaders like Brian Faulkner, James Molyneaux and David Trimble were deeply sceptical regarding the UK government's intentions in Northern Ireland. This distrust often presaged a difficult and even frosty personal relationship with the SOSNI. With regard to Faulkner, both Whitelaw and Rees underlined their respect for his professionalism, and both recognised in their memoirs that Faulkner's position was highly compromised in the aftermath of Sunningdale. After the power-sharing Executive's position became untenable and Faulkner tendered his resignation, Rees made it clear that 'he had been extremely honourable throughout and [...] I admired his courage. British governments had expected too much of him: he had been obliged to go into a political no man's land with his troops left far behind.'[62] Faulkner has tended to be viewed as somewhat reserved, and self-possessed, but there is a consensus surrounding his competence and willingness between 1972 and 1975 to take risks in exploring potential ways to resolve the crisis in Northern Irish politics. The comparisons with David Trimble, a future UUP leader, also involved in a period of transition to new political arrangements, are hard to resist. Analysing the memoirs of SOSNI from the different eras permits an interesting picture to be drawn; it might be said that had SOSNI from the 1990s and 2000s been more aware of the judgments of their predecessors, with respect to the problems that bedevilled UUP leaders in trying to lead their members and supporters towards a politics of accommodation, some of the obstacles and frustrations that attended the post-Belfast Agreement period could have been avoided, or at least minimised.

Even though David Trimble had expressly demanded her resignation in the summer of 1999, Mowlam's memoir showed some appreciation for the difficulty he had in convincing his party to engage fully in the peace process. There was, however, a sense of damning with faint praise in Mowlam's discussion of Trimble: she recollected that 'my early concern was that I didn't think he [Trimble] had the courage and determination to lead the Ulster Unionists in the difficult times ahead.' Still, as the negotiations progressed, her opinion altered, and 'David showed an iron will to keep going with, at times, very little support. He was very impressive.'[63] There was certainly speculation that Mowlam's informal style jarred with Trimble's rather awkward social interaction, and Jonathan Powell recorded that as early as August 1997, Trimble had expressed 'no confidence' in Mowlam as SOSNI.[64] In the memoirs of Mandelson, it is perhaps less surprising that Trimble is judged very positively; after all, Mandelson had been appointed, at least in part, with a brief to recalibrate the position of SOSNI, moving towards allaying unionist fears, rather than seeking to engage more closely with republicans, as Mowlam had been seen to do. Mandelson argued that he consciously sought a different tone from Mowlam in his dealings with Trimble, and he empathised with his predicament in a way that his predecessor had not, or had not *been seen to*. Trimble proved himself a 'politician of conviction, dedication and considerable guts', in Mandelson's judgment.[65] In a telling passage, which underlines the complexity of relations between SOSNI and the NIO on one hand, and the office of the Prime Minister, on the other, during the post-Belfast Agreement negotiations, Jonathan Powell revealed that his role changed after Mandelson replaced Mowlam:

> Peter had taken to heart our request that he cultivate the Unionists, but he rather overdid it, and became their favourite Secretary of State since Roy Mason [...] As a result Peter fell into the Northern Ireland Secretary trap in the opposite way to Mo [Mowlam], and I ended up having to manage relations with slighted Republicans rather than Unionists.[66]

One lesson that can be drawn from a close reading of SOSNI memoirs is the significance attached to the tone and character of inter-personal relationships, as well as the substance of political values and ideas. This highly personalised form of political decision-making was perhaps particularly in evidence during the fraught hours and days of close-quarters negotiating during the peace process, but it was also a function of a close-knit political community in which 'symbols can be more important than substance.'[67]

If SOSNI often found that their relations with unionists were fraught with misunderstanding and mutual distrust, then it perhaps came as less of a shock that relations with Irish nationalists in the SDLP, and later on with republicans in SF, could also be problematic. Broadly speaking, British SOSNI recognised the importance of the SDLP to the prospects for any possible forward movement in Northern Ireland, and there was considerable appreciation in the 1970s of the difficulties faced by a nationalist party working within the constraints imposed by both the Provisionals' armed campaign, and the unionists' perceived intransigence. Much of the commentary on the SDLP from British ministers focused upon the personality clashes and political disagreements within the party, which abated somewhat after Gerry Fitt's resignation, and John Hume's domination in the 1980s. In the 1990s, the position of the SDLP as the privileged interlocutor for negotiation with the Catholic nationalist population was progressively undermined, as securing and maintaining the IRA ceasefire brought relations with the Provisional movement increasingly to the fore. In addition, the SDLP under Hume had placed greater significance on constructing close relationships with the Dublin government, and the US administration. For these reasons, it is interesting to note that the SDLP tends not to feature as prominently in SOSNI memoir-writing in the post-1998 period. Although Mowlam paid tribute to the risks run by John Hume in initiating contacts with Gerry Adams in 1988 ('I think his contribution to the peace process will never be forgotten'), and she was clearly impressed by the qualities of Seamus Mallon (the Deputy First Minister in 1999–2000); nonetheless, even in her sympathetic account, the focus on the SDLP was soon replaced by a concentration upon the coming force of SF.[68]

For many SOSNI, the idea of meeting personally with leaders of the Irish republican movement was anathema. Of course, Whitelaw had secretly met with a delegation from the IRA in 1972, including Adams and McGuinness, but according to his memoir, the meeting served only to prove that the republican movement was uninterested in a negotiated settlement at that stage. However, the failure of the talks, and the British understanding of the intransigence of the republican demands, did at least allow for a strengthening of security policy. After the renewed IRA ceasefire in 1997, Mowlam was the first SOSNI to engage in a prolonged and serious fashion with SF leaders. Her impressions were that Adams and McGuinness were 'two very serious, committed human beings', but that they never really relaxed during talks. Afterwards, there was some small talk: 'Martin [McGuinness] is a more open person than Gerry [Adams], and we talked about our respective families.'[69] Both Mandelson and Powell made the point that Mowlam's capacity to develop personal ties with the SF leaders was important in getting talks underway, and keeping them going, even during periods of intense disagreement. Mandelson, as has been noted, approached his task from a different perspective, and was less concerned to 'establish personal chemistry – that would come, or not, over the course of the negotiations – than to build a bedrock of trust' with Adams and McGuinness.[70] The key was to act consistently with both sides, although Mandelson did express to the SF leaders his personal commitment to the union, something that Mowlam had not done. Perhaps inevitably, there was still a frisson attached to meetings with individuals who had for many years been vilified in the public mind in Britain. Typically, Mandelson reported his first meeting with Adams in terms that would burnish his own reputation: 'I could sense that he [Adams] was used to playing on his reputation for toughness and guile to get what he wanted. As we both recognised going into our first encounter, so was I.'[71]

Hain had been sympathetic to republicanism well before it became fashionable to laud the leadership skills of SF, and therefore it was not too surprising that

> Adams and McGuinness were the most professional and tough negotiators I had encountered in politics. Well-read and meticulously prepared, they were courteous and straightforward […] I got on with them well, they were informal with a good sense of humour and would invariably end telephone conversations or leave meetings with a "God bless."[72]

Hain made clear that he understood the road that Adams and McGuinness had travelled, and like Mowlam and Jonathan Powell, he subscribed to their portrayal of a fissiparous movement that was always on the verge of splintering, particularly during the long 'decommissioning' crisis from 1999 to 2005.[73] The notion that such an interpretation permitted Adams and McGuinness to constantly attempt to wring further concessions from the British is not discussed by Hain or Mowlam, although Powell does recognise the existence of such a dilemma. Given his radical background, Hain recognised that Adams was not averse to appealing to this supposed affinity between them. In Hain's account, however, he found it more difficult to relate directly to Adams; he 'often seemed tired. There was a sense with him that if we did not succeed in getting a settlement in this phase, then he might have little more to offer'.[74] By contrast, McGuinness had an interest in sport, and he and Hain found it easier to communicate at the margins of talks, something which should not be discounted in interpretations of the long peace-building endeavour. For SOSNI from an earlier era, such as Mason, the idea that a British SOSNI might enjoy 'friendly relations' with SF leaders was unthinkable. Even after the 1998 Agreement, Mason remained deeply concerned by the security threat, both in general but also in relation to his own personal circumstances. He remained highly sceptical regarding the prospects for a sustained peace. For Mason and his family, this entailed 'a strange existence, halfway between freedom and imprisonment'.[75]

Conclusion

The memoir-writing of successive SOSNI can be utilised by researchers to illuminate significant aspects of Westminster governments' engagement with the political life of Northern Ireland, whether under 'direct rule' or during the protracted inter-party negotiation on either side of the Good Friday Agreement. Some of these memoirs were published soon after incumbency (as with Mowlam and Prior), whilst others were composed with the benefit of a long period of reflection (for instance, Mason and Whitelaw). Of course, it is an obvious, but crucial, point that a very important variable in judging these texts concerns the state of Northern Ireland's political and security environment: those ex-SOSNI writing during a sustained period of peace tend to display a very different set of priorities from those who were primarily dealing with the ongoing violent conflict. Hain acknowledged the truth of this observation during his tenure in 2005, when the Provisional IRA finally declared its armed campaign at a definitive end: 'The morning of the statement, I made calls to my predecessors [as SOSNI] explaining what would happen. Each probably allowed themselves a "He's a lucky bugger, why not on my watch?" thought, though all were full of congratulations.'[76]

Another recurring theme in these memoirs is the scope for autonomy associated with the SOSNI role, but also the problems sometimes associated with prime ministerial involvement in the making of policy towards Northern Ireland. Of course, as with all Cabinet posts, the Prime Minister clearly has ultimate authority, and SOSNI had no option but to recognise this reality. For some SOSNI, however, there was ample scope to pursue their own initiatives, provided they stayed within the limits of overall government policy. By contrast, for others there was effectively a parallel administration, with the SOSNI and NIO largely bypassed in favour of a direct intervention by No. 10 (and special advisors working directly within the PM's office) to negotiate with the parties in Northern Ireland. If real power is seen to reside elsewhere than the NIO, or if the parties in Belfast take the view that they might procure a more favourable outcome by seeking to play off the SOSNI and No. 10, then this can cause real instability, or even deadlock. In a similar vein, the increasing importance of British government relations with the Dublin government, and the potential for this to involve communication that takes place over the head of SOSNI, has also reduced their possible scope for autonomous action. Prior and Mowlam, in diverse circumstances, both complained vociferously about their marginalisation at the hands of their respective prime ministers. Even Mandelson, the quintessential 'New Labour' insider, was often at loggerheads with No. 10's point man, Jonathan Powell, during his short period in office. Hain argued that he had learned this lesson on taking up his post:

One of the first crucial changes I made was to insist on being present at every one of Tony Blair's meetings [concerning Northern Ireland], especially with Gerry Adams and Martin McGuinness, whom he had cultivated and customarily met on his own with Jonathan Powell, his chief of staff, an indispensable cog in the negotiating process.[77]

Hain stressed that he had been aware that his predecessors had been excluded from 'all but the most routine of these meetings, almost relegated to a bit part in the grand scheme of the peace process; Mo Mowlam reported making the tea at one summit. I could not see how my job could be properly done on that basis.'[78] There may be some element of gender politics involved in this construction of roles, but Mowlam herself confirmed the extent to which she believed she had been bypassed in her memoir. Clearly, the direct engagement of No. 10 in the policy process in Northern Ireland, and particularly the inter-party talks process, could be a double-edged sword for any SOSNI. It often felt like an intrusion into the SOSNI's domain, or even a usurpation of their role, but it could also signal the significance attached to Northern Ireland, something which previous SOSNI would have found hard to credit.

One other aspect of the SOSNI memoir-writing that should be mentioned is the importance attached to the administrative relations that ministers needed to construct in an unfamiliar environment. Although there is not space to analyse these relations from the perspective of the civil servants engaged in administering government in Northern Ireland (a surprising number of whom have written memoirs of their own), it is worth briefly examining the SOSNI view of this question. Forging a good working relationship with the departmental civil service is, of course, a central task for any incoming Cabinet minister. In the case of SOSNI, where the incumbent was often inexperienced in the political affairs of the province, and the particularities of governing in the constitutional oddity that was Northern Ireland, building close relations in the NIO were critical. During a Cabinet sub-committee at which some fellow ministers had exposed their ignorance of the politics of Northern Ireland, Rees reflected that the 'distance between Whitehall and Stormont could be measured in light years'.[79] He noted that ministers tended to form unusually close bonds with their NIO officials: 'we were operating far from the Whitehall scene, living cheek by jowl and dealing with a tense political situation. It created a working opportunity that a Secretary of State could use if he wished.'[80] Interestingly, one of those civil servants working for Rees remembered his tenure in a much less flattering light: Maurice Hayes described him as an 'irritating man to work for'.[81] Hurd drew an important distinction between the bulk of the civil servants, who he worked well with on practical matters, and who were 'in a vague way unionist by background and inclination', and the Unionist politicians, who were much more likely to be recalcitrant and unwilling to search for flexible solutions.[82]

In conclusion, we can perhaps draw some parallels between the experiences of SOSNI, as recorded in their memoir-writing, and wider public attitudes in Britain towards the complex political problems of Northern Ireland. In some respects, SOSNI may represent these broader interpretations in microcosm: a small number became fascinated by the province and its politics, and retained a strong affiliation with and affection for Northern Ireland; while for the majority of earlier SOSNI, their time was marked by frustration and the futility of the search for political progress.

Since the restoration of devolved power-sharing in 2007, and its apparent stability since then, the role of SOSNI has been somewhat downgraded. However, the memoirs of SOSNI from 1972 through until 2007 may provide researchers with a key resource for a fuller understanding of the lived experience of 'direct rule', from the perspective of those with primary responsibility for implementing policy in Northern Ireland. Finally, the significance of the position of SOSNI to the people of Northern Ireland is summed up in an anecdote told by Peter Mandelson: speaking at a UUP constituency meeting in Portadown, in support of David Trimble's efforts to shore up his position as leader in the run-up to the creation of devolved government involving SF in autumn 1999, Mandelson was given a hostile reception. As he left the hall, surrounded by his security personnel, a unionist protester shouted at him: "'There are only two models of Northern Ireland Secretary: Mo Mowlam and Roy Mason […] If you know what's good for you, you'd better be Mason, not Mowlam. Got the message?'"[83]

Chapter 9

Journalists, the Northern Ireland 'Troubles' and the Politics of Memoir-Writing

Introduction

This chapter investigates a number of recent memoirs by a range of journalists who have reported on the Northern Ireland conflict, and develops an interpretation of these sources based upon several prominent themes: first, the extent to which the author may be understood as an 'insider' or an 'outsider' with regard to the political life of Northern Ireland; second, the particular spatial dimension of the journalist's experience of the conflict; third, the temporal dimension of this experience, both in the sense of the period of their reporting from or within Northern Ireland, and the distance between their professional day-to-day engagement with the conflict, and the act of memoir-writing; fourth, the degree to which the writing is genuinely autobiographical, reflecting upon the changing internal life of the author and the development of that life, or whether the focus is more squarely upon the external events and deeds that the author was reporting; and, finally, the extent to which these publications reflect upon the role of the journalist (whether primarily operating in the print or the broadcast media) in the specific conditions of the Northern Ireland conflict, and the wider lessons that might be drawn regarding journalism in conflict zones.

My War Gone by, I Miss it so …[1]

A number of journalists with extensive experience of Northern Ireland have written important and influential historical analyses of particular aspects of the conflict. Of the high-profile journalists who have reported from Belfast, a small number have written genuinely ground-breaking works alongside their mainstream reportage. For instance, Ed Moloney has published a popular history of the Provisional IRA, as well as a biography of the unionist leader, Ian Paisley.[2] David McKittrick has published several volumes of collected journalism, but is best-known for the monumental 1,600-page *Lost Lives,* detailing the deaths of the almost 3,700 people killed as a result of the conflict.[3] Chris Ryder has written well-received histories of the Royal Ulster Constabulary (RUC), the Ulster Defence Regiment (UDR) and the prison service in Northern Ireland.[4] Henry McDonald and Jim Cusack have written detailed studies of several of the major paramilitary groups engaged in the conflict, including the Ulster Volunteer Force (UVF) and the Ulster Defence Association (UDA).[5] Susan McKay has contributed a wide-ranging investigation into the diversity of opinion within the Protestant unionist population in Northern Ireland after the Belfast Agreement, and a moving reflection upon the legacies of violence, and the effects upon the victims and bereaved.[6] Other journalists have also written historical and political analyses of particular aspects of the conflict, including Robert Fisk, Peter Taylor, Martin Dillon and Toby Harnden. However, the focus of this chapter is not upon the more general contribution made by journalists to the historiography of the Troubles, which is undoubtedly impressive, but the specific study of their memoir-writing.

Among those journalists who have written memoirs of their experiences living and working in Northern Ireland during the Troubles, this chapter concentrates upon the following: John Conroy's *War as a Way of Life: A Belfast Diary* (1988); Mark Devenport's *Flash Frames: Twelve Years Reporting Belfast* (2000); Henry McDonald's *Colours: Ireland – From Bombs to Boom* (2005); Malachi O'Doherty's *The Telling Year: Belfast 1972* (2007); and Kevin Myers' *Watching the Door: Cheating Death in 1970s Belfast* (2008). These sources have been selected not because they are fully representative of the sub-genre, but because they encapsulate a range of perspectives and help to underline the diversity of journalistic experience. In terms of the general approaches taken, these narratives tend to be written in a broadly chronological fashion, and several share a focus on the early to mid-1970s, a period when the violent conflict was at its height. Only Conroy's memoir was written and published before the major paramilitary ceasefires were called in 1994 (and, in the IRA's case, renewed in 1997, after the breakdown of the first cessation in February 1996). Although it is described in the sub-title as a *diary,* it is in fact written in a similar narrative style to the other memoirs under consideration. Rather than being written contemporaneously, as is the usual diaristic norm, Conroy's work appears to qualify as a memoir composed at some remove from the events it recounts.

It is also worth noting that these journalists were (and in some cases still *are*) all based in Belfast, and although they travelled extensively around Northern Ireland reporting on aspects of the conflict elsewhere, they were primarily engaged, both professionally and personally, in the 'cockpit of the struggle'. The political atmosphere in Belfast, perhaps especially in the early 1970s, was paranoid and claustrophobic, and these memoirs often reflect a sense of the city's pervasive ethno-religious residential segregation.[7] Still, different areas of Belfast experienced the political conflict in different ways, and those individual districts of the city often exhibited significant changes over the course of the conflict, in terms of the intensity of violence, and the local responses to the prevailing political conditions. The chapter returns to this spatial dimension of these memoirs below. First, we turn our attention to the personal and professional backgrounds of these memoirists.

'Blow-Ins' and Belfastmen

Of the journalists considered here, both Malachi O'Doherty and Henry McDonald can clearly be considered as 'insiders', raised respectively on the Riverdale estate on the edge of Andersonstown in West Belfast, and in the Markets district close to the city centre.[8] Both were raised in what would conventionally be called 'Catholic nationalist' families, although both suggest, in diverse ways, that this simplifies the complex reality of political allegiances within Northern Ireland, and within their respective families. For McDonald, 'I grew up surrounded on one side by portraits of the Sacred Heart of Jesus and the busts of Marx and Lenin on the other.'[9] The McDonald household was situated in an area dominated in the early 1970s by the left-wing Official republican movement, and he describes the regular violence that took place in the area as an integral part of the physical and mental universe of his childhood. However, whilst McDonald bemoans the loss of the 'social cohesion and solidarity that pervaded the area through the worst days of the Troubles', he also argues that his perspective now is one that refuses to become 'sentimental or misty-eyed about those formative years spent in the maelstrom of incipient civil war'. In spite of the occasionally nostalgic tone of his reminiscences of what might be termed the 'social world' of the Troubles (in particular, his memories of the 'handsome, physically courageous and immaculately dressed' Joe McCann, a leading Official IRA gunman who used the McDonald home as a safe house), the adult McDonald insists that the insurgents' violence was counter-productive and a 'criminal adventure'.[10]

O'Doherty has a similar 'insider' status, but his rejection of the paramilitary violence that surrounded him in his late teens was unambiguous, and marked him out from many of his peers at that early stage of the Troubles. O'Doherty's father was from Donegal, and was a traditional republican, one who 'never felt the need to take seriously anyone who disputed' the central tenets of that ideology.[11] His mother, however, was not supportive of republicanism, and O'Doherty tended to side with her views. Before the publication of his memoir, O'Doherty had also written an insightful critique of the Provisional IRA.[12] In this work, he also included an autobiographical chapter, setting out his early 'annoyance with the IRA for the way they treated nonmembers like me in the housing estates of West Belfast'. He makes an interesting comment on his reasons for including this personal information: 'If you know my baggage, and the inclination of my prejudices, then you can take them into consideration when weighing up my ideas. I won't pretend to have no such prejudices, but I will make an honest effort to disclose them.'[13] As well as the burgeoning influence of republican paramilitary groups, and the regular rioting of the early 1970s, both McDonald and O'Doherty were also marked by their youthful encounters with the British Army. For the latter, though he 'feared and detested the army more than anyone [...] I thought that the best way to get rid of them was to stop shooting at them'.[14] O'Doherty explicitly saw journalism as a way of avoiding the street fighting, which he was temperamentally unsuited for, but still having a 'place in the game'.[15]

The other authors under consideration can all be thought of as 'outsiders' to a greater or lesser extent. Mark Devenport, an English trainee journalist with the BBC in the mid-1980s, ended up in Belfast on a temporary placement; there was a good deal of competition amongst the trainees for this posting as Northern Ireland was viewed as 'the one area in the UK where you were guaranteed a lot of news'.[16] Although he acknowledges some 'personal baggage', as his family is 'Catholic with distant Irish roots', nonetheless Devenport 'never intended to be anything more than a passing "blow-in"'.[17] However, he states in his introduction that after more than a decade of television news and features reporting from Belfast, 'my friends, my professional experience and a fair slab of my life are rooted in Northern Ireland [...] I instinctively see the world through a Northern Irish looking-glass. The place just won't let go. Which is why, I suppose, I am writing this book.'[18] On completion of his posting, Devenport decided to apply for a permanent job, and worked until 1989 as a news reporter on local television, before a move to the Northern Irish current affairs programme *Spotlight* (1989–94), and eventually a prestigious post as the BBC's Ireland Correspondent.

Kevin Myers argues in his preface that the publication of *Lost Lives* was the catalyst for his decision to write a memoir of his experiences as a journalist in Northern Ireland during the 1970s, providing him with both the 'moral compulsion and the documentary material'.[19] But Myers is also clear from the outset that he had both political and personal reasons for his undertaking; he wished to hold up to the light the 'reality of what violence does', both to the victims and the perpetrators, but also to those who 'saw murder face to face, and heard the keen of bereaved and broken hearts'.[20] A key theme for many of these journalists looking back on their experiences is the difficulty in balancing their human and emotional reactions to the violence they witnessed, and the sense of professional detachment that was necessary to get the job done. Myers was indeed an outsider in Northern Ireland, born and raised in Leicester in the East

Midlands, but to parents from Dublin. His father, unbeknownst to the family until after his death, had been in the 'old IRA' during the War of Independence (1919–21), but 'far from being raised a republican, I had not even been raised in any real sense as Irish, just Catholic, although Ireland remained a constant drumbeat to my heart from over the horizon.'[21] After the sudden death of his father, from a heart attack, Myers became, by his own admission, a troubled adolescent. He managed to win a place at University College Dublin, and immersed himself in the radical student political milieu of the late 1960s. Myers recalls his naivety with a jaundiced though comic eye; he is disparaging about his younger self's political posturing, a part of which was an early infatuation with the communal violence and rioting which had followed swiftly upon the civil rights movement in Northern Ireland. Serendipitously, Myers found himself accepted in 1971 as a junior news reporter for the Irish national broadcaster, RTÉ, based in Belfast; this despite his self-acknowledged lack of professional training, skills or 'the least morsel of knowledge which would have qualified me in any way for the job'.[22] Myers is disparaging about Belfast and its denizens; indeed, his memoir begins with the following sentence: 'It is never the ambition of a wise person, who knows anything about the place, to live and work in Belfast and I was no exception.'[23]

John Conroy, an American who was plainly an 'outsider' in Belfast, nevertheless wound up living in the highly dangerous district of Clonard in West Belfast, in an area that was on the frontline in the battle between the Provisionals and the British Army in the early 1980s. Conroy's first experience of Belfast was brief; as part of a summer vacation trip around Britain and Ireland in 1972, he 'took the ferry to the North from Scotland and arrived at Belfast early in the morning. I was so unsettled by what I saw that I left the city by noon'.[24] As a journalist for the Chicago *Daily News* Conroy returned in 1977, and was surprised to learn that there was no permanent US press presence in Northern Ireland. It was primarily to fill that gap that Conroy decided to return for a year-long immersion in the life of the city in 1980, and he regularly went back in subsequent years. Although he filed regular news reports, his avowed intention was to write a fuller account of 'ordinary life' in the 'war zone'. Initially, at least, he was the object of suspicion from all sides, and Conroy resisted the idea of moving into Clonard when the opportunity arose: 'I don't mind being scared once in a while, but I didn't want to be scared for twenty-four hours a day for the rest of the year.'[25] He was also concerned from a professional standpoint; he was worried that his perceived neutrality would be compromised in the eyes of the state authorities (British Army and RUC), and amongst the Protestant unionist community if it became known that he was living in such a hostile district. Although he states that he 'never wanted to be more than an observer', it is clear that he was progressively drawn into the life of the area, and ultimately he closely identified with the people of Clonard, with whom he eventually lived as an accepted, albeit exotic, 'insider'.[26]

Forgive Us Our Press Passes: Political Space and Journalism

As Peter Shirlow and Brendan Murtagh argue, 'an extensive tradition of research into the effects of conflict in Northern Ireland on spatially segregated communities exists.'[27] However, in the research into the realities of the politicisation of territory in Northern Ireland, and Belfast in particular, there has not been an acknowledgement of the significance of this spatial dimension for those journalists reporting the Troubles. It is surely important to know both the institutional background and affiliation of journalists, but also *where* they were living and working when they reported from Northern Ireland. It is a commonplace that there was an enormous diversity of experience of the conflict in different parts of Northern Ireland, but it is still of great significance for a proper evaluation of these sources. Unlike many of the memoirs by direct protagonists of the violent conflict, who are deeply committed to and 'embedded' within a particular political and geographic community, we could expect journalists to have travelled extensively around the conflict zone, and to be aware of these 'different "worlds"' of the Troubles.[28] But, all the same, it is also probable that journalists are more familiar with particular locales than with others, and that this inevitably means that their memoirs, as well as their reportage, are redolent of the political atmosphere and social milieu in which they operated.

Both McDonald and O'Doherty have a finely-tuned awareness of the sectarian sensitivities of place in Belfast, and a nuanced understanding of the significance of social and communal background when weighing up individuals. This native appreciation of the terrain of conflict affords them distinct advantages compared with those journalists who often arrived in Belfast with only a rudimentary knowledge of the city. However, both McDonald and O'Doherty, remembering their early bravado and youthful arrogance which belied their deep-seated fear, sometimes found themselves in dangerous situations, encountering either the British Army on patrol, or loyalist vigilantes. O'Doherty recalled venturing to East Belfast one night in 1971, on hearing reports of gunfire from around the Short Strand, a small Catholic district surrounded by fiercely loyalist areas; he and his fellow reporter ran into a roadblock manned by loyalists, and were warned to leave immediately. 'Months later, when the murder of Catholics became routine, I would have been unable to do this; I would have been sure I was going to die.'[29] For McDonald, as a teenage supporter of local North Belfast football team Cliftonville, part of the thrill of following the team in the late 1970s was the prospect of venturing 'into the enemy's lair, to where the Fenians were never supposed to go'.[30] Although he subsequently recalled the youthful excesses and casual sectarianism of his 'hooligan' years with a sense of shame, nonetheless it is striking that one of the elements that attracted McDonald was clearly the opportunity to subvert the established sectarian boundaries, both social and geographical, that had become rigid by the late 1970s.

Mark Devenport lived for a time in a shared house in Ravenhill Park in South Belfast, before moving to Dub Lane, on the southern outskirts of the city just off the respectable middle-class Upper Malone Road. However, straight across the road was the tough loyalist estate of Taughmonagh; generally, the residents had little to do with each other, segregated by class in this instance, except when 'youths from the estate came across and tried to steal our cars'.[31] Myers engaged in a dissection of the sectarianism of Belfast, and even almost forty years on his ambivalent sense of both fascination and repulsion for the city is evident. After a short period in a bed-and-breakfast, Myers moved into a shared flat in a house in Eglantine Avenue, near to Queen's University. Myers was disparaging about the 'unutterable boredom' and ennui of life in Belfast, where on Sundays in particular 'nothing opened – shops, pubs, cinemas, supermarkets, even chip shops'.[32] He was scathing about the 'strange melancholy' of the city centre:

> Belfast is a lie. It is unreal. The consensual agreement that shapes and cements other urban communities is absent from this city. At best, people agree not to disagree, matter and anti-matter mingling and yet declining to eliminate one another [...] But they do not define themselves or their city in a common language, with common feelings or common meanings.[33]

By the same token, however, he recognised that rioting and political violence made the city exciting for a young journalist. According to Myers, who wishes to portray himself as rapidly acquiring an 'insider' status, as someone who clearly understood the fundamental social divisions at work in shaping the character of Belfast, riots were 'one of the most honest and defining features of the city, kept secret from most visitors but not from me.[34] In the central shopping district people would maintain an uneasy tolerance of 'the other side', but in the ghettos 'they could freely indulge in Belfast's most powerful indigenous art form, the sculpting of ancient grievances into a dynamic life-force.'[35] However, Myers is self-critical enough to acknowledge that his real understanding was limited: he exposed his ignorance by asking a driving instructor *who* Ben Madigan was![36]

Occasionally, it is difficult not to believe that Myers consciously plays upon his naivety and foolhardiness in the face of the intensifying conflict; the (perhaps) unintended consequence of some of his anecdotes is a romanticisation of the role of the war journalist. As his familiarity with the city and its people increased, so Myers came to recognise a key lesson about Northern Ireland: there are not just two 'tribes', and interpreting the lived experience of the Troubles is a hugely complex undertaking. As well as those often brave individuals who refused to choose sides, or renounced their presumed affiliation, he also saw the subtle variations *within* the tribes, based upon religious and geographical distinctions: 'Ardoyne Catholics were quite different from Andersonstown Catholics: for the former were more quick-tempered, prone to violence, rasher, and generally less competent.'[37] Myers later moved into a notoriously dangerous area in north Belfast, off the Antrim Road, partly as a response to threats from loyalist paramilitaries; paradoxically, he thought he would feel safer in an area of more intensive violence, because the army and police were more likely to discourage the presence of loyalists bent on retribution. However, Myers was also signalling his bravado; a devil-may-care response to the growing threat of random assassination in the mid-1970s.

While Myers' attitude bordered on the reckless, John Conroy made no secret of his ever-present fear of living in the heart of a conflict zone:

> when I first moved into Clonard I didn't know who or what should be feared [...] In the beginning, a visit to any of the shops in the district was a challenge, and I could feel people acting differently when they realized a stranger was in their midst. It took me some time to work out who was a threat and who was not.[38]

Conroy is keen to impress upon his American audience just how distinctive different areas of the city were: only two days after Bobby Sands' funeral, which had been accompanied by widespread rioting and disorder in Catholic districts, Conroy is amazed by the serene spectacle of the Lord Mayor's annual parade in the city centre. Visiting the Divis flats, Conroy noted that 'not more than a few hundred yards from the city centre, a whole different world existed.'[39] These memoirs can certainly help to elucidate the different social worlds of the Troubles, and they can serve as reminders of the essential localism (or even parochialism) of much of the violent conflict. These authors each reflect a very strong sense of the politicisation of all public space in Belfast during the Troubles, and much domestic or private space also. As Zwicker argues, with respect to her analysis of Gerry Adams' autobiographical fiction, there are 'intimate imbrications of politics with streetscapes in Catholic West Belfast'.[40] These journalists demonstrate the extent to which the violent conflict impinged upon the quotidian life of the city and its people.

Confronting the Past: Distance and Denial

These considerations illustrate some important issues concerning the specificity of the experiences related in these journalists' memoirs. For both 'insiders' and 'outsiders' the intensity of the violence during the period 1972–6 made Belfast a claustrophobic and paranoid city in which to live and work. Only at some considerable temporal distance, and after the ending of the worst aspects of political violence, do O'Doherty, McDonald and Myers feel able to confront this period, and its effects upon them personally. However, all three continue to be professionally concerned with political developments in Northern Ireland, as does Mark Devenport. All of these journalists have found that Northern Ireland, whether during the 'long war' or the 'long peace' that followed, has shaped their professional careers to a very great extent. It is also worth noting that the *type* of violence that predominated in the early to mid-1970s was different from that experienced by Devenport in the mid and late 1980s; the era of deadly street battles was largely over, and successful electronic surveillance techniques, as well as infiltration of the paramilitary groups by the intelligence arm of the state, meant that the use of violence had not only diminished significantly, but that the republican movement concentrated its effort upon strategic or symbolic targets. The number of successful 'operations' had been reduced very substantially over the course of this period.

John Conroy wrote his narrative at less of a temporal remove from the events he recounts (only seven years separated his year in Clonard in 1980–1 from publication, and he continued to make regular visits to Northern Ireland up to 1985), but he is more clearly an 'outsider', or at least he started off as such. Indeed, Conroy continued to feel ill at ease during his year in Clonard:

> I found it very hard to be a reporter in west Belfast. I felt I looked suspicious – an American employed not by some well-known magazine or newspaper, but by a foundation no one had ever heard of living not in a pleasant hotel like the rest of the American journalists, but in a boarding house in a grim neighbourhood. I would have been suspicious of such a stranger myself.[41]

With respect to Conroy's period spent living in Clonard, by the early 1980s the local population had, to some degree at least, become inured to the situation they were living in and through, and it was true that for many of them, unlike Conroy, the threat of violence was nothing new, and moreover, this threat had diminished in comparison to the early and mid-1970s. However, the conflict was still ongoing, and it was potentially socially dangerous and psychologically damaging for those living *within* the conflict to dwell upon the violence, and its effects on both individuals and the wider community. As Marie Breen Smyth has noted, 'denial, as a coping mechanism, is widespread among populations living with armed conflict. People living in ongoing violent conflicts will typically say, for example, that things are not as bad as they appear, that everyone is learning to live with the situation.'[42] Journalists, whether born and brought up in the conflict zone, or simply working there temporarily, are not entirely immune from this tendency towards stoicism and world-weariness, which can sometimes even manifest itself as cynicism, but some of these memoirs, written with the benefit of hindsight, recognise this normalisation or routinisation of violence. This may well present difficulties for all those who lived through intense violence in adjusting to the *ending* of such conflict, or at least its substantial reduction. Only in the aftermath of violent conflict might those who have lived through it begin to exhibit the symptoms of their distress. So, Kevin Myers, for instance, looked back with a mixture of scorn and perplexity on his younger self's apparent inability to appreciate the gravity of the situation that was developing in Northern Ireland, and he described himself as 'almost immune' to the intensifying violence.[43]

Telling *the* Story and Telling *one's* Story

An important aspect of interpreting these memoirs is to interrogate their representativeness. What can they reveal about the journalistic experience of violent conflict, and what light can they shed upon the professional and personal reactions of reporters to the cataclysm that unfolded in front of them, and sometimes touched them directly? Journalists may be expected to be interested primarily in the 'story', and those covering the violent conflict in Northern Ireland had plenty of stories to keep them occupied, particularly when the Troubles were at their most intense. Indeed, as Kevin Myers noted of his descent into the whirlwind of Belfast in 1972, 'in our various newsrooms we were being overwhelmed by a blizzard of facts and atrocities, lies and propaganda, from all sides, and it was simply impossible to tell truth from fantasy, fact from fiction.'[44] An important function of these memoirs is the piecing together of information about events that had been shrouded in mystery and controversy hitherto; only with the advent of the paramilitary ceasefires was it possible to revisit some of these murky episodes and untold stories. Therefore, journalists may well revisit stories that they reported on several years previously, or follow up stories that were neglected at an earlier juncture. Although Myers saw himself at the time not as a 'serious chronicler' of events, but rather as an 'avid witness', still he returns to these events in the present in order to make sense of this unfinished business.[45] However, if we might reasonably expect that the primary purpose of these memoirs is to revisit the *events* themselves, seeking to provide an authentic interpretation of the world of the Troubles, then it is also true that these middle-aged memoirists are often profoundly interested in looking back at their own younger selves, and their personal experiences of those turbulent years.

Henry McDonald begins his book with an explicit recognition of the potential problem of revisiting his memories of growing up in the Markets: 'this is more than just a memoir; it is an exercise in time travel. The time machine I use here has only two gears: one to reverse into the past of my childhood and youth, the other to go forward to the present.'[46] He argued that he attempted to avoid associating history with his own self and his own story, 'hence the move in most chapters from the personal anecdote to larger intricately connected themes'. He would not be 'arrogant enough to try to, let alone assert that I do, speak for a certain age group who grew up, endured and survived Ulster's Troubles'.[47] Nevertheless, as with all of the memoirists studied here, it is clear that McDonald, while disclaiming his credentials as a representative individual of wider social significance, believed that his personal story could tell the reader some important details of this period. Although he was writing at a considerable distance from the events of his early years, nonetheless McDonald was confident he could present an accurate picture.

> I am equally blessed and cursed with a strong recall for events that have marked my life over the last 35 years [...] All of that which is dredged up from my personal story actually happened, although it is seen at times through the dark and often kaleidoscopic filter of times past.[48]

As we have noted, McDonald was at pains to convince the reader that he was not nostalgic for the social world of the Markets during the Troubles, given the havoc that was caused, but he could not prevent an elegiac note from creeping in to his reminiscences. He bemoaned the 'atomised' state of the contemporary district, with 'the present generation retreating into their own privatised little worlds [*sic*]'. He contrasted this 'drabness' with 'the sense of social cohesion and solidarity that pervaded the area through the worst days of the Troubles'.[49] There is an air of regret that runs throughout McDonald's remembrances, both for what has been lost in terms of political and social activism (notwithstanding the spillover of such utopian dreams into brutalising violence), and for the 'social vacuum' that has replaced it. Ultimately, the memoir ends on a sombre note, with an epilogue that mourned the squalid killing of Robert McCartney in 2005 by members of the Provisional republican movement: for McDonald, 'the men on both sides who started this war three and a half decades ago have sent this destructive force into the world, shown its malign example and set out a pattern of violence, intolerance and sectarian confrontation that continues to be followed.'[50]

If McDonald's attitude towards the past occasionally betrays some ambivalence, then Malachi O'Doherty tends to be less prone to any hint of nostalgia. Despite (or because of) the fact that his job was becoming 'more adventurous and dangerous' in the autumn of 1972, O'Doherty took the decision to leave Northern Ireland, believing that 'this war would go on a very long time and not be resolved.'[51] He was amazed then that so many of his former schoolmates appeared willing to face imprisonment and the danger of death through joining up with the paramilitaries. He was cold-eyed in his portrayal of the republican movement as an organisation that had no viable political project but which, having embarked upon the path of 'armed struggle', was determined to maintain its campaign of violence no matter its growing futility, for fully three more decades. 'Nothing in my life since has made me wish I had done it their way [and joined the IRA]. I wonder if many of them wish they had done it mine.'[52] O'Doherty looked back on his decision as one of a 'fraught and frightened young man, who might instead have cut down on his drinking, held his nerve and survived'. But, although he was escaping from Belfast to an uncertain future beginning with a spell on the dole, still he reasoned, 'better that any day [...] than the misery of a city saturated with murder, in which the only relief was the unsustainable fantasy that you understood.'[53]

However, O'Doherty also recognised that the reasons he gave himself for leaving were not as strong as he had thought; the violence had in fact reached a peak in its intensity during the summer of 1972 (though he could not know this at the time); also, he was making his way as a young journalist in a political environment that was a centre of global interest; and, ultimately, Belfast was home: 'My older self says to my younger one: *Stay. Your vocation is journalism and this is the story. Surely there is someone who can advise you on how to get a flat in a safe area, and manage your life [...] Get serious about your work.*'[54] But, in the end, the voice of his older self also advised that he was right to leave, and find some maturity in an environment where he was less likely to get killed in the meantime. In recreating his young self, and looking back from the vantage point of a successful career (variously as editor of the Northern Ireland current affairs magazine, *Fortnight*, as columnist for the *Belfast Telegraph*, and as author and commentator), O'Doherty gives the reader a glimpse into the contingencies of a life, the regrets at the roads not taken, but also a measured judgment concerning how the violent conflict took hold, and its effects upon an individual who rejected it, but nonetheless remained committed to Belfast and its often maligned people. Both O'Doherty and McDonald look back with a certain bemusement at what happened to their city, and their people, but they also interrogate their own emotions at the time, and subsequently. The approach is genuinely autobiographical, but their sense of self is intimately connected to the development of the political and violent environment in which they attempted to negotiate a personal and professional existence.

Kevin Myers made the telling point that he pitied friends of his in Dublin in the early 1970s, living their lives in a peaceful world of 'utter eventlessness'.[55] As far as he was concerned, at that time, Northern Ireland and its benighted people really were at the centre of the universe. Unlike both O'Doherty and McDonald, he displayed no great fondness for most of the inhabitants of Belfast, many of whom he viewed as either active protagonists in the worsening sectarian violence or, at best, 'passive accomplices', a phrase he also uses about his own relationship to the conflict.[56]

Myers does not spare his younger self from this fiercely critical approach. He started working for US news corporation NBC in 1975, preparing short radio reports. A year earlier he had resigned from his previous job with the *Observer*, as he planned to leave Belfast for a job in London; he was suffering from nightmares, and he began 'to realize that I could no longer take the endless killings, increasingly meaningless, increasingly purposeless, increasingly cyclical'.[57] Circumstances (a debilitating illness suffered by his girlfriend) conspired against him, and he ended up staying in Northern Ireland, even though he had already sensed that 'there was no logical end to this horror – that it had enough energy to fuel an absolutely goalless war for years to come.'[58] As the violence intensified once again in 1975, with the notorious Shankill Butchers gang terrorising Catholic districts, and a feud between different wings of the republican movement causing further distress in those areas, Myers judged that he had become anaesthetised to its effects: 'my new employers were news-hungry: the more of my bulletins they used, the more I got paid; the more misery and bloodshed there was in Northern Ireland, the richer I became.'[59] In his jaundiced style, Myers poured scorn on what others might regard as his 'professionalism': he 'felt like filth for a day or so at such blood money, until a fresh wave of killings swept over us, and I lost all power of introspection or analysis, and returned to producing my perky little forty-second slots about mayhem and murder for NBC news across the USA.'[60]

Myers' account is particularly anguished with regard to his failure to act upon a hunch that a 'riot' in the Markets area was in fact the pretext for an Official IRA ambush, which saw Corporal Robert Bankier shot dead in May 1971. Bankier's death haunted Myers for many years, and in many ways the writing of his memoir is an effort to cauterise his feelings of guilt at what he terms his 'passive complicity' in one of the early deaths of the Troubles. Although Myers reasoned that 'there was and is no resolution to my moral dilemma', regarding whether he should have alerted the British Army to his intuition before the incident took place, still it is clear that, of all the killings of those years, Myers has been marked indelibly by this event: 'I remember his face, I remember his eyes, I remember the stricken cry of his mates.'[61] Ultimately, whilst Myers' ostensible, publicly-declared purpose in writing the memoir was to provide a 'slightly sharper moral eyesight about the wickedness and folly of political violence on this island', it is evident that he has his own internal moral and emotional agenda, aimed squarely at his younger self, a 'naive young man in pursuit of the adrenaline of war'.[62] For the middle-aged Myers, a self-declared contented man in a comfortable job, this younger self seems at once both alien, almost a different person, but also a constitutive element of what he has now become: 'the darkness of my time there [in Belfast] is now a vital part of my being.'[63]

Neither John Conroy nor Mark Devenport appeared to have any similar anguish to exorcise through their memoir-writing. In the end, however, Conroy found that he was drawn into the life of Clonard, and felt an emotional investment in its fortunes, and those of its struggling people. Even in the epilogue, what the reader does not find out much about is Conroy's own personal thoughts and feelings about the aftermath of the hunger strikes, and his experience of living as a partial 'insider' in this republican community. Written at only a few years' remove from these events, it is perhaps unsurprising that Conroy did not use his book to reflect a great deal upon his personal reactions and his interior life. However, what all of these memoirists do share is an interest in the relationship between their professional role as journalists covering political conflict, and their individual, human reactions to the violence they witnessed.

Reflections on Reporting Political Violence

All of the journalists considered here have spent significant time reporting from Northern Ireland, and their experiences, as reflected in their published memoirs, can be contrasted with the many jobbing journalists who merely passed through. In several of these memoirs, these experienced and knowledgeable journalists express their sense of frustration with the prevailing view of their news organisations concerning the conflict. Given the seemingly endless cycle of violence, London or New York based editors were often dismissive of the news value of yet more bloodshed in Belfast; after all, from their perspective, and indeed from the point of view of many of their readers (or those watching on television or listening to radio), 'news' must necessarily be out of the ordinary. However, violence, deaths and injuries in Northern Ireland were no longer abnormal. As Conroy noted, the public in Great Britain very rarely, if ever, had the conflict in Northern Ireland at the top of its political agenda; the 'full-scale living room invasion' which might have been expected, given the fact that the Westminster government was directly responsible for policy after 1972, simply did not materialise.[64] Conroy's explanation is based on multiple factors, including press and television censorship, restrictions placed on information-gathering by the military authorities, and the deep-rooted perception that Northern Ireland, whilst technically part of the United Kingdom, was in reality a 'place apart'.

However, perhaps the most dispiriting aspect of Conroy's contemplation of the paucity of coverage afforded to the conflict was the 'willing blindness' of a majority of the British public, and its refusal to seek out more detailed sources analysing both the origins and the conduct of the conflict. He quoted *Guardian* reporter Anne McHardy:

> It's not that they [the British public] seem to be just bored by it [Northern Ireland]. It seems most people have a will not to know about it. They refuse to read about Northern Ireland, and when you talk to them about it, they greet you with stares of total disbelief.[65]

Mark Devenport was promoted to become the BBC's Ireland correspondent for radio in 1994, just in time for a period of frantic activity leading to the paramilitary ceasefires and the developing peace process. He is at pains to point out the significant differences between reporting to a nationwide audience across the UK, many of whom are largely ignorant of and perhaps uninterested in the Northern Irish political situation, and working as a regional broadcaster, where every nuance and quirk of language is analysed with a fine toothcomb by the competing factions. Both Conroy and Myers also complain that the major news organisations in the United States were largely uninterested in anything more analytical concerning the nature of the conflict; Conroy's purpose in seeking to spend a year immersed in the life (and death) of the Troubles was prompted by his surprise that no US newspaper in the late 1970s had a bureau in Belfast. Ultimately, these memoirs have finally permitted their authors to address this sense that a fuller understanding of the conflict was missing from earlier accounts, which were often 'two or three-paragraph casualty reports taken from wire copy, or combat stories and accounts of personal tragedy'.[66]

Mark Devenport also reflected critically upon some of the journalistic values that he saw at work during the Troubles. After the infamous attack in 1988 by loyalist Michael Stone at the funerals of three IRA members killed in Gibraltar by the SAS, Devenport recalled seeing

> some journalists over from London celebrating with a large magnum of champagne. They weren't happy about the killings, just wanting to mark a journalistic "job well done". But the gesture seemed insensitive and didn't impress me or my colleagues based in Belfast, who were all too aware that nothing happens in Northern Ireland without a reaction.[67]

In the aftermath, at the subsequent funerals of Stone's victims, two British Army corporals were killed after driving, apparently inadvertently, into the cortege. Devenport arrived at the incident only later and, in an example of the kind of professional dilemma that Myers also discusses, he bemoaned the fact that he had 'missed' the story, which would have been 'the biggest of my career to date'.[68] However, in the end Devenport was relieved as the BBC faced a delicate decision about whether to hand over the video recording of the incident to the RUC, who were gathering evidence against some of the republican crowd. This was a classic illustration of the dilemmas and difficulties facing broadcasters: on the one hand, Devenport incurred the wrath of loyalists in East Belfast shortly afterwards, when the corporation was accused of aiding republicans to avoid justice, given its unwillingness to be seen as an arm of the police authorities by simply handing over the relevant footage to investigators; on the other, several BBC staff who had been subpoenaed to vouch for the authenticity of the tapes (which were eventually seized from the BBC office by the RUC) were subject to an orchestrated campaign of intimidation by republicans, and some felt constrained to leave Northern Ireland.

The political sensitivities of filming and reporting on Troubles-related deaths and funerals are also broached by Devenport; in terms of even-handedness, it was argued that the BBC could not be seen to condone a hierarchy of victimhood, and therefore *all* deaths needed to be covered, but this caused discomfort to Devenport, who 'felt very uneasy about turning up at what, by rights, should have been very private occasions for those who lost loved ones [...] we were often filming where we weren't wanted.'[69] Later in 1988, following the IRA's Ballygawley bus bombing which killed eight soldiers, the British government introduced measures (popularly known as the 'broadcasting ban') which restricted the news organisations' ability to transmit statements from or interviews with representatives of illegal paramilitary organisations. Devenport was unsympathetic to the new regulations, which he saw as being aimed at the government's 'liberal' enemies in the media, as much as against the 'terrorists' themselves. Whilst he defended the reputation of his fellow journalists for impartiality, nonetheless Devenport concluded that the ban probably did have an 'insidious impact'.[70]

A critical issue tackled by these memoirists is how to come to terms with the effects of proximity to intense political violence. Related to this is the thorny question of how to balance the professional duties and functions of the journalist with the human reactions of an individual sometimes caught up in traumatic events. Susan McKay discussed the harmful psychological effects of covering this grief at close quarters on journalists such as herself:

> from the early 1990s on, I covered the North as a reporter. I met many bereaved people, often in the immediate aftermath of a murder. We journalists would record the harrowing stories told by heartbroken wives, parents and children in the first throes of their grief, and then we'd leave. It was extraordinary work, privileged and damaging.[71]

Her instinctive empathy for the bereaved in such melancholy circumstances led her to experience from time to time a 'sudden shaft of bleakness', as if she had no right to her relative happiness when surrounded by such darkness. However, it was also the fact that these deaths only touched journalists briefly, in passing, which caused psychological disorientation:

those close to the murdered person had been plunged into horror. We were workers with a job to do, a job we'd chosen. Often, by the time our reports of a murder were published or broadcast, the ghastly story of the Troubles would have moved on and there would be another door to knock.[72]

Of course, for those journalists who were born and raised in Northern Ireland, or who spent a lengthy period making their lives there, the risk also existed that one might know victims of the violence, and their families, personally. This opened up a further breach in the effort to maintain a hermetic seal between a professional, detached approach and a human, emotional response to tragedy. Malachi O'Doherty recalled how he was working in the office of the *Sunday News* one Saturday in October 1972 when the name of a young Catholic killed the previous night in loyalist East Belfast was released by the RUC press office; it happened to be the brother of a close friend of his, Terence Maguire, who had been working at a temporary summer job in a lemonade factory, where the two brothers had begun seeing local Protestant girls, which was considered highly dangerous at this time. O'Doherty reacted as a friend, trying (unsuccessfully) to contact the surviving brother before he heard the news on the radio, and he recounts that 'there was a strangely awkward divide now between professional and personal interests.'[73] Eventually, O'Doherty's friend did make contact by phone, and asked whether Malachi was writing up the 'story'; he replied that he wasn't: 'I had simply forgotten [...] I had forgotten that I was a reporter.' His editor did not prove very sympathetic: '"Fuck", said Jim. "What were you thinking of?"'[74] Mark Devenport also captured a similar sense of ambivalence concerning his professional role and his emotional reaction when he was involved in reporting on the Omagh bombing in 1998: 'I don't claim to have been traumatised by Omagh [...] I did not lose a brother, mother or daughter. I still have the use of all my limbs. But nobody could cover anything of that scale without feeling a dark cloud pass over them.'[75] Later, Devenport vowed that he would attend the memorial service held for the victims at St Anne's Cathedral in Belfast, not as a journalist, but rather as an ordinary member of the public:

I was a "blow-in" but, by now, I felt I owed some kind of duty to the community I had lived in for so many years [...] After days broadcasting about the bombing, I felt like a citizen doing what a citizen ought to do rather than a journalist peering in from the outside.[76]

The ethical dilemmas posed by working *and* living in the heart of a conflict zone are explored in great depth in these memoirs, and they afford the reader a genuine insight into these attempts to integrate both professional and personal reactions. Kevin Myers explores another related issue that has exercised journalists covering the conflict: how to deal with sensitive, potentially incriminating information that they come to hold? Co-operation with the authorities (whether of the state or non-state variety) and disclosure of sources could be fatal, but Myers is unable to see a clear resolution to this kind of dilemma:

> Journalists are not intelligence agents; but nor are we moral theologians, able to tease out the ethical threads of consequence and responsibility. As journalists become enmeshed in a story, any story, we are no longer mere witnesses but participants. When that participation is merely political, the conscience can remain aloof: but when innocents die, especially when journalists have kept vital information to themselves, conscientious aloofness is no longer possible.[77]

Conclusion

The increasing willingness of erstwhile protagonists of the conflict to publish their stories of the Troubles has become a significant element in the public engagement with the politics of the past in Northern Ireland. And yet this area of study has been under-researched in the academic treatment of this complex subject in the post-ceasefire era. As we have pointed out in the introduction, this relative neglect stems from a number of factors: one is the surprising dearth of interest among scholars from a range of disciplines in the genre of memoir or autobiography in the Irish (and Northern Irish) context more broadly conceived; a second is the understandable scepticism with which historians and political scientists have tended to approach the unverifiable aspects of life-writing, even taking into consideration the 'biographical turn' in the social sciences over recent times; a third reason relates to the problematic nature of defining the parameters of the genre of 'memoir' or 'autobiography', a difficulty which is no less apparent in the sub-genre of 'political memoir'. All in all, the intrinsically inter-disciplinary nature of 'memory studies', including the study of political memoir-writing, may also help to explain the relative dearth of scholarly interest in this field. Here, it is argued that notwithstanding this lack of critical attention, the study of these sources, such as journalistic memoirs, can help to illuminate hitherto shadowy aspects of the Troubles, and contribute to the wider prospects for a societal reckoning with the past. Equally, a key advantage of studying the legacies of conflict through the life-writing of some of the major protagonists is the opportunity offered to understand in real depth the multi-layered relationship between the roles played by the individual and the politics of the collective. Furthermore, this focus can potentially permit researchers to grasp the genuine complexity of the lived experience of the Troubles, and the efforts made to address its difficult personal and social aftermath. The argument is that the study of memoir-writing permits an appreciation of the myriad reactions in Northern Ireland to the traumatic effects of violent conflict, which may help to condition a series of negotiations with its legacies.

Chapter 10

Victims and Memoir-Writing:
Leaving the Troubles Behind?

Introduction

This chapter investigates a distinctive dimension of the recent growth in memoir-writing by concentrating upon the publications of some of those victims/survivors who were intimately affected by the violence of the Troubles. Perhaps counter-intuitively, some victims, despite the fact that they have suffered intensely as a result of the conflict (whether in terms of physical injury and/or psychological trauma, or bereavement), have been less concerned than some other categories of memoirists with shaping the wider political and historical narrative of conflict. We can hypothesise that very often victims' memoirs reflect a personal desire to come to terms with a traumatic past event and to gain public recognition of the suffering endured, but the scope of such an endeavour is usually relatively circumscribed. Unlike those (ex-)protagonists who were intimately involved in the political and violent conflict, it might be speculated that at least some of these victims/survivors can look back at the past through a less ideological prism, without the same filter of organisational commitment and loyalty felt by political representatives or paramilitary actors. Many such victims' memoirs are based more closely on the individual experience of conflict, and its legacies; these 'humanising' stories of the costs of violent conflict may have resonance with wider society, in part *because* these individuals are perceived as very ordinary and as reluctant protagonists thrust into the spotlight, in contrast to political leaders, and even paramilitary figures (who whilst operating in clandestinity, nonetheless often traded upon their notoriety). If it is possible, though unusual, for republicans or loyalists to engage in genuinely self-critical remembrance of their part in the conflict, nonetheless the act of self-writing by these authors often tempts them onto the path of 'vindication, exculpation and the byways of personal interest'.[1] For victims/survivors, especially those around whom can be formed a consensus regarding their status as 'innocent', this may be less problematic. Marie Breen Smyth has recognised the paradoxical potential power of the stereotypical victim, viewed as 'innocent, passive, suffering, bereft, powerless, helpless, dependent, absolved from responsibility, needy and morally entitled to help.'[2] She goes on to cite L. M. Thomas' idea of the victim as a 'moral beacon', an individual for whom 'great suffering carries in its wake deep moral knowledge.'[3] However, whilst the status of some victims/survivors is clearly unassailable, in the circumstances of a deeply divided society this will not be the case for all.

Perhaps those who could be identified primarily as victims of the violence might provide through their memoir-writing a less overtly politicised retrospective stance, even if it is highly problematic to ascribe any sort of 'objectivity' to such reminiscence. In short, these memoirs are worth the attention of researchers for the light they may shed upon the historical narratives put forward by other memoirists of the conflict. For all the difficulties associated with 'personal historiography' of this type, the 'potential for honesty, accuracy and insight remains'.[4] This chapter investigates a range of victims' memoirs by a number of authors, including Gordon Wilson's *Marie: A Story from Enniskillen* (1990), Colin and Wendy Parry's *Tim: An Ordinary Boy* (1994), Rita Restorick's *Death of A Soldier: A Mother's Search for Peace in Northern Ireland* (2000), Stephen Travers and Neil Fetherstonhaugh's *The Miami Showband Massacre: A Survivor's Search for the Truth* (2007), and Timothy Knatchbull's *From a Clear Blue Sky: Surviving the Mountbatten Bomb* (2009). The chapter then develops an interpretation of these sources based upon several prominent themes: first, there is an examination of the extent to which the author may be understood as an 'insider' or an 'outsider' with regard to the political life of Northern Ireland; second, the chapter interrogates the temporal dimension of this experience, both in the sense of the specific historical context of the violent events that the author recounts, and the distance (both temporal and psychological) between their experience of the conflict and the act of memoir-writing; third, the attitudes of these memoirists to those who perpetrated the violent acts that affected them (and their families); and, finally, the conclusion reflects upon the extent to which these publications express the diversity of experience amongst victims/survivors in the specific conditions of the Northern Ireland conflict, and some of the wider lessons that might be drawn regarding conflict transformation.

There is a range of potential ways in which victims/survivors of the conflict in Northern Ireland could be characterised and categorised, and this has proved to be one of the most contentious aspects of the wider questions associated with the legacy of the violence. In its most restricted definition, direct victims of the violence must include those who were killed or injured directly in conflict-related incidents. Approximately 3,700 people died as a result of the conflict.[5] Even more approximately, it has been estimated that 40,000 people were physically injured during the Troubles, some much more seriously than others.[6] However, there are no accurate figures or even estimates for the number of people who have been psychologically affected by the violence, but broader definitions must surely take into consideration those who have suffered harm, emotional distress or traumatic disequilibrium as a result of bereavement or proximity to violent events. There is insufficient space here to rehearse the ongoing debate concerning the definition of 'victimhood' in the Northern Ireland context, but many of the authors studied favour a relatively inclusive, if not universal, interpretation. As Morrissey and Smyth acknowledge, the difficulties with a universalist or over-inclusive definition are not simply that practical provision for victims would become impossible to target adequately, but also moral equivalence between different *types* of victim may serve to create further grievance.[7] How one should distinguish between clearly deserving or legitimate victims and less deserving or even illegitimate victims depends on one's judgment regarding the causes of conflict (i.e. who was primarily responsible for instigating violence?); this is a profoundly political question, and one which cannot hope to elicit a consensual response in Northern Ireland. In many victims' memoirs, however, this problem is often only discussed tangentially or indirectly; this may be a conscious decision to avoid controversy, or alternatively it may be an implicit belief that the answer is too evident to warrant discussion.

Insiders and Outsiders: The 'Different Worlds' of the Troubles[8]

Researchers can distinguish the memoirs of victims/survivors in a number of ways, one of which is with reference to the relationship of the writer to Northern Ireland. Of the books under consideration here, Gordon Wilson's is most clearly written from the perspective of someone who was intimately familiar with the social and political environment of the Northern Ireland conflict. Although Wilson traced the roots of his family to Manorhamilton in Co. Leitrim (and more distantly, to Scottish settlers in Ulster), he moved to work in the family's drapery store in Enniskillen, Co. Fermanagh, in 1945. Although from a 'fervently Methodist' background, Wilson came to appreciate the subtleties and complexities of communal identity formation in the local area.[9] Through his work in the shop, 'serving the whole community', Wilson soon learned 'how people were thinking and behaving, on both sides of the house'.[10] Still, 'some attitudes surprised me, and in certain cases they shook me.' In response, he eschewed political and religious conversation, and 'was happy to try to be a friend to all, and an enemy of none'. He was willing to pay the price of being thought 'wishy-washy' by refusing to take sides, and not identifying himself with either 'tribe', but nevertheless he professed that he 'would hate to give the impression that Gordon Wilson thought that he was better than anyone else'.[11]

After the murder 'by terrorists' of the father of one of his daughter's close friends, Wilson contemplated leaving Northern Ireland, but in the end the family felt too at home in Enniskillen, with its 'familiar touchstones'. This very strong attachment to home and the deep sense of connection to the landscape and society of Fermanagh thus overcame the 'hardening tribalism' of the Troubles. In sum, Gordon Wilson was clearly an insider, with a very strong understanding of the rhythms of life in Northern Ireland, but he was also at pains to portray himself as a rather unusual insider; this was a man with a certain sense of distance from the more visceral *political* divisions of the society to which he nonetheless felt intimately connected. Ultimately, Gordon Wilson's story and his credentials as an emblematic victim of the conflict are partly conferred by his steadfast refusal to engage in the more partisan political and sectarian divisions of his hometown. Interestingly, however, Alf McCreary (the professional journalist who collaborated in the writing of *Marie*), in his introduction, places the 1987 Enniskillen bombing (in which Wilson's daughter, Marie, was killed along with ten others and Gordon severely injured), squarely within the context of the crucial significance of Remembrance Day, and particularly the collective memory of the Somme, which has been so important for Protestant unionists in modern Northern Ireland.[12]

Of the other memoirs studied here, the authors are much more evidently 'outsiders' in the context of the Troubles. Stephen Restorick was an English soldier killed in 1997 by an IRA sniper in Bessbrook, Co. Armagh, and his mother Rita bemoaned the fact that so many people in Great Britain had little knowledge of or interest in the political situation in Northern Ireland, and the role of the army there. However, Restorick questions whether such uninvolved or indifferent citizens can really be altogether innocent 'bystanders'; can civilians in Great Britain or the Republic of Ireland be assigned an entirely neutral status, when many of them turned a 'blind eye' to the conflict, and simply wished Northern Ireland and its Troubles would disappear? After her son's death, Rita Restorick engaged in a 'crash course in the history of Ireland and the background to the conflict [...] Like many English people, I didn't even know the names of the six counties of Northern Ireland before Stephen's death caused me to take a deeper interest.'[13] When she wrote to political leaders encouraging them to make the necessary compromises for peace during the negotiation of the Good Friday Agreement in 1998, she argued 'we had all been guilty, even those like the English public who shut their eyes and ears to the situation and allowed it to continue for so long.'[14] Of course, although few would question Rita Restorick's status as a bereaved mother, the same cannot be said of her son's presence in Northern Ireland. In her memoir, Rita recounts her son's belief that 'he was there to prevent violence and to protect Catholics and Protestants.'[15] As the book proceeds, however, we find her confronting alternative interpretations put forward by Irish nationalists/republicans.

Stephen Travers is a survivor of the Miami showband killings of 1975, which took place in Co. Down on the road between Banbridge and Newry, for which the UVF claimed responsibility. Although the band included a mix of Catholics and Protestants, northerners and southerners, Travers hailed from a devout Catholic family in Carrick-on-Suir, Co. Tipperary. Timothy Knatchbull was fourteen when he was badly injured in an IRA bombing in August 1979, in Mullaghmore, Co. Sligo, in which his twin brother Nicholas was killed, along with his grandfather Lord Mountbatten and his grandmother, and a fifteen-year-old boy from Enniskillen, Paul Maxwell. Although he had travelled regularly for summer holidays in Sligo, he was only dimly aware at the time of the political violence that was taking place in Northern Ireland. Tim Parry (aged twelve) was killed, along with Johnathan Ball (two), by an IRA bomb in Warrington in 1993, and had no connection with Northern Ireland. As children with no relationship to Northern Ireland, the status of these victims may be universally recognised as entirely innocent, and this may partly explain the depth of public reaction to these deaths (and, indeed, to the memoir of Colin and Wendy Parry).

Of these victims/survivors, Colin and Wendy Parry, and Rita and John Restorick (as bereaved parents), and Timothy Knatchbull and Stephen Travers (as injured victims of traumatic events in which family and friends were killed), are (or perhaps more accurately, were) clearly 'outsiders' to a very large extent, and in this they share one of the aspects of victimhood that means their status as 'legitimate' or 'innocent' victims is viewed by many as unassailable. This contrasts very strongly with those who were clearly 'insiders', and sometimes protagonists involved in the conflict, who were thereby implicated in the use of violence. Employing an inclusive definition of victimhood, former paramilitaries may be conceived as victims of circumstance, as well as perpetrators. Yet, there is surely a distinction to be drawn between this broadening of responsibility (and by extension a widening of the category of 'victim') and those 'outsiders' who, by reason of their age or status, have cast-iron claims to the title of legitimate victim.[16]

Memoir-Writing and the Question of Timing

The motivation for and timing of the decision to write and publish a memoir is likely to be complex and dependent upon a variety of factors, some of which will be explored below. As the Healing Through Remembering civil society grouping of victims/survivors and memory workers has pointed out, 'storytelling' about the conflict (which includes the publication of written memoirs, but can also be understood more broadly) can serve a number of functions: one is 'to record the "stories" of individuals' experiences of the conflict as an historical resource and a way of enabling society to examine the wealth of meanings and learning connected to the conflict.'[17] In this view, the 'external' motive is emphasised: explaining the circumstances of the historical events which have affected the author, in the hope that political and social benefits will accrue (however these might be defined by the particular memoirist or storyteller). Another interpretation gives precedence to the 'internal' motive; the potential therapeutic benefits that could arise from these 'personal narrative projects'. In practice, the memoirs studied here tend to combine both of these elements in a nuanced fashion.

For those individuals who have suffered physical injury and psychological trauma through their experiences, we can speculate that there is often a significant distance between the events that have marked them so strongly, and the capacity and/or willingness to confront the effects through thinking and writing about them. For instance, Stephen Travers attempted for a lengthy period after the bombing to simply continue with his busy life as a musician; the associations were too painful to contemplate, and he resented being associated with the 'Miami massacre'. The identity of 'victim' or 'survivor' offered only a truncated identity as he sought to rebuild his life. As with Gordon Wilson, Stephen Travers occasionally uses the third person in his memoir in order to distinguish the 'victim' from the fuller personality.[18] This coping mechanism began to be eroded, but it was not until the twentieth anniversary of the bombing (in 1995, during a period of relative peace in Northern Ireland, which is surely significant) that he began, in a tentative fashion at first, to revisit the past. He was deeply anxious that the memoir project might 'turn out to be the key that releases a renewed terror.'[19] But Travers was driven to continue with his reckoning with the past for two primary reasons: first, to pay a belated tribute to his dead friends, and to tell their story truthfully and accurately; secondly, he wished to find out more about the bombing, which had long been surrounded by suspicions of British security force collusion, and the motivation of those who caused such devastation. Travers was twenty-four at the time of the bombing, and the timing of his decision may also have something to do with his growing into middle age, a more reflective period in many lives.

In a similar vein, Timothy Knatchbull decided with trepidation to return to Sligo in 2003, twenty-four years after the attack (although he had returned briefly once before, in 1987) which still weighed him down with unresolved questions. He had been only fourteen at the time of the bomb, and his parents had attempted to shield him somewhat from the terrible reality of the event. Subsequently, however, he felt that he had not been able to grieve properly, and although his motivation for writing the memoir was not 'prescriptive', he did want to tell his story now in order to potentially help others navigate similarly traumatic events. As with Travers, Knatchbull makes plain that his decision to delve again into the past was aided by the ending of widespread paramilitary violence. He also alerts the reader to his purpose in placing the story in the public domain: he does not want to engage in an analysis of the Troubles, or of the IRA; 'I went to engage in a human process, not a political one. I went to understand my twin's death.'[20]

In a partial contrast, both the Parrys and Rita Restorick published their stories relatively soon after the traumatic events that saw their sons killed (one year and three years later, respectively). Both wished to pay tribute to the 'special nature' of their sons, but both were also moved to use their memoirs to provide an impetus towards a wider peace; to give voice to 'ordinary people' in Britain and both parts of Ireland who yearned for an end to the violence. Rita Restorick wanted to act as a 'focal point for all mothers who wanted an end to violence'.[21] She left her paid employment in order to devote herself completely to this cause; to 'make Stephen's death a focus, to do my utmost to make it mean something, to be a symbol of all the other victims in Northern Ireland.'[22] This desire not to allow her son to become just another forgotten victim led to a very active approach, writing letters to political leaders, visiting Northern Ireland regularly, and taking the opportunities offered by media interest in her story, in order to push her message that this tragedy needed to be a 'turning point' in the broader history of the Troubles. Many of these memoirs oscillate between such hope that the suffering will not be in vain, and a crushing sense of futility if other violent acts supervene. Publishing the memoir thus becomes imperative, and Restorick is scathing of the larger publishers who rejected her manuscript, before Blackstaff Press (a smaller independent company based in Belfast) stepped in. However, Rita Restorick also recognised that her campaign could be met with cynicism in some quarters: 'We had hoped that Stephen's death would be the last in the conflict in Northern Ireland. That was a naïve and futile hope [...] In a way it was an insult to all those others who had died, to think that our Stephen was different, that his death should mean something.'[23]

Gordon Wilson also published his memoir only three years after the Enniskillen bomb. He was careful to assure readers that he recognised his family's suffering was by no means unique; he stated that 'at no time, then or since, did I regard myself as a "spokesman" for Enniskillen,' but he did agree to undertake a gruelling round of interviews, believing that the story needed to be told, and furthermore that 'if sufficient people were shocked by what happened in Enniskillen this might help to make them say "enough is enough", and to bring this country to its senses.'[24] Gordon Wilson saw himself not as *the* 'voice of Enniskillen', but one voice, among many, in favour of an end to conflict. He cited three reasons for publishing the memoir: first, as a lasting written memorial to Marie; second, to 'share his experiences in the hope that they might bring encouragement and comfort to others'; third, 'as a therapy for himself by talking through some of his deepest and perhaps unspoken feelings'.[25] Although Wilson's book was published in 1990 (quickly selling out and being reprinted), whilst the violence remained at an intensive level (with eighty-four deaths caused by the

Troubles that year, rising to 102 in 1991), he was astute enough to realise that there were stirrings of changed thinking, particularly among republicans. Perhaps it is not too fanciful to believe that Wilson's book helped to encourage a wider perception that the violence had reached a stalemate.

Certainly, there is evidence that Gordon Wilson's approach to his victimhood had a strong impression on many subsequent victims. Before Stephen's killing, Rita Restorick remembered only a few high-profile cases of victims in Northern Ireland, including Lord Mountbatten, Airey Neave MP, Marie Wilson and Tim Parry. Joan Wilson, Marie's mother, had written to Rita soon after Stephen's death, including a copy of Gordon's memoir, which helped her a lot. Rita met with Joan Wilson in Enniskillen, and also became friends with the Parrys, attending the opening of the peace centre in Warrington. For Rita, these three victims 'seemed to form a kind of trinity: a young woman from Northern Ireland [Marie Wilson], an English boy [Tim Parry], and Stephen who was a young man but also a soldier'.[26]

Victims and Perpetrators: Towards Understanding?

There is by no means a consensus amongst victims/survivors regarding attitudes to those who committed the violent acts that caused death, injury and bereavement, but the memoirists analysed here do share certain traits, and in more than one case the memoir is structured around a search for understanding that involves meeting those engaged personally in the violent incident, or talking to the paramilitary organisations to which those individuals belonged. Even among these memoirists the reader can discern oscillating feelings and a genuine sense of uncertainty about how to respond. Sometimes this question can rather reductively be narrowed to one of 'forgiveness' or 'retribution'. Of course, these personal stories have their echoes in the wider societal question of how to forge a post-conflict reconciliation in Northern Ireland, and arguably, they are crucial signposts for the shape and character of this broader debate.[27] Memoirs by prominent or emblematic victims have helped to set the parameters of the public discourse regarding a post-conflict reckoning. Certain voices, like Gordon Wilson's, have come to be regarded as symbolic, due to the nature and extent of the pain and suffering endured, but also due to their apparent capacity to articulate a vision for both individual and societal healing. In some respects, this dominant discourse conforms to the notion of certain victims as 'moral beacons', guiding society towards a reconciled future. This does not necessarily require an endorsement of a hierarchy of victimhood, or a denigration of those who have experienced their victimhood differently, but it is undeniable that some victims/survivors have felt marginalised by the sense that some testimonies have become dominant narratives, at the expense of other voices. Jim Dixon, also badly injured at Enniskillen, was 'full of righteous indignation' that Gordon Wilson should take it upon himself to 'forgive' the bombers.[28]

Gordon Wilson's response in the immediate aftermath of the bombing, and the death of Marie, has indeed been characterised as one of 'forgiveness' for those who perpetrated the attack. Interestingly, Wilson himself pointed out that he 'did not use the word "forgive" in that broadcast, nor in any later one'; his position was more nuanced, and informed by his deep Christian beliefs.[29] He was at pains to point out that his words were not intended as 'a statement of theology or righteousness', but 'those who have to account for this deed will have to face a judgement of God which is way beyond the forgiveness of Gordon Wilson.'[30] Joan Wilson expressed the wish to meet the bombers, and ask them what their justification for such acts could be, but in his memoir Gordon Wilson stated that, 'for my part I have no desire to meet these people [the bombers], and as far as I am concerned it would serve no purpose.'[31] However, in 1993, Gordon Wilson did agree to meet with representatives of the IRA, in order to plead for an end to their armed campaign. He professed himself disappointed with the outcome, and his decision was met with significant criticism in some quarters.[32]

For Stephen Travers, there was a nagging desire to find out more about the circumstances of the Miami bombing, and there remained highly controversial questions about the alleged role of the British security services in the UVF attack.[33] After a long period in which they had had no contact, Travers met with Helen McCoy (widow of Brian McCoy, who had been killed in the attack) and her son Keith, and their conversation was partly about the nature and motivation of the attackers. Keith was implicitly critical of Stephen's desire to meet with those responsible, arguing that 'those guys knew exactly what they were doing and they deliberately set out to do it [...] I'm worried sometimes that we let them off the hook a little bit by trying to understand their motives or by using phrases like "it was nothing personal."'[34] Stephen contemplated the nature of forgiveness; concluding that perhaps 'not carrying it around on my shoulders, like some kind of grudge, enabled me to live a relatively normal life.'[35] Helen and Keith pointed out that Stephen was able to resume his life, after his recovery, but with the death of Brian, their lives were 'cut short'. Keith questioned the 'forgiveness' of Gordon Wilson, asking at what point forgiveness becomes forgetting. For Travers, the perpetrators were also always seen as victims, but victims of 'stupidity and ignorance'.[36] Ultimately, this exchange illustrates the degree to which victims/survivors of violent events react in highly personal ways, and their conception of the perpetrators may evolve over time.

Although advised by many people not to proceed with a meeting with the UVF, Travers managed, through an intermediary, to set up a meeting with a senior UVF commander, known in the book only by the pseudonym 'the Craftsman'. Stephen hoped before the meeting for some recognition from the

UVF of the error of their ways, and an assurance that a similar incident would not occur again. Although it was clear that the commander was not proud of the Miami attack, he did attempt, to Stephen's chagrin, to deflect some of the responsibility. This public relations and damage limitation exercise was flatly contradicted later on by RUC detectives who had worked on the case. Despite this, Stephen and the Craftsman did make progress in agreeing the necessity of leaving the violent past behind.[37] At the end of the meeting, Travers felt pleased to have represented his friends who were killed, and whilst he was unimpressed by the 'explanation' offered by the UVF, he was nonetheless convinced by the sincerity of the Craftsman's desire to never return to those dark days.

Rita Restorick began her memoir by stating that she was helped to avoid becoming 'overtaken by bitterness' at her son's death by the actions of a young Catholic mother from Bessbrook, Lorraine McElroy, whose car had been stopped at the checkpoint manned by Stephen Restorick, and who was also slightly injured by the sniper's bullet that killed him.[38] She had travelled with him in the ambulance, and comforted him. Afterwards, she talked about the human tragedy of the killing, and she 'made all but hardline republicans see beyond the uniform of a British soldier to the person within and a family who would be devastated by his death'.[39] Later, the two women met, and this was clearly a very significant element in Rita's subsequent approach to her bereavement. Attending the opening day of the talks process in September 1997 (after the restoration of the IRA's ceasefire), Rita met with politicians from several parties, but she felt the pain was still too raw to meet Sinn Féin (SF) leaders, even though she was committed to the necessity of their inclusion in the process. Subsequently, at an event in Derry, she did shake hands with members of the SF delegation, but away from the gaze of the media.[40] On the first anniversary of Stephen's killing, Rita found herself contemplating the motivation of the IRA man who pulled the trigger: 'he only knew he had killed a figure of hate, someone he believed should not be in his country [...] did he think of friends of his who had been killed? Was he seeking revenge as well as a united Ireland? Or just revenge?'[41]

Timothy Knatchbull reported a similar set of questions arising when he contemplated returning to Sligo. He discussed his attitudes towards the attackers with John Maxwell, the father of Paul (the 15-year-old boatboy killed at Mullaghmore), who argued that he would like to confront the bombers, in order to gauge whether there was a sense of remorse. Timothy's mother Patricia had said that she did not feel bitter towards the bombers because she regarded them as 'sub-human, a race apart', but John Maxwell pointed out, to Timothy's distress, that although the bombers were not local people, 'they obviously had considerable support.'[42]

Conclusion

Many of the memoirs studied here reveal a desire to eschew what the authors might regard as the 'politicisation' of their victimhood, in favour of a humanising story of the Troubles. Following the example set by Gordon Wilson, several have come to embody symbolic positions, often invoked by others as emblematic of the capacity for individuals, and by extension society more generally, to embrace concepts such as 'forgiveness', 'reconciliation' or 'peace'. As has been regularly pointed out in the debate over victimhood in post-conflict Northern Ireland, there is an ever-present danger of the 'instrumentalisation' of victims/survivors, and their stories.[43] It is understandable, therefore, that victims are wary of presenting themselves as political or historical protagonists, or as 'spokespersons' for anything other than their own experiences. Indeed, the legitimacy of these stories, in the eyes of the broader public (perhaps especially *outside* Northern Ireland) is partly conferred by this refusal to engage with the core political dispute. Nevertheless, such an approach can only be partially successful; it is simply not feasible, within Northern Ireland at least, where division regarding the *causes* of the violent conflict is nigh on impossible to resolve, for an entirely apolitical reception of these stories to take root. Ideas of victimhood, of survival, and of healing (whether in terms of personal 'forgiveness' or societal 'reconciliation'), cannot be wholly extricated from the ongoing meta-conflict.

It is interesting to note that, Gordon Wilson apart, there has been a relative dearth of memoirs by victims/survivors based in Northern Ireland, although there has (since 1998) been a good deal of 'storytelling' in other formats.[44] One explanation may be the commercial priorities of publishers, but perhaps more significant is the political sensitivity of such writing within a society that remains deeply divided, and in which there are many categories of victim. However, it may be the case that the memoirs studied here, even (or *especially*) those by 'outsiders', can contribute to a blurring or softening of the protracted and largely circular debate concerning inclusive/exclusive definitions of victimhood (and responsibility). An appreciation of the complexity of victimhood as a category may be easier to forge in the field of life-writing (where individuals may seek to empathise with other, even opposed, viewpoints) than in the field of public policy, as demonstrated by the fraught reaction to official attempts to address the issue of 'recognition' payments to victims/survivors, as part of the broader question of how to tackle the legacy of conflict in Northern Ireland.[45]

Chapter 11

Chroniclers of the Conflict

This book has examined two related dimensions of political memoir-writing concerning the Troubles in Northern Ireland. First, it has attempted to discuss aspects of memoir-writing as a specific genre for studying political conflict. Second, it has also investigated in some depth the particular function and impact of political memoir in the context of Northern Ireland's past, and the efforts to better understand that past. A careful reading and interpretation of these memoirs can provide genuine insights into the lived experience and retrospective judgments of some of the key protagonists of the conflict. It may also permit analysis of the rhetorical strategies employed by these authors, designed to shape and influence the ways in which the conflict is remembered and presented. As the violent conflict moves further into the past, it is probable that the political narratives that have been produced to explain and interpret the Troubles will play an even more significant role for future generations. As those individuals with personal memories and a sense of the lived experience of conflict grow old and die, then arguably it is in the cultural production of collective or social memory that future interpretations will be grounded. Memoir-writing is but one dimension of the current ad hoc approach to 'dealing with the past' in Northern Ireland, but in the absence of any consensus regarding an overarching 'truth recovery' process, this is likely to be the pattern for the foreseeable future.

For many (ex-)protagonists of the conflict, whether in conventional political parties or associated with paramilitary groups, attitudes and opinions with regard to the *meta-conflict* (i.e. what the Northern Ireland conflict was about, what were its key origins and, by extension, which groups in society bear primary responsibility for it) remain polarised. As Cillian McGrattan has argued, the period of peace that has endured for approximately two decades has been based upon an 'uneasy calm' in Northern Ireland.[1] Of course, it is also true that this has been a *relative* peace, and ongoing political violence has directly caused more than a hundred deaths since 1997 and the restoration of the Provisional IRA's ceasefire. Both directly and indirectly, the legacy of the conflict continues to blight many lives in Northern Ireland, and beyond. The communal divisions that continue to structure the party system, as well as being built into the institutional settlement of the Good Friday Agreement, also exercise a strong grip on most aspects of social life. They revolve partly around the contemporary competition for socio-economic resources, but, perhaps of even greater importance, these divisions exist and are regularly reinforced by disputes over how to interpret the past. It may be thought, or even hoped, that relative peace would have allowed less constricted discourses to flourish within Northern Ireland; where it was once unacceptable, and potentially dangerous, to question the moral probity of one's 'own side', or sympathise with the 'enemy', now perhaps a loosening of these restrictions might occur. However, this process, where it does occur, is likely to be a lengthy one, involving the gradual construction of greater trust between individuals and communities. Such willingness to vacate the 'battlefield' of competing discourses about the past is fragile, and may well be subject to deep-rooted pressures; many people will continue to inhabit 'contested ideological territories', partly because they are habituated to them, and partly because they are nervous that, in a polarised society, even the ending of violence from the 'other side' is a political trap.[2]

Whether in terms of selective victimhood, or strategies for shaping the narrative 'telling' of the conflict, the Protestant unionist and Catholic Irish nationalist communities can appear locked into exclusive and self-justifying discourses. In such circumstances, many (ex-)protagonists of the conflict have utilised a post-conflict language of societal reconciliation in order to mask a strategy that actually seeks to score rhetorical victories, to discomfort traditional enemies, and reassure traditional supporters that 'our side' is winning ground (or, at least, not losing it), and 'them 'uns' are in political, social and cultural retreat. In this pessimistic reading, cultural production in Northern Ireland in the contemporary era, including the publication of many of the memoirs studied in this work, is likely to comprise 'remembering at' the other community, summoning up the dead to re-fight, or continue fighting, 'undignified battles'.[3] In this reading, memoir-writing may be studied as a useful microcosm of the impulse towards self-justification, both for individuals and at the communal level.

The argument presented here is that the 'exemplary' lives and careers of political actors, as mediated through their memoir-writing, can serve as a significant element in the construction of such cultures of remembrance and commemoration. It has been argued that in the production of collective memory, agents of the state have a 'central role and a special weight because of their power in relation to establishing and developing an "official history/memory"'.[4] The public management of memory and the attempt to create a 'master narrative' for the population has been a crucial facet of state formation. The purpose of such memorial strategies is to define and reinforce feelings of belonging, with the aim of creating and maintaining social cohesion and defending symbolic (or actual) borders. In the process, heroes must be mythologised, and their flaws overlooked, in order to present an exemplary or immaculate face to the world.

As we have noted, certain life-stories, as exemplified through memoir literature, are held up by political parties and movements as emblematic; they may become a 'personalised form of official party history'.[5] This attempt by states to establish canonical master narratives of their history, through the exemplary lives of key individuals, is always a dynamic process, and there are usually subaltern political forces that seek to challenge aspects of the master narrative, and deny its hegemonic power. This general insight may also be applied to parties/ movements within deeply divided societies like Northern Ireland, where the very idea of a 'national' consensus regarding the region's history is highly problematic. Clearly, one could read the memoirs of Secretaries of State for Northern Ireland as examples of attempts to establish a British state-sponsored master narrative, which seeks to portray the British as a 'neutral arbiter' forced to intervene in the antagonistic inter-communal sectarian struggle.

However, unionists and nationalists, as well as republicans and loyalists have contested this narrative, though from very different perspectives, and memoirists from these political traditions have attempted to put forward their own 'official' narratives. But, as we have seen in the case of 'dissident' republican memoir-writing, these 'party narratives' may also be scrutinised and challenged in their turn. During periods of political transition or 'openness', alternative voices and memories may be heard and jostle for supremacy in the public marketplace for historical ideas. In the context of Northern Ireland, the post-Belfast Agreement era may be understood as such a transitional period. The struggle over the control of the narrative parameters within which the conflict is interpreted may involve almost all (ex-)protagonists, but it can also engage many in the general population, which remains unusually highly politicised. The disputes and street protests over Belfast City Council's decision to restrict the flying of the Union flag over City Hall in December 2012 is a good illustration of the degree to which symbolic representations of this cultural struggle are viewed as critical by many 'ordinary' citizens. Insofar as political memoirs are widely read, and discussed, in Northern Ireland, they have played a significant role in this broader cultural process of creating a 'rhetorical history' of the Troubles.[6]

On the other hand, there may also be countervailing forces at work. For the political settlement to endure in the longer term, more is required than well-rooted institutions, which rather than fostering a genuine effort to share power, have often been criticised for cementing communal and sectarian difference (in a *share-out* of power).[7] What a successful settlement would require is the construction of an overarching cross-community culture in Northern Ireland, one based upon mutual respect and understanding at the level of the individual citizen, and a search for some degree of consensus regarding the past as well as the future. One facet of such a cultural process is the necessity to be able to appreciate and interpret the discourses of the 'other side'. The memoirs studied here may provide the potential for such access, particularly those that seek to do more than simply appeal to a monocultural sectarian audience, thereby reinforcing pre-existing versions of the past. What this work has tried to do is to distinguish between those memoirs that genuinely seek to make sense of the author's past actions (and inactions or complicities) in the Troubles and to present self-critically his or her understanding of the political context in which this life was lived, and, by contrast, those that tailor the narrative to fit an expedient 'story', in which the complexities of individual and collective experience are restricted by the imposition of an ideological straightjacket. Paul Arthur has argued that 'telling stories, creating narratives, is non-threatening.'[8] In this view, what has been called 'the gentle art of reperceiving' permits communication between previously closed communities: constructing these narratives 'was about establishing networks and understandings and ultimately changing hardened opinions'.[9] However, it is clear from this study that whilst memoir literature certainly can contribute to such a 'reperceiving', the stories that are told may also rest upon the brutal art of reinforcing the conflict.

Some of these memoirists may be understood as akin to those 'memory entrepreneurs' that Elizabeth Jelin has argued are necessary to put particular narratives of the past into the public domain.[10] These individuals are leaders or social agents who mobilise their supporters, and rally them to the cause of propagating an historical narrative. Henry Rousso used a similar concept of 'militants of memory', though Jelin points out that memory entrepreneurs may be distinguished from 'militants' because they 'generate projects, new ideas, expressions and creative initiatives – rather than repeating time and again the same script'.[11] In this book, we have examined examples of both kinds of cultural production. There is always a danger of appearing to endorse the self-projection of memoirists, but the intention here has been to critically examine their claims in order to build a fuller understanding of how and why Northern Ireland was permitted, and permitted itself, to be torn apart by violent conflict for so long. Several of the foregoing chapters have concentrated upon the detailed memories of protagonists from the period of the late 1960s up until the mid-1970s, and arguably this was the critical juncture, both in terms of the origins of the violent struggle, and the failure of initial efforts to bring it to an end. After the failure of the power-sharing Executive in 1974, the pattern of the conflict, if not its intensity, was established for the next two decades. 'Dealing with the past' has often been conceived in terms of hoped-for gains at the level of individual 'healing' and social reconciliation, but this study suggests that this aspiration in Northern Ireland may be viewed as highly ambitious and potentially destabilising. And yet, some effort to destabilise the reheated and rehearsed antagonisms associated with sectarian reaffirmations of the past may be thought necessary for political progress to genuinely take root. As more of the scarred 'survivors' of this bloody mess feel the time is right for them to compose their narratives, and tell their stories, there is at least the possibility for a fuller picture of the nature of this struggle to emerge. In this sense, whether motivated primarily by ideas of reconciliation or not, these 'people's remembrancers'[12] deserve to be widely read and studied, both across the generations in Northern Ireland, as well as by academic observers.

Notes and references

Notes to Chapter 1: The Study of Political Memoir and the Legacy of the Conflict in Northern Ireland

1 Such a process prevailed for decades after the Spanish Civil War, in the notion of the 'pact of forgetting' (*pacto de olvido*). See Paloma Aguilar, *Memory and Amnesia: The Role of the Spanish Civil War in the Transition to Democracy* (New York: Berghahn, 2000).

2 Marie Breen Smyth, *Truth Recovery and Justice after Conflict: Managing Violent Pasts* (Abingdon: Routledge, 2007), pp. 20–1.

3 Katrina Goldstone, 'Thanks for the Memory', *Irish Times*, 21 January 1998. Cited in Paul Arthur, 'Memory, Forgiveness and Conflict: Trust-Building in Northern Ireland', in *Commemorating Ireland: History, Politics, Culture* ed. by Eberhard Bort (Dublin: Irish Academic Press, 2004).

4 Peter Shirlow and Brendan Murtagh, *Belfast: Segregation, Violence and the City* (London and Ann Arbor, MI: Pluto Press, 2006), p. 2.

5 Smyth, *Truth Recovery and Justice after Conflict*, p. 21.

6 Arthur, 'Memory, Forgiveness and Conflict', p. 76.

7 Shirlow and Murtagh, *Belfast*, p. 29.

8 Ibid.

9 Paul Arthur, 'Memory and Reconciliation', paper delivered at the conference Pathways to Reconciliation and Global Human Rights, Sarajevo, 2005. He cites from Padraig O'Malley, *Biting at the Grave: The Irish Hunger Strikes and the Politics of Despair* (Belfast: Blackstaff Press, 1990), p. 8.

10 For a recent discussion of the use of political memoir in British political studies, see Patrick Diamond and David Richards, 'The Case for Theoretical and Methodological Pluralism in British Political Studies: New Labour's Political Memoirs and the British Political Tradition', *Political Studies Review*, 10 (2012), 177–194.

11 Ben Yagoda, *Memoir: A History* (New York: Riverhead Books, 2009), p. 1.

12 Ibid. Emphasis in original.

13 Claire Lynch, *Irish Autobiography: Stories of Self in the Narrative of a Nation* (Bern: Peter Lang, 2009), p. 1.

14 George Egerton, 'The Anatomy of Political Memoir: Findings and Conclusion', in *Political Memoir: Essays on the Politics of Memory* ed. by George Egerton (London:

Frank Cass, 1994), p. 342.

15 Ibid, p. 346. Egerton uses the work of Roy Pascal to support this characterisation. Roy Pascal, *Design and Truth in Autobiography* (Cambridge, MA: Harvard University Press, 1960).

16 In an earlier work analysing similar themes, the term 'autobiography' was used, so it should be recognised that there is a good deal of overlap. See Stephen Hopkins, 'Fighting without Guns? Political Autobiography in Contemporary Northern Ireland', in *Modern Irish Autobiography: Self, Nation and Society* ed. by Liam Harte (Basingstoke and New York: Palgrave Macmillan, 2007).

17 Ken Bloomfield, *We Will Remember Them* [Report of the Northern Ireland Victims' Commissioner] (Belfast: HMSO, 1998).

18 Leigh Gilmore, *The Limits of Autobiography: Trauma and Testimony* (Ithaca, NY and London: Cornell University Press, 2001), p. 1. Emphasis in original.

19 Yagoda gives several examples of 'the seemingly endless stream of memoir scandals', particularly in the United States, but he also cites figures from Nielsen Bookscan which suggest that there was a 400% increase in sales in the sub-genres of personal memoirs, childhood memoirs and parental memoirs between 2004 and 2008 (Yagoda, *Memoir: A History*, p. 7).

20 Andrew Gamble, 'Political Memoirs', in *British Journal of Politics and International Relations*, 4.1 (2002), p. 142.

21 Liam Harte, 'Introduction: Autobiography and the Irish Cultural Moment', in *Modern Irish Autobiography: Self, Nation and Society* ed. by Liam Harte (Basingstoke and New York: Palgrave Macmillan, 2007), p. 1.

22 James Olney, *Autobiography: Essays Theoretical and Critical* (Princeton, NJ: Princeton University Press, 1980), p. 4. Cited in Lynch, *Irish Autobiography*, p. 8.

23 Lynch, *Irish Autobiography*, p. 34.

24 Ibid., p. 34.

25 Ibid., p. 42.

26 Kevin Morgan, 'Parts of People and Communist Lives', in *Party People, Communist Lives: Explorations in Biography* ed. by John McIlroy, Kevin Morgan and Alan Campbell (London: Lawrence and Wishart, 2001), p. 10.

27 Ibid.

28 Jochen Hellbeck, *Revolution on My Mind: Writing a Diary under Stalin* (Cambridge, MA: Harvard University Press, 2006), xi. (Italics in original). For further discussion of the comparison between communist life-histories and, in particular, the Irish republican movement, see Stephen Hopkins, 'Comparing Revolutionary Narratives: Irish Republican Self-Presentation and Considerations for the Study of Communist Life-Histories', *Socialist History*, 34 (2009), pp. 52–69. For a fuller review of Hellbeck's work, see Stephen Hopkins, 'Review Essay: The Soviet Politics of the Self', *Labour History Review*, 73 (2008), pp. 336–47.

29 Ben Yagoda, *Memoir*, pp. 95–6.

30 Ibid., p. 96.

31 Ibid., p. 167.

32 Ibid., p. 102.

33 Ibid., p. 102.

34 Gerry Adams, *Hope and History: Making Peace in Ireland* (London and Dingle: Brandon, 2003), p. 2.

35 Jorge Semprún, *Literature or Life* (New York: Viking Penguin, 1997), pp. 123–4. For further details on Semprún's writing, see Stephen Hopkins, 'Still a Spanish Red? The Communist Past and National Identity in the Writing of Jorge Semprún', *Twentieth Century Communism*, 3 (2011).

36 Susan Rubin Suleiman, *Crises of Memory and the Second World War* (Cambridge, MA/London: Harvard University Press, 2006), p. 149. She cites Charlotte Delbo, *Auschwitz and After* (New Haven, CT and London: Yale University Press, 1995), p. 1.

37 Yagoda, *Memoir*, p. 101.

38 There has been a long-running legal battle regarding the Boston College archive material; the Police Service of Northern Ireland has demanded that transcripts of interviews conducted with the Republican, Dolours Price, be made available, given claims that had been made in relation to the killing of Jean McConville by the IRA in 1972. This demand has been resisted by the directors of the archive project.

39 Ed Moloney, *Voices from the Grave: Two Men's War in Ireland* (London: Faber and Faber, 2010), p. 8.

40 Ibid., p. 6.

41 Ibid., p. 107.

42 Yagoda, *Memoir*, p. 103.

43 Gamble, 'Political Memoirs', p. 142.

44 Egerton, 'The Anatomy of Political Memoir', p. 347.

45 Ibid., p. 348.

46 Ibid., p. 347. See also Roy Foster, *Telling Tales and Making it up in Ireland* (London: Penguin, 2002), p. 1

47 Foster, *Telling Tales*, p. xi.

48 Ibid., xi + xiv–v.

49 Lynch, *Irish Autobiography*, p. 9.

50 Ibid., p. 10.

51 Ibid., p. 19.

52 Ibid., p. 24.

53 See, *inter alia*, John Hermon, *Holding the Line: An Autobiography* (Dublin: Gill and Macmillan, 1997); Alan Barker, *Shadows: Inside Northern Ireland's Special Branch* (Edinburgh: Mainstream, 2004); Johnston Brown, *Into the Dark: 30 Years in the RUC* (Dublin: Gill and Macmillan, 2005).

Notes to Chapter 2: Provisional Republican Memoir-Writing

1 R. Alonso, *The IRA and Armed Struggle* (London: Routledge, 2007), p. 8.

2 Ibid., p. 8. Alonso cites the work of B. Cordes, 'When Terrorists do the Talking:

Reflections on Terrorist Literature', in *Inside Terrorist Organizations* ed. by D. Rapoport (New York: Columbia University Press, 1988), pp. 150–71.

3   L. McKeown, *Out of Time: Irish Republican Prisoners Long Kesh 1972–2000* (Belfast: Beyond the Pale Publications, 2001), p. 233.

4   D. Breen, *My Fight for Irish Freedom* (Dublin: Anvil, 1989 [1st edition, 1924]); E. O'Malley, *On Another Man's Wound* (Dublin: Anvil, 1979 [1st edition, 1936]) and *The Singing Flame* (Dublin: Anvil, 1978); T. Barry, *Guerrilla Days in Ireland* (Dublin: Anvil, 1989 [1st edition, 1949]).

5   R. Foster, *The Irish Story: Telling Tales and Making it up in Ireland* (London: Penguin, 2002), xi.

6   R. English, *Armed Struggle: A History of the IRA* (London: Macmillan, 2003), p. 115.

7   D. Morrison, *Then The Walls Came Down: A Prison Journal* (Dublin: Mercier Press, 1999), p. 291.

8   English, *Armed Struggle*, p. 115.

9   G. Adams, *Hope and History: Making Peace in Ireland* (Dingle: Brandon, 2003), pp. 38–9.

10 Alonso, *The IRA and Armed Struggle*, p. 120.

11 From the nineteenth century, see John Mitchel's *Jail Journal* (1854) or Jeremiah O'Donovan Rossa's *Irish Rebels in English Prisons* (Dingle: Brandon, 1991 [revised edition]); in more recent generations, there have been prison memoirs by, *inter alia*, E. Boyce, *The Insider: The Prison Diaries of Eamonn Boyce, 1956–62* (Belfast: Lilliput Press, 2007); R. McLaughlin, *Inside an English Jail* (Dublin: Borderline, 1987), as well as the iconic jail writings of hunger striker Bobby Sands, *One Day in My Life* (Cork and Dublin: Mercier, 1983). For a sympathetic academic treatment of Republican prison writing, see L. Whalen, *Contemporary Irish Republican Prison Writing: Writing and Resistance* (Basingstoke: Palgrave Macmillan, 2008).

12 See the thought-provoking study by E. Jelin, *State Repression and the Struggles for Memory* (London: Latin America Bureau, 2003), ch. 3.

13 M. L. R. Smith, *Fighting for Ireland? The Military Strategy of the Irish Republican Movement* (London and New York: Routledge, 1995), p. 14.

14 Ibid., p. 227.

15 Ibid., p. 227.

16 G. Herrmann, *Written in Red: The Communist Memoir in Spain* (Chicago, IL: University of Illinois Press, 2010), xii.

17 S. Hopkins, 'Comparing Revolutionary Narratives: Irish Republican Self-Presentation and Considerations for the Study of Communist Life-Histories', *Socialist History*, 34 (2009), pp. 52–69.

18 Although he did not publish a memoir as such, Brendan Hughes gave extensive interviews to an oral history archive at Boston College, and after his death in 2008, these reminiscences formed the basis of an edited collection by Ed Moloney, *Voices from the Grave: Two Men's War in Ireland* (London: Faber and Faber, 2010).

19 Ibid., p. 35.

20 Brendan Hughes interviewed in K. Bean and M. Hayes (eds.), *Republican Voices*

(Monaghan: Seesyu Press, 2001), p. 32.

21 Brendan Hughes interviewed in Moloney, *Voices from the Grave*, p. 36.

22 R. O'Rawe, *Blanketmen: An Untold Story of the H-Block Hunger Strike* (Dublin: New Island, 2005), p. 77.

23 G. Bradley with B. Feeney, *Insider: Gerry Bradley's Life in the IRA* (Dublin: O'Brien Press, 2009), p. 38.

24 Ibid., pp. 39–40.

25 K. Morgan, 'An Exemplary Communist Life? Harry Pollitt's *Serving My Time* in Comparative Perspective', in *Making Reputations: Power, Persuasion and the Individual in Modern British Politics* ed. by R. Toye and J. Gottlieb (London: I.B. Tauris, 2005), p. 56.

26 G. Adams, *Before the Dawn: An Autobiography* (London: William Heinemann and Dingle: Brandon Books, 1996), p. 22.

27 Ibid., p. 23. See also D. Sharrock and M. Devenport, *Man of War, Man of Peace? The Unauthorised Biography of Gerry Adams* (London: Macmillan, 1997), pp. 13–20.

28 Alonso, *The IRA and Armed Struggle*, pp. 9–23. According to Alonso, in 1975 60–70% of Republicans arrested and prosecuted were under 21 years of age.

29 Adams, *Before the Dawn*, p. 22.

30 See, *inter alia*, D. Morrison, *All the Dead Voices* (Cork and Dublin: Mercier Press, 2002); *West Belfast* (Cork: Mercier Press, 1989); *On the Back of the Swallow* (Cork, Mercier Press, 1994); *The Wrong Man* (Cork: Mercier Press, 1996); *Rebel Columns* (Belfast: Beyond the Pale, 2004).

31 Morrison, *All the Dead Voices*, pp. 33–43.

32 Adams, *Before the Dawn*, p. 73.

33 Ibid., p. 50. The display of the Irish tricolour was illegal under the Stormont government's Flags and Emblems Act (1954).

34 Ibid., pp. 51–2.

35 Sharrock and Devenport, *Man of War, Man of Peace?*, p. 33.

36 Bean and Hayes, *Republican Voices*, p. 30.

37 See D. McKittrick, S. Kelters, B. Feeney and C. Thornton, *Lost Lives: The Stories of the Men, Women and Children Who Died as a Result of the Northern Ireland Troubles* (Edinburgh: Mainstream, 1999), pp. 33–4.

38 Ibid., p. 32. See also Moloney, *Voices from the Grave*, pp. 18–20, 41.

39 I. Halfin, *Terror in my Soul: Communist Autobiographies on Trial* (Cambridge, MA: Harvard University Press, 2003), p. 27.

40 G. Adams, 'A Republican in the Civil Rights Campaign', in *Twenty Years On* ed. by M. Farrell (Dingle: Brandon, 1988), p. 47.

41 See, for example, the interviews conducted with founding members of the Provisionals by Kevin Bean and Mark Hayes, *Republican Voices*, who title the first chapter of their book, 'The Ashes of Bombay Street: Formative Influences and Political Motivations' (pp. 25–43).

42 See T. Shanahan, *The Provisional Irish Republican Army and the Morality of Terrorism* (Edinburgh: Edinburgh University Press, 2009), pp. 11–39. Also, M. O'Doherty

sustains a concerted critique of the Provisional narrative of August 1969, and its aftermath; see *The Trouble with Guns: Republican Strategy and the Provisional IRA* (Belfast: Blackstaff Press, 1998), pp. 34–61.

43 Adams, *Before the Dawn*, p. 104.

44 Ibid., pp. 106–7. For alternative readings of the events in the Lower Falls during the night of 14/15 August 1969, see H. Patterson, *The Politics of Illusion: A Political History of the IRA* (London: Serif, 1997), pp. 125–8; Sharrock and Devenport, *Man of War, Man of Peace?*, pp. 56–63.

45 P. Shirlow and B. Murtagh, *Belfast: Segregation, Violence and the City* (London and Ann Arbor, MI: Pluto Press, 2006), p. 21.

46 Ibid., p. 17.

47 G. Adams, *Falls Memories: A Belfast Life* (Dingle: Brandon, 1982), pp. 4–5.

48 H. Zwicker, 'Gerry Adams, Moving Target', *Canadian Journal of Irish Studies*, 27.2/28.1 (Fall 2001-Spring 2002), p. 91.

49 L. Duffy cited in McKeown, *Out of Time*, pp. 31–2.

50 E. MacDermott cited in K. Bean and M. Hayes (eds.), *Republican Voices*, p. 54.

51 S. Mac Stíofáin, *Revolutionary in Ireland* (Edinburgh: Gordon Cremonesi, 1975), p. 128.

52 Bradley with Feeney, *Insider*, p. 87.

53 Ibid., p. 11.

54 Ibid., pp. 50–1.

55 A. Maillot, *New Sinn Féin: Irish Republicanism in the Twenty-First Century* (London: Routledge, 2005), p. 98.

56 A telling illustration of this cult of personality was provided in the Provisional movement's newspaper, *An Phoblacht/Republican News*, in its report of the 1986 *ard fheis*: 'At 11.32 and 25 seconds, Gerry Adams lit his pipe. That was the signal that we were really down to business.' (6 November 1986). Cited in E. O'Malley, 'Populist Nationalists: Sinn Féin and Redefining the "Radical Right"', unpublished paper.

57 A. McIntyre, 'And Goodbye Adams?' *Parliamentary Brief*, April 2008. See also M. O'Doherty, 'Could Gerry Adams be Living on Borrowed Time?' *Belfast Telegraph*, 16 May 2008.

58 See K. Morgan, 'Parts of People and Communist Lives' in *Party People, Communist Lives: Explorations in Biography* ed. by J. McIlroy, K. Morgan and A. Campbell (London: Lawrence and Wishart, 2001), pp. 9–28.

59 Ibid., p. 13. On French Communist Party approaches to leaders' memoirs, and Thorez's *Fils du peuple* in particular, see C. Pennetier and B. Pudal, 'Les autobiographies des "Fils du peuple": de l'autobiographie édifiante à l'autobiographie auto-analytique', in *Autobiographies, autocritiques, aveux dans le monde communiste* ed. by C. Pennetier and B. Pudal (Paris: Belin, 2002), pp. 217–46.

60 Zwicker, 'Gerry Adams, Moving Target', p. 82.

61 Ibid., p. 82.

62 Adams, *Before the Dawn*, p. 18.

63 Ibid., pp. 33, 47.

64 Bradley with Feeney, *Insider*, p. 118.

65 Adams, *Before the Dawn*, p. 122.

66 Ibid., p. 124.

67 Ibid., p. 126.

68 Adams' claim not to have been present at either meeting has been contested by several participants; see Moloney, *Voices from the Grave*, p. 69.

69 Sharrock and Devenport, *Man of War, Man of Peace?*, pp. 64–5. See also Adams, *Before the Dawn*, p. 128.

70 Foster, *The Irish Story*, 177.

71 Ibid., 176.

72 *Irish Independent*, 30 September 2003.

73 C. Thornton, 'Vintage Adams: His Life in Books', *Belfast Telegraph*, 29 September 2003.

74 G. Adams, *Cage Eleven* (Dingle: Brandon, 1990), p. 14.

75 S. MacDonogh, 'Introduction', in G. Adams, *Selected Writings* (Dingle: Brandon, 1994), x-xii. See also G. Adams, *The Street and Other Stories* (Dingle: Brandon, 1992).

76 Adams, *Before the Dawn*, p. 168.

77 Zwicker, 'Gerry Adams, Moving Target', p87.

78 F. O'Toole, 'The Premature Life of Gerry Adams', *Irish Times*, 28 September 1996.

79 A. Aughey, 'The Art and Effect of Political Lying in Northern Ireland', *Irish Political Studies*, 17.2 (2002), pp. 7–11; A. McIntyre, 'The Battle against Truth', *The Blanket*, 19 August 2007.

80 B. Hughes cited in Moloney, *Voices from the Grave*, p. 107.

81 English, *Armed Struggle*, p. 110. See also Sharrock and Devenport, *Man of War, Man of Peace?*, p. 116; C. Keena, *Gerry Adams: A Biography* (Dublin and Cork: Mercier, 1990), pp. 53, 72–3, 79; K. Kelley, *The Longest War: Northern Ireland and the IRA* (Dingle: Brandon, 1983), p. 128; C. de Baróid, *Ballymurphy and the Irish War* (London, 2000 [revised edition]), p. 33; Smith, *Fighting for Ireland?*, p. 145; P. Taylor, *Provos: The IRA and Sinn Féin* (London: Bloomsbury, 1997), pp. 201–2.

82 E. Moloney, *A Secret History of the IRA* (London: Allen Lane, 2002), pp. 172–3.

83 F. O'Toole, 'The Taming of a Terrorist', *New York Review*, 27 February 2003, p. 14; Foster, *The Irish Story*, pp. 177–8. McIntyre chose a metaphor from closer to home when he compared Adams' omission of his IRA career as akin to George Best telling his life-story but failing to mention that he had played for Manchester United. Cited in R. Dudley Edwards, 'Gerry the Liar', *Spectator*, 27 July 2002; in another metaphor, Roy Foster argued that it was about as credible as Paul McCartney denying his past membership of the Beatles, *Financial Times Magazine*, 23 October 2005.

84 O'Toole, 'The Taming of a Terrorist', p. 14.

85 Ibid., p. 14.

86 'Victims Ask Adams: Where is our Truth?', *Newsletter*, 11 August 2007. See also B.

Feeney, 'Adams Calls for Truth but Keeps Past Secret', *Irish News*, 16 August 2007; *An Phoblacht*, 16 August 2007.

87 Foster, *The Irish Story*, p. 181.

88 O'Toole, 'The Premature Life of Gerry Adams'.

89 Adams, *Before the Dawn*, Foreword, p. 2.

90 D. Sharrock, 'Adams Signs £400,000 Deal for New Book', *Daily Telegraph*, 10 October 2001.

91 O'Toole, 'The Premature Life of Gerry Adams'. Suzanne Breen argues that in his 'studied attempt to exhibit emotion and sincerity' Adams' veers between 'statesmanlike' and 'folksy' throughout ('The Many Tales of Gerry Adams', *News Letter*, 2 October 2003).

92 Thornton, 'Vintage Adams'.

93 Adams, *Hope and History*, p. 2.

94 G. Adams cited in P. Leahy, 'Trimble Knows the Old Days are Over', *Sunday Business Post*, 28 September 2003. Emphasis added.

95 See the extensive interview with Adams conducted by Nick Stadlen (*Guardian*, 12 September 2007). Asked whether the IRA's armed struggle was justified, given what was on offer at Sunningdale in 1973, and what Republicans settled for in the 1998 Agreement, Adams replied, 'Well, you can only – at the risk of scaring the Unionist horses – you can only make that judgment at the end, and the end in my view will be a united Ireland.'

Notes to Chapter 3: Departing the Republican Movement: Memoir-Writing and the Politics of Dissent

1 For a fuller treatment of the question of abstention, and the development of republican attitudes, see B. Lynn, 'Tactic or Principle? The Evolution of Republican Thinking on Abstentionism in Ireland, 1970–1998', *Irish Political Studies*, 17.2 (2002).

2 Although it has been denied by both groups, many commentators have argued that the 'political wing' of CIRA is *Republican* Sinn Féin (RSF), which was inaugurated in 1986, after a group of Provisional SF members departed the movement following the *ard fheis* decision to end abstentionism for elections to Dáil Éireann. The President of RSF from its inception until his retirement in 2009 was Ruairí Ó Brádaigh; one of the historic figures of Irish republicanism, he had been Chief-of-Staff of the IRA during the Border campaign in the early 1960s, and served as President of Provisional SF from 1970 to 1983, when he was replaced by Gerry Adams. See R. W. White, *Ruairí Ó Brádaigh: The Life and Politics of an Irish Revolutionary* (Bloomington, IN: Indiana University Press, 2006).

3 The 'political wing' of RIRA is the 32 County Sovereignty Movement (32CSM), which publishes *The Sovereign Nation* as a bi-monthly periodical.

4 K. Bean, *The New Politics of Sinn Féin* (Liverpool: Liverpool University Press, 2007), pp. 120–1.

5   McIntyre has proved to be one of the most prolific and tenacious critics of the Adams leadership. For a representative collection of his articles, see A. McIntyre, *Good Friday: The Death of Irish Republicanism* (New York: Ausubo Press, 2008). McIntyre completed a PhD on the Provisional movement's trajectory, and has contributed a number of sharply-argued chapters and articles to academic works examining the Provisionals. He also felt constrained to leave his home in West Belfast, after it was picketed by SF supporters.

6   The dissident organisations have been the subject of growing academic interest; see P. M. Currie and M. Taylor (eds.), *Dissident Irish Republicanism* (London: Continuum, 2011); M. Frampton, *Legion of the Rearguard: Dissident Irish Republicanism* (Dublin: Irish Academic Press, 2011); J. Tonge, '"They Haven't Gone Away, Y'Know": Irish Republican "Dissidents" and "Armed Struggle"', *Terrorism and Political Violence*, 16.3 (2004), pp. 671–93.

7   Of course, those 'dissidents' who are engaged in trying to reconstruct an organisation capable of continuing with the 'armed struggle', now that the Provisionals have vacated the battlefield, have not been able (or perhaps wanted) to publish memoirs or other forms of life-writing thus far.

8   Brendan Hughes cited in E. Moloney, *Voices from the Grave: Two Men's War in Ireland* (London: Faber and Faber, 2010), p. 292.

9   A. McIntyre, *Good Friday*, p. 199. This interview was originally published in *Fourthwrite*, 1 (March 2000).

10 Ibid., p. 200.

11 Although McKearney has not published a memoir as such, there are elements of personal reflection in his book *The Provisional IRA: From Insurrection to Parliament* (London: Pluto Press, 2011). For the League of Communist Republicans, see L. McKeown, *Out of Time: Irish Republican Prisoners, Long Kesh 1972–2000* (Belfast: Beyond the Pale, 2001), pp. 161–6.

12 G. Bradley with B. Feeney, *Insider: Gerry Bradley's Life in the IRA* (Dublin: O'Brien Press, 2009), p. 8.

13 R. O'Rawe, *Blanketmen: An Untold Story of the H-Block Hunger Strike* (Dublin: New Island, 2005); see also R. O'Rawe, *Afterlives: The Hunger Strike and the Secret Offer that Changed Irish History* (Dublin: Lilliput Press, 2010). See also S. Hopkins, 'The Chronicles of Long Kesh: Irish Republican Memoirs and the Contested Memory of the Hunger Strikes', *Memory Studies*, 7.4 (2014, forthcoming).

14 Moloney, 'Foreword' in O'Rawe, *Afterlives*, x.

15 O'Rawe, *Blanketmen*, Prologue (no pagination). See also O'Rawe, *Afterlives*, p. 7.

16 O'Rawe, *Blanketmen*, prologue (no pagination).

17 O'Rawe, *Afterlives*, pp. 12–3.

18 Ibid., p. 104.

19 Ibid., p. 105.

20 Ibid., p. 117.

21 S. O'Doherty, *The Volunteer: A Former IRA Man's True Story* (London: Fount, 1993).

22 Ibid., pp. 208–11.

23 M. McGuire, *To Take Arms: A Year in the Provisional IRA* (London: Macmillan, 1973), pp. 9–10.

24 M. L. R. Smith, *Fighting for Ireland? The Military Strategy of the Irish Republican Movement* (London and New York: Routledge, 1995), p. 113.

25 S. MacStíofáin, *Revolutionary in Ireland* (Edinburgh: Gordon Cremonesi, 1975).

26 Smith, *Fighting for Ireland*, p. 113.

27 Ibid., p. 113; McGuire, *To Take Arms*, p. 73.

28 McGuire, *To Take Arms*, p. 116.

29 MacStíofáin, *Revolutionary in Ireland*, ix and pp. 306–7.

30 White, *Ruairí Ó Brádaigh*, p. 192. There has been an interesting recent exchange regarding the Provisional movement and sectarianism, involving Prof. White and Prof. Henry Patterson; see R. W. White, 'The Irish Republican Army: An Assessment of Sectarianism', *Terrorism and Political Violence*, 9.1 (1997); H. Patterson, 'Sectarianism Revisited: The Provisional IRA in a Border Region of Northern Ireland', *Terrorism and Political Violence*, 22.3 (2010); R. W. White, 'Provisional IRA Attacks on the UDR in Fermanagh and South Tyrone: Implications for the Study of Political Violence and Terrorism', *Terrorism and Political Violence*, 23.3 (2011). There were further replies from Patterson and White in the same volume.

31 Ibid., pp. 178, 192.

32 McGuire, *To Take Arms*, p. 9.

33 See D. McKittrick, *Independent*, 6 December 2008.

34 S. O'Callaghan, *The Informer* (London: Bantam Press, 1998).

35 Ibid., pp. 62–8, 70–7. The two killings that O'Callaghan later confessed to were those of a UDR Greenfinch, Eva Martin, who died during a gun and grenade attack on the UDR base at Clogher, and the shooting of RUC Detective Inspector Peter Flanagan who was killed in a pub in Omagh. See also D. McKittrick, S. Kelters, B. Feeney and C. Thornton, *Lost Lives: The Stories of the Men, Women and Children Who Died as a Result of the Northern Ireland Troubles* (Edinburgh: Mainstream, 1999), pp. 443, 472–3.

36 Ibid., p. 81.

37 Ibid., p. 81.

38 Ibid., p. 85.

39 Ibid., pp. 89–92.

40 Ibid., pp. 233–7. See also McKittrick et al., *Lost Lives*, pp. 1013–14.

41 See D. Godson, *Himself Alone: David Trimble and the Ordeal of Unionism* (London: Harper Collins, 2004), pp. 309–10.

42 M. McGartland, *Fifty Dead Men Walking* (London: Blake, 1997) and M. McGartland, *Dead Man Running* (Edinburgh: Mainstream, 1998); R. Gilmour, *Dead Ground: Infiltrating the IRA* (London: Little, Brown, 1998).

43 O'Callaghan's anti-Provisional revelations were met with sustained efforts to denigrate his reputation, even before the publication of his memoir; see, for example, B. Campbell, 'O'Callaghan – The Truth', *An Phoblacht/Republican News*, 27 February 1997.

44 E. Collins (with M. McGovern), *Killing Rage* (London: Granta, 1997).

45 Ibid., p. 43.

46 Ibid., pp. 44–5, 49–53. For further details of the killings in Newry, see McKittrick et al., *Lost Lives*, p. 108.

47 Ibid., p. 46.

48 For further discussion of this developing campaign for 'political status', see F. Stuart Ross, *Smashing H-Block: The Rise and Fall of the Popular Campaign against Criminalization, 1976–1982* (Liverpool: Liverpool University Press, 2011), p. 68 (fn 66). See Collins and McGovern, *Killing Rage*, p. 58.

49 Collins and McGovern, *Killing Rage*, p. 148.

50 Ibid., p. 148. Emphasis in original.

51 Ibid., p. 213.

52 Ibid., p. 214.

53 Ibid., p. 220. Many in the leadership of the South Armagh area had for a lengthy period been suspicious of the direction taken by the Belfast leadership, particularly Gerry Adams. According to many accounts, Michael McKevitt and his partner, Bernadette Sands-McKevitt (a sister of hunger striker, Bobby Sands) were two of the key individuals who opposed the Adams/McGuinness leadership, and subsequently split with the Provisionals, creating the 32 County Sovereignty Movement in 1997. The 'Real IRA' is usually understood to be the military wing of the 32CSM. See *inter alia* T. Harnden, *'Bandit Country': The IRA and South Armagh* (London: Hodder and Stoughton, 1999), pp. 310–23; Frampton, *Legion of the Rearguard*, pp. 90–1.

54 Collins and McGovern, *Killing Rage*, pp. 225–32.

55 Ibid., p. 248.

56 Ibid., p. 314.

57 The documentary was entitled *Confession* (dir. Stephen Scott), and was broadcast on ITV in 1995. According to the director, Collins 'laid bare the black heart of Irish republicanism. But what made him so dangerous to the IRA was his clear analysis of the futility of it all. Long before Gerry Adams, Eamon Collins concluded that the armed struggle was going nowhere.' See S. Scott, 'Dead Man Talking', *Guardian*, 31 January 1999.

58 Collins was killed, aged 47, by unknown assailants whilst he was out walking his dogs outside the family farm in Camlough, near Newry. The IRA denied responsibility for his death, and both Gerry Adams and Martin McGuinness expressed regret, but pointed out that Collins had created many enemies over the years. See Scott, 'Dead Man Talking', *Guardian*, 31 January 1999. It has also been speculated that 'dissident' republicans in the Real IRA had a motive for killing Collins, given his excoriating criticism of the organisation in the wake of the Omagh bomb in 1998.

59 Collins and McGovern, *Killing Rage*, p. 362.

60 Ibid., p. 361. In a revealing interview shortly before the publication of the memoir (which was serialised over three days in the *Guardian*), Kevin Toolis recognised a similar ambiguity: 'in a sense, Collins is still psychologically in thrall to the IRA.

He believes he was cast out unfairly [...] and the pain of that rejection has stirred him into writing Killing Rage. The book's publication is an act of Lutheran defiance, the stand of an outcast who will be heard regardless of the consequences to himself or to his enemies – a prophet in the darkness.' See K. Toolis, 'A Prophet from the Darkness', *Guardian Weekend*, 5 April 1997, p. 23.

61 Toolis, 'A Prophet from the Darkness', p. 18.

62 *Guardian*, 28 January 1999.

63 See McKeown, *Out of Time*, xv.

64 B. Hughes cited in S. Breen, 'Decommissioned: Provos on Scrapheap of History', *Sunday Tribune*, 16 April 2006, p. 12. See also A. McIntyre, 'Provisional Republicanism: Internal Politics, Inequities and Modes of Repression', in *Republicanism in Modern Ireland* ed. by F. McGarry (Dublin: University College Dublin Press, 2003), p. 189.

65 McKeown, *Out of Time*, p. 3. Emphasis added.

66 McIntyre, 'Provisional Republicanism', p. 192.

67 Tommy McKearney cited in McIntyre, 'Provisional Republicanism', p. 193.

68 For detailed discussion of these issues, see McKeown, *Out of Time*, especially the conclusion.

69 Ibid., p. 230.

70 Ibid., p. 234.

71 The quotation is from John Nixon's book review of *Out of Time*, in *Fourthwrite*, 8 (Winter 2001), p. 23. Nixon is a long-standing member of the Irish Republican Socialist Party, and highly critical of the Provisionals' recent direction.

72 McKeown, *Out of Time*, p. 8.

73 Collins and McGovern, *Killing Rage*, p. 367.

74 Ibid., p. 368.

75 Adams, *Before the Dawn*, p. 247.

76 Ibid.

77 Ibid., pp. 318, 279.

78 Tommy Gorman, cited in McIntyre, 'Provisional Republicanism', p. 193.

Notes to Chapter 4: Loyalist Paramilitarism and the Politics of Memoir-Writing

1 G. Gillespie, 'Noises Off: Loyalists after the Agreement', in *A Farewell to Arms: Beyond the Good Friday Agreement* ed. by M. Cox, A. Guelke and F. Stephen (Manchester: Manchester University Press, 2006), p. 139.

2 B. Faulkner, *Memoirs of a Statesman* (London: Weidenfeld and Nicolson, 1978).

3 See *inter alia*, R. Harbinson, *No Surrender: An Ulster Childhood* (Belfast: Blackstaff Press, 1960); J. Boyd, *Out of My Class* (Belfast: Blackstaff Press, 1985); J. Boyd, *The Middle of My Journey* (Belfast: Blackstaff Press, 1990).

4 See S. Thompson, *Three Plays: Over the Bridge, The Evangelist, Cemented with Love* (Belfast: Lagan Press, 1997).

5 See *inter alia* G. Mitchell, *As the Beast Sleeps* (London: Nick Hern Books, 2001),

which is based on a Ulster Defence Association (UDA) unit in a district not unlike Rathcoole; G. Mitchell, *Tearing the Loom* and *In a Little World of our Own* (London: Nick Hern Books, 1998); G. Mitchell, *Loyal Women* (London: Nick Hern Books, 2003).

6 P. Johnston, *The Lost Tribe in the Mirror: Four Playwrights of Northern Ireland* (Belfast: Lagan Press, 2009), p. 160. This book provides a useful comparative critical treatment of several playwrights from the Protestant tradition, including Sam Thompson, Stewart Parker and Gary Mitchell.

7 G. Mitchell, cited in *South Belfast News*, 13 February 2007.

8 G. Mitchell cited in *Guardian*, 21 December 2005. *Remnants of Fear* was staged in Belfast in February 2007.

9 M. Leitch, *Silver's City* (London: Secker and Warburg, 1981).

10 See A. Finlay, 'Defeatism and Northern Protestant "Identity"', *Global Review of Ethnopolitics*, 1.2 (2001), pp. 3–20; A. Aughey, 'Learning from "The Leopard"', in *Aspects of the Belfast Agreement* ed. by R. Wilford (Oxford: Oxford University Press, 2001).

11 J. Newsinger, *Dangerous Men: The SAS and Popular Culture* (London: Pluto Press, 1997), p. 39.

12 See *inter alia* N. Curtis, *Faith and Duty: The True Story of A Soldier's War in Northern Ireland* (London: Andre Deutsch, 2003); R. Lewis, *Fishers of Men* (London: Hodder and Stoughton, 1999); J. Rennie, *The Operators: Inside 14 Intelligence Company – The Army's Top Secret Elite* (London: Century, 1996).

13 There are several important memoirs from leading figures within the RUC; see *inter alia* J. Hermon, *Holding the Line: An Autobiography* (Dublin: Gill and Macmillan, 1997); J. Brown, *Into the Dark: 30 Years in the RUC* (Dublin: Gill and Macmillan, 2005); A. Barker, *Shadows: Inside Northern Ireland's Special Branch* (Edinburgh: Mainstream, 2004); R. Latham, *Deadly Beat: Inside the Royal Ulster Constabulary* (Edinburgh: Mainstream, 2001).

14 Newsinger, *Dangerous Men*, p. 39.

15 A. McIntyre, 'Uncharted Waters', *The Other View*, Autumn 2003.

16 See J. Cusack and H. McDonald, *UVF* (Dublin: Poolbeg Press, 1997); H. McDonald and J. Cusack, *UDA: Inside the Heart of Loyalist Terror* (Dublin: Penguin Ireland, 2004); P. Taylor, *Loyalists* (London: Bloomsbury, 1999).

17 S. McKay, *Northern Protestants: An Unsettled People* (Belfast: Blackstaff, 2000); G. Beattie, *We Are the People: Journeys through the Heart of Protestant Ulster* (London: Heinemann, 1992).

18 Among recent works see P. Shirlow, *The End of Ulster Loyalism?* (Manchester: Manchester University Press, 2012); C. Gallaher, *After the Peace: Loyalist Paramilitaries in Post-Accord Northern Ireland* (Ithaca, NY: Cornell University Press, 2007); J. McAuley, *The Politics of Identity: A Loyalist Community in Belfast* (Aldershot: Avebury, 1994); S. Bruce, *The Edge of the Union: the Ulster Loyalist Political Vision* (Oxford: Oxford University Press, 1994); C. Crawford, *Inside the UDA: Volunteers and Violence* (London: Pluto, 2003); I. Wood, *Crimes of Loyalty: A History of the*

UDA (Edinburgh: Edinburgh University Press, 2006); G. Spencer, *The State of Loyalism in Northern Ireland* (Basingstoke: Palgrave, 2008).

19 A. McIntyre, 'Uncharted waters', no pagination.

20 R. Garland, *Gusty Spence* (Belfast: Blackstaff, 2001). Spence (1933–2011) was one of the key figures in the contemporary reformation of the UVF. The original UVF had been formed to resist Home Rule proposals in 1913, and had been led by Edward Carson. Spence served eighteen years for the murder of a Catholic barman in 1966, an event sometimes viewed as the start of the renewed Troubles, and was the commander of the UVF in the cages of Long Kesh. He regularly argued in favour of ceasefires by the paramilitary groups from the late 1970s, and he read the CLMC ceasefire statement in 1994.

21 Ervine (1953–2007) was interviewed extensively for the Boston College archive project, which involved frank interviews with ex-paramilitaries from both republican and loyalist backgrounds. After Ervine's death from a heart attack, an edited version of his interview was published, along with a similar set of recollections from ex-Provisional IRA man, Brendan Hughes; see E. Moloney, *Voices from the Grave: Two Men's War in Ireland* (London: Faber and Faber, 2010). In addition, there is also a biography of Ervine available; H. Sinnerton, *David Ervine: Uncharted Waters* (Dingle: Brandon, 2002).

22 See A. Little (with R. Scott), *Give a Boy a Gun: One Man's Journey from Killing to Peace-Keeping* (London: Darton, Longman and Todd, 2009). Little, a teenager at the time, was sentenced at the Secretary of State's pleasure for the murder of a Catholic civilian, James Griffen, in 1975. See D. McKittrick, S. Kelters, B. Feeney and C. Thornton, *Lost Lives: The Stories of the Men, Women and Children Killed as a Result of the Northern Ireland Troubles* (Edinburgh: Mainstream, 1999), p. 589. He was released on licence in 1988, and has subsequently been engaged with various reconciliation initiatives involving ex-paramilitaries. The film version of this story was broadcast in 2009 as *Five Minutes of Heaven* (dir. Oliver Hirschbiegel). The screenplay, by Guy Hibbert, was based in part on interviews with Little and the younger brother of the man he had killed, Joe Griffen.

23 M. Stone, *None Shall Divide Us* (London: John Blake, 2003). Michael Stone (born 1955), who had been associated with the UDA in East Belfast, was convicted of several counts of murder after his attack on a republican funeral at Milltown cemetery in Belfast in 1988; he was released in 2000 as part of the early release programme of the Belfast Agreement. In November 2006, Stone was arrested following an attempt to enter the Stormont parliament with a replica firearm and explosives; he was subsequently convicted of attempted murder and sentenced to sixteen years in 2008. For further biographical details of Stone, see M. Dillon, *Stone Cold: The True Story of Michael Stone and the Milltown Massacre* (London: Hutchinson, 1992).

24 J. Adair (with G. McKendry), *Mad Dog* (London: John Blake, 2007). See also the collective biography of Adair and 2nd Battalion C Company of the UDA: D. Lister and H. Jordan, *Mad Dog: The Rise and Fall of Johnny Adair and 'C Company'*

(Edinburgh: Mainstream, 2003). Johnny Adair (born 1963) became an infamous loyalist leader in the late 1980s, and was convicted of directing terrorism in the late 1990s.

25 C. Anderson, *The Billy Boy: The Life and Death of LVF Leader Billy Wright* (Edinburgh: Mainstream, 2004). Wright was killed by two Irish National Liberation Army (INLA) inmates inside the Maze prison in 1997.

26 F. Meredith, 'Rounded, Intelligent, Articulate, Human and Murderous', *Fortnight*, 412 (2003).

27 Ibid., no pagination.

28 *Sunday Life*, 8 June 2003; *Belfast Telegraph*, 29 August 2003; *An Phoblacht/Republican News*, 29 May 2003.

29 *Observer*, 21 May 2006.

30 *Belfast Telegraph*, 31 October 2006.

31 G. Egerton (ed.), *Political Memoir: Essays on the Politics of Memory* (London: Frank Cass, 1994), p. 344.

32 Ibid., p. 347.

33 Wood, *Crimes of Loyalty*, p. 150.

34 Lister and Jordan, *Mad Dog*, acknowledgements, unpaginated.

35 Ibid.

36 Ibid., p. 18.

37 Ibid., p. 18.

38 Wood, *Crimes of Loyalty*, p. 171.

39 Adair and McKendry, *Mad Dog*, xiii.

40 Ibid., xiii.

41 J. Horgan, 'Foreword' in Adair and McKendry, *Mad Dog*, vi.

42 Ibid., xi.

43 K. McManus, 'Introduction' in Stone, *None Shall Divide Us*, xi.

44 *Belfast Telegraph*, 11 June 2003.

45 Garland, *Gusty Spence*, ix.

46 Ibid., p. 311.

47 R. Scott, 'Acknowledgements' in Little and Scott, *Give a Boy a Gun*, p. 7.

48 M. Smyth and M.-T. Fay (eds.), *Personal Accounts from Northern Ireland's Troubles: Public Conflict, Private Loss* (London: Pluto, 2000), p. 133.

49 For a full treatment of the feud, and Adair's eventual expulsion, see Wood, *Crimes of Loyalty*, ch.11.

50 Adair and McKendry, *Mad Dog*, xiii.

51 Wood, *Crimes of Loyalty*, p. 215.

52 Adair and McKendry, *Mad Dog*, pp. 185–6.

53 Wood, *Crimes of Loyalty*, p. 165.

54 Martin Snodden is another ex-UVF member who was strongly influenced by Gusty Spence, during a fifteen-year period in jail for his part in a pub bombing which killed two people. Snodden has, since his release in 1990, become a worker for conflict resolution; he has been on the board of trustees of both the Mediation Network

(NI) and the cross-community civil society group Healing through Remembering. He also founded the Ex-Prisoners Interpretive Centre (EPIC), an NGO committed to the reintegration of ex-UVF prisoners after release. Although he has not published a memoir, a short piece of life-writing by Snodden is included in a collection edited by Peace Direct, *Unarmed Heroes: The Courage to Go beyond Violence* (London: Clairview, 2004), pp. 30–41.

55 Billy Hutchinson is a key leader of the PUP, and was one of its elected representatives to the Northern Ireland Assembly after 1998. His memoir was scheduled for publication in the late 1990s, but it was subsequently shelved.

56 John White was a key political adviser to Adair in the late 1990s and early 2000s, and was elected to the Northern Ireland Forum for the UDP in 1996. In this capacity he had been part of the UDP negotiating team that met PM John Major in Downing Street that year. He had been imprisoned (from 1978–1992) for one of the most notorious murders of the Troubles, the stabbing to death of Irene Andrews and SDLP Stormont Senator Paddy Wilson. See McKittrick et al., *Lost Lives*, pp. 371–74.

57 John McMichael was a leading figure in the UDA in the 1980s, and was viewed as one of the foremost political thinkers in the organisation. He helped to found the short-lived Ulster Loyalist Democratic Party (a forerunner of the UDP) in 1981, and was a prime mover behind the UDA's most developed policy document, *Common Sense*, in 1987. He was killed by an IRA car-bomb later that year.

58 Ray Smallwoods was Chairman of the UDP and a leading exponent of political loyalism at the time of his killing by the IRA in July 1994 (shortly before the paramilitary ceasefires of the IRA and the CLMC). He had served a lengthy jail term for his part in the attempted murder of Bernadette McAliskey (née Devlin) in 1981.

59 See P. Shirlow and B. Murtagh, *Belfast: Segregation, Violence and the City* (London: Pluto, 2006).

60 See E. Longley, 'What do Protestants Want?', *Irish Review*, 20 (1997), pp. 104–20.

61 For the NILP, see A. Edwards, *A History of the Northern Ireland Labour Party: Democratic Socialism and Sectarianism* (Manchester: Manchester University Press, 2011).

62 Adair and McKendry, *Mad Dog*, pp. 19–23.

63 Garland, *Gusty Spence*, pp. 244–5.

64 D. Ervine cited in Moloney, *Voices for the Grave*, p. 367.

65 Ibid., p. 368.

66 Stone and McManus, *None Shall Divide Us*, xiv.

67 M. Stone cited in McKittrick et. al., *Lost Lives*, p. 1119.

68 Stone and McManus, *None Shall Divide Us*, xvii.

69 See *News of the World*, 11 February 2007.

70 M. Dillon, *The Trigger Men* (Edinburgh: Mainstream, 2004).

71 Stone and Adair were reported as trading insults regarding the quality and truthfulness of their respective memoirs; see *Sunday Life*, 4 June 2006.

72 Little and Scott, *Give a Boy a Gun*, p. 11.

73 Ibid., p. 11.

74 Snodden in *Unarmed Heroes*, p. 31. Snodden came from the Suffolk estate, a small Protestant enclave surrounded by nationalist/republican districts in west Belfast.

75 Adair and McKendry, *Mad Dog*, p. 2.

76 Little and Scott, *Give a Boy a Gun*, pp. 18–19.

77 Adair and McKendry, *Mad Dog*, p. 23.

78 Little and Scott, *Give a Boy a Gun*, pp. 60–3. Little did join the British Army, even though he had recently been arrested and charged by the RUC with obstructing the police and disorderly behaviour. However, during his basic training in 'Sutton Coalfield' (*sic*), he found that he was subject to anti-Irish prejudice, and when his superior officer found out about his conviction back home, he was forced to sign discharge papers: 'I was deeply shaken by this turn of events. This treatment wasn't what I had expected of the British Army. I thought I'd be welcomed in with open arms. I was a loyal subject, committed to the Crown and to everything British, and yet I was treated as an unwelcome foreigner. I left without ceremony, disoriented and aggrieved.' Adair (*Mad Dog*, pp. 23–4) claimed that he tried to join the UDR part-time as an eighteen-year-old, wanting 'to do more than be a street-fighter, as I was sure I had other skills to offer'. However, this effort to do 'something legitimate to fight our corner' was stymied by Adair's string of convictions, and he was rejected.

79 Ibid., p. 53.

80 Ibid., p. 71.

Notes to Chapter 5: Memoir-Writing and Moderation? Ulster Unionists Face the Troubles

1 There have been a number of important biographical studies of leading unionists, both within the UUP and DUP. See *inter alia*, D. Godson, *Himself Alone: David Trimble and the Ordeal of Unionism* (London: Harper Collins, 2004); H. McDonald, *Trimble* (London: Bloomsbury, 2000); S. Bruce, *Paisley: Religion and Politics in Northern Ireland* (Oxford: Oxford University Press, 2009).

2 J. O'Neill, *Blood-Dark Track: A Family History* (London: Granta, 2002), p. 330.

3 T. O'Neill, *The Autobiography of Terence O'Neill* (London: Rupert Hart-Davis, 1972), xi.

4 Ibid., p. 20.

5 B. McIvor, *Hope Deferred: Experiences of an Irish Unionist* (Belfast: Blackstaff Press, 1998), p. 1.

6 K. Bloomfield, *Stormont in Crisis: A Memoir* (Belfast: Blackstaff Press, 1994), p. 71.

7 W. D. Flackes and S. Elliott, *Northern Ireland: A Political Directory, 1968–1993* (Belfast: Blackstaff Press, 1994), p. 255; O'Neill, *The Autobiography*, p. 45.

8 O'Neill, *The Autobiography*, p. 54.

9 Ibid., p. 67.

10 Bloomfield, *Stormont in Crisis*, p. 93.

11 O'Neill, *The Autobiography*, p. 103.

12 Bloomfield, *Stormont in Crisis*, p. 97.

13 Ibid., p. 100. The five-point plan included: the introduction of an impartial 'points' system for allocation of public housing; the appointment of an ombudsman to investigate complaints of unfair treatment; the abolition of the 'company' vote in local elections; the replacement of the Londonderry local authority with a Development Commission; and a review of the 1922 Special Powers Act, and its provision for internment without trial.

14 O'Neill, *The Autobiography*, p. 107.

15 The significance of this speech is evident and in the following year O'Neill published a book devoted to its themes of cross-community support for a moderate programme of reform, whilst maintaining the Stormont system of government. See T. O'Neill, *Ulster at the Crossroads* (London: Faber and Faber, 1969).

16 M. Mulholland, *Northern Ireland at the Crossroads: Ulster Unionism in the O'Neill Years, 1960–9* (Basingstoke: Macmillan, 2000), p. 172.

17 O'Neill, *The Autobiography*, pp. 107–8.

18 B. Faulkner, *Memoirs of a Statesman* (London: Weidenfeld and Nicolson, 1978), pp. 16–17. For a description of the two UUP Ministers' relationship, see A. Gailey, *Crying in the Wilderness – Jack Sayers: A Liberal Editor in Ulster, 1939–69* (Belfast: Institute of Irish Studies, 1995), p. 90. Gailey states 'as with many political enemies, they had much in common.'

19 Faulkner, *Memoirs of a Statesman*, p. 39.

20 Bloomfield, *Stormont in Crisis*, p. 84.

21 Faulkner, *Memoirs of a Statesman*, p. 41.

22 Mulholland, *Northern Ireland at the Crossroads*, p. 109.

23 See Gailey, *Crying in the Wilderness*, p. 115.

24 Bloomfield, *Stormont in Crisis*, p. 85.

25 Faulkner, *Memoirs of a Statesman*, p. 41.

26 Gailey, *Crying in the Wilderness*, p. 115.

27 J. Sayers cited in A. Gailey, *Crying in the Wilderness*, p. 117.

28 T. O'Neill cited in Bloomfield, *Stormont in Crisis*, pp. 107–8.

29 The Commission was chaired by Lord Cameron and reported in September 1969, after O'Neill's resignation. The findings were highly critical of the inaction of the 'hidebound' and 'complacent' Stormont government. See Flackes and Elliott, *Northern Ireland: A Political Directory*, pp. 111–12.

30 Faulkner, *Memoirs of a Statesman*, pp. 50–1.

31 Ibid., p. 51.

32 F. Cochrane, '"Meddling at the Crossroads": The Decline and Fall of Terence O'Neill within the Unionist Community' in R. English and G. Walker (eds.), *Unionism in Modern Ireland* (Basingstoke: Macmillan, 1996), p. 163. See also H. Patterson, *Ireland Since 1939: The Persistence of Conflict* (Dublin: Penguin Ireland, 2006), p. 208.

33 Bloomfield, *Stormont in Crisis*, p. 103.

34 Faulkner, *Memoirs of a Statesman*, p. 52.

35 Ibid.

36 Ibid.

37 Mulholland, *Northern Ireland at the Crossroads*, p. 178.

38 According to Bloomfield, O'Neill voted for Chichester-Clark and not Faulkner in the leadership election after his resignation. Despite the fact that Chichester-Clark had resigned as Minister of Agriculture in late April 1969, thereby precipitating the final crisis in O'Neill's premiership, the latter preferred 'the man who had brought him down the previous week [Chichester-Clark] to the man who had been trying to bring him down for the past several years [Faulkner]'. (Bloomfield, *Stormont in Crisis*, pp. 109–10). O'Neill himself thought Chichester-Clark's action a 'stab in the back', although he was more willing to forgive Chichester-Clark than Faulkner, due to the former's 'unpolitical mind' (O'Neill, *The Autobiography*, pp. 127, 129).

39 K. Bloomfield, *A Tragedy of Errors: The Government and Misgovernment of Northern Ireland* (Liverpool: Liverpool University Press, 2007), p. 178.

40 Ibid.

41 Faulkner, *Memoirs of a Statesman*, p. 52. Bloomfield reinforced this judgment to some extent when he argued that 'at the time, perhaps inevitably, I shared to some degree O'Neill's rather paranoid notion that Faulkner was continually conspiring against him.' (Bloomfield, *A Tragedy of Errors*, p. 239.)

42 Ibid., p. 53.

43 McIvor, *Hope Deferred*, p. 45.

44 Ibid., p. 3.

45 Ibid., pp. 6, 17. There are some interesting parallels to be drawn between the memoir-writing of McIvor and another Methodist from Co. Fermanagh, Gordon Wilson. See A. McCreary, *Gordon Wilson: An Ordinary Hero* (London: Marshall Pickering, 1996) and G. Wilson with McCreary, *Marie: A Story from Enniskillen* (London: Marshall Pickering, 1990).

46 Ibid., p. 51. For a fuller treatment of the internal organisation of the UUP, see G. Walker, *A History of the Ulster Unionist Party: Protest, Pragmatism and Pessimism* (Manchester: Manchester University Press, 2004).

47 Bloomfield, *A Tragedy of Errors*, p. 239.

48 Faulkner, *Memoirs of a Statesman*, p. 87.

49 McIvor, *Hope Deferred*, p. 38. There are evident echoes of John Hewitt's well-known poem, 'The Coasters', which cast a jaundiced eye on such liberal Protestants. See F. Ormsby (ed.), *The Collected Poems of John Hewitt* (Belfast: Blackstaff Press, 1991), pp. 135–7.

50 Ibid., p. 52.

51 Ibid.

52 Ibid., p. 55.

53 Faulkner, *Memoirs of a Statesman*, p. 76.

54 On the killing of Seamus Cusack and Desmond Beattie, see McKittrick, S. Kelters, B. Feeney and C. Thornton, *Lost Lives: The Stories of the Men, Women and Children*

Who Died as a Result of the Northern Ireland Troubles (Edinburgh: Mainstream, 1999), pp. 75–7. An unofficial enquiry, chaired by the English QC Lord Gifford was held into the killings. This found that neither man had been armed, or carrying weapons or explosives. The army refuted this version, and did not participate in the enquiry. For further details of this crucial incident, see T. Hennessey, *The Evolution of the Troubles, 1970–72* (Dublin: Irish Academic Press, 2007), pp. 103–7.

55 Faulkner, *Memoirs of a Statesman*, pp. 107–8.
56 Ibid., p. 110.
57 Ibid., p. 114.
58 Ibid., p. 119.
59 Ibid.
60 Ibid., pp. 118–19.
61 Hennessey, *The Evolution of the Troubles*, p. 126.
62 Faulkner, *Memoirs of a Statesman*, p. 137.

Notes to Chapter 6: Northern Nationalists and Memoir-Writing: The Social Democratic and Labour Party and the Troubles

1 See B. Devlin, *The Price of My Soul* (London: Pan Books, 1969). Devlin won the Mid-Ulster seat as a Unity candidate in the March 1969 by-election, was returned as an independent with an increased majority in 1970, but lost her seat (after the SDLP contested the constituency) in February 1974. From this point until 2001, no woman was elected for a Westminster seat from Northern Ireland. See W. D. Flackes and S. Elliott, *Northern Ireland: A Political Directory, 1969–1993* (Belfast: Blackstaff Press, 1994), pp. 214–16.

2 P. Devlin, *Straight Left: An Autobiography* (Belfast: Blackstaff Press, 1993).

3 P. O'Hanlon, *End of Term Report* (Newry: Paddy O'Hanlon Publishing, 2011). O'Hanlon's memoir was published posthumously, and edited by journalist Brian Feeney.

4 A. Currie, *All Hell Will Break Loose* (Dublin: O'Brien Press, 2004).

5 Hume (born 1937) was leader of the SDLP from 1979 until 2001, and although he has published a volume devoted to the Northern Ireland conflict, it is not strictly a memoir; see J. Hume, *A New Ireland* (Boulder, CO: Roberts Rinehart, 1996). This chapter will make occasional reference to the autobiographical material in the opening chapters of *A New Ireland*. In addition, there have been several biographical studies of Hume: see B. White, *John Hume: Statesman of the Troubles* (Belfast: Blackstaff Press, 1984); G. Drower, *John Hume: Man of Peace* (London: Victor Gollancz, 1995); P. Routledge, *John Hume* (London: Harper Collins, 1997).

6 Fitt (1926–2005) was leader of the SDLP from its inception in 1970 until his resignation from the party in 1979. Fitt wrote no memoir, but there are two biographies available: C. Ryder, *Fighting Fitt* (Belfast: Brehon Press, 2006); M. Murphy, *Gerry Fitt: A Political Chameleon* (Dublin: Mercier Press, 2007).

7 C. Parr, 'Managing his Aspirations: The Labour and Republican Politics of Paddy

Devlin', *Irish Political Studies*, 27.1 (2012), p. 112.

8 P. Devlin, *Yes We Have No Bananas: Outdoor Relief in Belfast, 1920–39* (Belfast: Blackstaff Press, 1981).

9 Hume, *A New Ireland*, pp. 25–6.

10 Currie, *All Hell Will Break Loose*, p. 19.

11 Devlin, *The Price of My Soul*, p. 49.

12 Ibid., p. 37.

13 Ibid., p. 51.

14 Currie, *All Hell Will Break Loose*, pp. 37–8.

15 Ibid., p. 38.

16 O'Hanlon, *End of Term Report*, p. 19.

17 Hume, *A New Ireland*, p. 23.

18 M. Elliott, *The Catholics of Ulster: A History* (London: Penguin, 2001), p. 397.

19 Currie, *All Hell Will Break Loose*, p. 63. Hume (standing as an independent) had defeated McAteer in the Foyle constituency at the Stormont general election in 1969. He described him as 'an honourable and highly respected man, who had been a natural leader of his generation. However, I felt that our generation was faced with a whole new situation'. See Hume, *A New Ireland*, p. 34.

20 For detailed analysis of the trajectory of the Nationalist Party, see B. Lynn, *Holding the Ground: The Nationalist Party in Northern Ireland, 1945–72* (Aldershot: Ashgate, 1997).

21 O'Hanlon, *End of Term Report*, p. 10.

22 Ibid., p. 18.

23 Ibid., p. 27.

24 Ibid.

25 Currie, *All Hell Will Break Loose*, pp. 28–9.

26 Ibid., p. 32.

27 Devlin, *The Price of My Soul*, pp. 58–9.

28 Ibid., p. 62. Emphasis in the original.

29 Currie, *All Hell Will Break Loose*, p. 125.

30 Ibid. At the end of 1974, Devlin was a founding member of the Irish Republican Socialist Party, although her involvement was short-lived. Later in the 1970s, she was active in the anti-criminalisation campaign that was waged on behalf of republican prisoners. In 1980–1, she was the main spokeswoman for the National H-Block/Armagh Committee; she survived a loyalist assassination attempt, along with her husband Michael McAliskey, in February 1981. See Flackes and Elliott, *Northern Ireland: A Political Directory*, pp. 215–16.

31 Hume, *A New Ireland*, pp. 25, 35–6.

32 Devlin, *Straight Left*, p. 22.

33 Ibid., p. 24.

34 Ibid., p. 29.

35 Parr, 'Managing his Aspirations', p. 112.

36 Ibid., p. 132.

37 Ibid., p. 134.

38 Ibid., p. 121.

39 Devlin, *Straight Left*, p. 48.

40 Ibid., p. 49. There are striking parallels between Devlin's experience and that of a loyalist prison leader, Gusty Spence, also a working-class autodidact who used his much lengthier period of incarceration to question his own half-formed views, and challenge those of fellow Ulster Volunteer Force (UVF) prisoners. See Chapter 4 on loyalist memoir, and R. Garland, *Gusty Spence* (Belfast: Blackstaff Press, 2001).

41 See C. McCluskey, *Up off Their Knees: A Commentary on the Civil Rights Movement in Northern Ireland* (no place: Conn McCluskey and Associates, 1989).

42 Currie, *All Hell Will Break Loose*, pp. 58–60.

43 Ibid., p. 61.

44 O'Hanlon, *End of Term Report*, p. 29.

45 Ibid., p. 30.

46 Currie, *All Hell Will Break Loose*, p. 68.

47 Ibid., p. 84.

48 Devlin, *Straight Left*, pp. 92–3.

49 Currie, *All Hell Will Break Loose*, p. 116.

50 Ibid.

51 Ibid., p. 117. See also H. Patterson, *Ireland since 1939*, p. 207. The march is generally described as the Burntollet march, after the bridge outside Dungiven where it was attacked by loyalists, including off-duty B Specials. The march was organised by the radical left group, People's Democracy (PD), which largely comprised students from Queen's University.

52 Devlin, *Straight Left*, pp. 93–5. In a telling example of the capacity for personal interests to intrude upon political strategy, it was surely significant for Devlin that his daughter, Anne, took part in the Burntollet march, and was one of those injured as a result of the loyalist assault.

53 Devlin, *The Price of My Soul*, p. 116.

54 Ibid., p. 119.

55 Ibid.

56 Devlin, *Straight Left*, p. 96.

57 O'Hanlon, *End of Term Report*, p. 27.

58 Currie, *All Hell Will Break Loose*, p. 118.

59 Devlin, *Straight Left*, p. 108.

60 O'Hanlon, *End of Term Report*, p. 32.

61 Ibid.

62 Devlin, *Straight Left*, pp. 108–9. In his analysis of this episode, Connal Parr makes the important point that Devlin was reflecting to some degree the 'staunchly nationalist views of his West Belfast constituents', and that he did so in similar situations in the coming years. Whether one can extrapolate from these occasions, and argue that Devlin essentially *shared* these views is more difficult to sustain. See Parr, 'Managing his Aspirations', pp. 119–20.

63 Currie, *All Hell Will Break Loose*, p. 119. Currie had helped to galvanise the civil rights protests when he led the squatting of a council house in Caledon, Co. Tyrone; see Ibid., pp. 90–9.

64 Ibid., p. 119. All of the memoirists included here recounted the impact of their political activities upon their families, particularly in terms of the intimidation and violence directed at them, either by republicans or loyalists. See Devlin, *Straight Left*, pp. 151–2, 167–8; O'Hanlon, *End of Term Report*, p. 32.

65 See I. McAllister, *The Northern Ireland Social Democratic and Labour Party: Political Opposition in a Divided Society* (London: Macmillan, 1977), pp. 29–32.

66 Currie, *All Hell Will Break Loose*, p. 152.

67 Devlin, *Straight Left*, p. 137.

68 Ibid., p. 138.

69 Ibid.

70 Ibid., pp. 140–2. See also Currie, *All Hell Will Break Loose*, p. 160.

71 O'Hanlon, *End of Term Report*, pp. 33–4.

72 Seamus Cusack and Desmond Beattie were shot in disputed circumstances: British soldiers claimed the men were armed, but civilian witnesses vehemently denied this. See Chapter 5, note 54.

73 Devlin, *Straight Left*, p. 155. It has been argued elsewhere that Devlin was consulted by telephone about the ultimatum, and agreed to it provided that, 'if the party did withdraw they would have to broaden the basis for leaving'; see Hennessey, *The Evolution of the Troubles*, p. 106. Currie backed up the claim that both Devlin and Fitt had been called by Hume, but although he agreed with the ultimatum, he was nervous about the reaction of the Belfast men; see Currie, *All Hell Will Break Loose*, p. 170. A biographer of Fitt agreed he had been informed, and quoted him as follows: "'Bollocks; I'm not going to any fucking meeting. I have lost constituents too. It's a Derry thing.'" See Murphy, *Gerry Fitt*, p. 167.

74 Ibid., p. 154. Devlin had welcomed the committee proposals as showing imagination, and described it as Faulkner's 'finest hour since I came into the house'. According to one biographer, 'even Hume, later to say he was "appalled" by Devlin's acceptance of the committee deal, was complimentary [at the time].' See White, *John Hume*, p. 112.

75 Ibid., p. 155.

76 Ibid., p. 156.

77 Currie, *All Hell Will Break Loose*, p. 170.

78 Ibid., p. 173.

79 Devlin, *Straight Left*, p. 155. In an interview with his biographer in 1989, Fitt went much further, and claimed that Hume was "'playing ball with the Provos'". See Murphy, *Gerry Fitt*, p. 168. This was an incendiary claim, and perhaps should be understood in the context of the bitterness that followed Fitt's resignation from the SDLP, and Hume's assumption of the leadership, in 1979.

80 Currie, *All Hell Will Break Loose*, p. 175.

81 Ibid., p. 175.

82 O'Hanlon, *End of Term Report*, pp. 36–9.

83 Devlin, *Straight Left*, p. 159.

84 Currie, *All Hell Will Break Loose*, p. 178.

Notes to Chapter 7: A Case-Study of Memoir-Writing and the Elusive Search for a Political Settlement: The 1974 Power-Sharing Executive and Sunningdale

 1 B. Faulkner, *Memoirs of a Statesman* (London: Weidenfeld and Nicolson, 1978), p. 152.

 2 Ibid., p. 147.

 3 P. O'Hanlon, *End of Term Report* (Newry: Paddy O'Hanlon Publishing, 2011), pp. 39–41. O'Hanlon reproduced sections of the minutes of a meeting between Stormont PM Faulkner and the Westminster government's Northern Ireland sub-committee (known as the G bundles).

 4 A. Currie, *All Hell Will Break Loose* (Dublin: O'Brien Press, 2004), p. 211.

 5 Faulkner, *Memoirs of a Statesman*, p. 167.

 6 Currie, *All Hell Will Break Loose*, p. 211. It was not made explicit which specific documents Currie was referring to, but it is worth noting that political figures have on occasion made use of official documents in their memoir-writing, once they are released into the public domain.

 7 Faulkner, *Memoirs of a Statesman*, p. 203.

 8 P. Devlin, *Straight Left* (Belfast: Blackstaff Press, 1993), p. 153.

 9 G. Gillespie, 'The Sunningdale Agreement: Lost Opportunity or an Agreement too Far?', *Irish Political Studies* 13 (1998), p. 101.

10 K. Bloomfield, *Stormont in Crisis: A Memoir* (Belfast: Blackstaff Press, 1994), p. 145.

11 Ibid., p. 147.

12 Ibid., pp. 148–9.

13 M. Hayes, *Minority Verdict: Experiences of a Catholic Public Servant* (Belfast: Blackstaff Press, 1995), pp. 132–4. It is surely not incidental that Hayes was a Catholic from Killough, Co. Down, who in 1971 was heading the Community Relations Commission. He had a clear understanding of the way in which internment would be received in the Catholic community, and this sense was unlikely to be shared by the vast majority of civil servants, who came from Protestant unionist backgrounds, such as Bloomfield.

14 Ibid., p. 137.

15 B. McIvor, *Hope Deferred: Experiences of an Irish Unionist* (Belfast: Blackstaff Press, 1998), p. 67.

16 Ibid., p. 70.

17 Ibid., p. 86.

18 O'Hanlon, *End of Term Report*, p. 50. See also Currie, *All Hell Will Break Loose*, p. 211.

19 Faulkner, *Memoirs of a Statesman*, p. 204.

20 Ibid., p. 204.

21 McIvor, *Hope Deferred*, p. 95. See also Faulkner, *Memoirs of a Statesman*, p. 204.

22 Devlin, *Straight Left*, p. 196.

23 Faulkner, *Memoirs of a Statesman*, p. 213.

24 Currie, *All Hell Will Break Loose*, p. 213; Faulkner, *Memoirs of a Statesman*, p. 205.

25 Ibid., p. 219. Currie stated that 'I could not believe that at this juncture, when progress towards the solution of the Northern Ireland problem was so dependent on Whitelaw, that the actions of the Prime Minister would be motivated by party political considerations.' In fact, Whitelaw was soon to be replaced by Francis Pym before the tripartite Sunningdale conference; almost all involved in the delicate inter-party talks seemed to concur that this was 'overhasty and ill-timed', or even a 'calamitous decision' by Heath. See Bloomfield, *Stormont in Crisis*, p. 186 and Faulkner, *Memoirs of a Statesman*, p. 226.

26 Ibid., p. 215.

27 McIvor, *Hope Deferred*, p. 97.

28 Faulkner, *Memoirs of a Statesman*, pp. 223–4.

29 Gillespie, 'The Sunningdale Agreement', p. 103.

30 Faulkner, *Memoirs of a Statesman*, p. 242. The phrase was Faulkner's description of the power-sharing Executive.

31 Ibid., p. 104.

32 H. Patterson, *Ireland since 1939: The Persistence of Conflict* (Dublin: Penguin Ireland, 2006), p. 240.

33 B. Faulkner, *Memoirs of a Statesman*, pp. 215–6.

34 Ibid., p. 229.

35 Ibid.

36 McIvor, *Hope Deferred*, p. 96.

37 Ibid., p. 103.

38 Ibid., p. 100.

39 Faulkner, *Memoirs of a Statesman*, pp. 236–7.

40 Devlin, *Straight Left*, p. 203.

41 Ibid., p. 210.

42 Currie, *All Hell Will Break Loose*, pp. 228, 241.

43 Ibid., p. 241.

44 In December 1973, at the Irish High Court, Kevin Boland, an ex-Fianna Fáil minister, had challenged the Cosgrave government's decision to sign the Sunningdale Agreement. Boland argued that by signing up to an effective recognition of Northern Ireland's current constitutional status (as part of the United Kingdom), the government in Dublin was reneging on its own constitutional claim over the territory (as expressed in Articles 2 and 3). Faulkner (*Memoirs of a Statesman*, pp. 246–7) recognised that 'this put the Dublin Cabinet in a very difficult position and they had to mount a technical defence claiming that they had not actually recognized Northern Ireland as being outside their jurisdiction. Naturally, this caused a sensation in Northern Ireland where many people who had thought the recognition side of Sunningdale a real step forward now began to doubt if it had any value.'

Despite efforts to paper over the cracks, 'the status issue, previously one of our trump cards, had been blurred.' See also, Gillespie, 'The Sunningdale Agreement', p. 108.

45 McIvor, *Hope Deferred*, p. 104.

46 P. Arthur, 'The Heath Government and Northern Ireland', in *The Heath Government, 1970–1974: A Reappraisal* ed. by S. Ball and A. Seldon (London: Longman, 1996), p. 256.

47 Bloomfield, *Stormont in Crisis*, p. 197.

48 Gillespie, 'The Sunningdale Agreement', p. 108.

49 Bloomfield, *Stormont in Crisis*, p. 200.

50 Ibid., p. 205.

51 Currie, *All Hell Will Break Loose*, p. 243.

52 J. Oliver, *Working at Stormont* (Dublin: Institute of Public Administration, 1978), p. 108.

53 Currie, *All Hell Will Break Loose*, p. 244. Oliver (*Working at Stormont*, p. 109) described Currie as 'young, fresh, hard-working and likeable', while Currie (Ibid.) appreciated the advice of a 'wise and wily old owl, and we got on extremely well at a personal level; some people commented that his attitude to me was almost paternalistic.'

54 Devlin, *Straight Left*, pp. 213–15.

55 Faulkner, *Memoirs of a Statesman*, p. 251.

56 Gillespie, 'The Sunningdale Agreement', p. 111.

57 Faulkner, *Memoirs of a Statesman*, p. 252.

58 Currie, *All Hell Will Break Loose*, p. 252.

59 Devlin, *Straight Left*, p. 226. For contesting every seat, including Mid-Ulster (held by Bernadette Devlin) and Fermanagh-South Tyrone (held by Frank McManus), the SDLP were accused by their republican opponents of splitting the non-unionist vote, and effectively handing these seats to unionists. Both seats were won by supporters of the UUUC loyalist coalition.

60 Faulkner, *Memoirs of a Statesman*, p. 253.

61 Murphy, *Gerry Fitt*, p. 198.

62 Devlin, *Straight Left*, p. 229.

63 Ibid., p. 230.

64 See Currie, *All Hell Will Break Loose*, pp. 259–61. He was particularly affected personally by the loyalist killing of two close family friends, Jim and Gertie Devlin, who lived in the same village. One of those convicted for the killings had worked on improving the security at Currie's home.

65 Ibid., p. 263.

66 Faulkner, *Memoirs of a Statesman*, pp. 256–7. See also M. Rees, *Northern Ireland: A Personal Perspective* (London: Methuen, 1985), pp. 60–1.

67 Bloomfield, *Stormont in Crisis*, p. 209.

68 McIvor, *Hope Deferred*, p. 118.

69 For further detailed treatment of the UWC strike, see D. Anderson, *Fourteen May Days: The Inside Story of the Loyalist Strike of May 1974* (Dublin: Gill and Macmillan,

1994).

70 Faulkner, *Memoirs of a Statesman*, p. 262.

71 Ibid., p. 263. Currie (*All Hell Will Break Loose*, p. 268) agreed with this judgment: 'I believe that the future of the Power-Sharing Executive was determined more in Lisburn, at the Headquarters of the British Army, than at Downing Street, or Stormont Castle.'

72 Rees, *Northern Ireland*, p. 64.

73 Currie, *All Hell Will Break Loose*, p. 265. Civil servants were also calm about the likely impact of the strike; Hayes (*Minority Verdict*, p. 186) recalled that he left Stormont on 14 May with no sense of 'impending doom'.

74 Devlin, *Straight Left*, p. 236.

75 Currie, *All Hell Will Break Loose*, p. 267.

76 Devlin, *Straight Left*, p. 236.

77 G. FitzGerald, *All in a Life: An Autobiography* (Dublin: Gill and Macmillan, 1991), p. 228.

78 Hayes, *Minority Verdict*, p. 187. Bloomfield (*Stormont in Crisis*, pp. 215–16) asserted that the security forces, under Westminster's control, had produced only 'flabby resistance' to the UWC, and that people who wished to get to work and ignore the strike were 'afforded no protection whatever by authority'. In such circumstances, 'it was hardly surprising that their resolution faded.'

79 McIvor, *Hope Deferred*, p. 118.

80 Rees, *Northern Ireland*, p. 89.

81 Bloomfield, *Stormont in Crisis*, pp. 214–15. Hayes (*Minority Verdict*, p. 200) compared the position of the unionist middle class to the last days of the Weimar Republic.

82 Gillespie, 'The Sunningdale Agreement', p. 112.

83 Currie, *All Hell Will Break Loose*, p. 266.

84 Rees, *Northern Ireland*, p. 89.

85 Faulkner, *Memoirs of a Statesman*, p. 278.

86 McIvor, *Hope Deferred*, p. 120.

87 Currie, *All Hell Will Break Loose*, pp. 281, 300.

88 Devlin, *Straight Left*, p. 253.

89 Ibid., p. 289.

90 Bloomfield, *Stormont in Crisis*, p. 220.

91 Hayes, *Minority Verdict*, p. 202.

92 K. Bloomfield, *A Tragedy of Errors: The Government and Misgovernment of Northern Ireland* (Liverpool: Liverpool University Press, 2007), p. 197.

93 Ibid.

94 Bloomfield, *Stormont in Crisis*, p. 221.

95 McIvor, *Hope Deferred*, p. 122.

96 Devlin, *Straight Left*, p. 251.

97 Ibid., p. 252.

98 W. Whitelaw, *The Whitelaw Memoirs* (London: Headline, 1989), pp. 144–5.

99 R. Ramsay, *Ringside Seats: An Insider's View of the Crisis in Northern Ireland* (Dublin: Irish Academic Press, 2009), p. 123.

100 Bloomfield, *A Tragedy of Errors*, p. 198.

101 Bloomfield, *Stormont in Crisis*, p. 222.

Notes to Chapter 8: British Ministers and the Politics of Northern Ireland: Reading the Political Memoirs of Secretaries of State

1 J. Callaghan, *A House Divided: The Dilemma of Northern Ireland* (London: Collins, 1973).

2 R. Needham, *Battling for Peace* (Belfast: Blackstaff Press, 1998).

3 See A. Gamble, 'Political Memoirs', *British Journal of Politics and International Relations*, 4.1 (2002), p. 142.

4 Of course, several SOSNI have not published memoirs, or at least have not yet done so. Amongst this group are Francis Pym (1973–4), Humphrey Atkins (1979–81), Tom King (1985–9), Peter Brooke (1989–92), Patrick Mayhew (1992–7), Paul Murphy (2002–5) and John Reid (2001–2). In some cases, these individuals spent significant periods of time in Northern Ireland, but in others they were a fleeting presence.

5 Norman Dugdale, a permanent secretary at the Department of Health and Social Security, and also a poet and translator, composed a poem, 'Provincia Deserta', that summed up the feelings of many locals about the attitude and outlook of the average SOSNI:

> Well, here it is: not Botany Bay
> But a penal settlement all the same,
> The sentence life without remission – saving,
> Of course, Sir, such as yourself, gentlemen newly come
> To live here at the Governor's Lodge. Two years from now
> You will be safely home again and dining out
> On your bizarre experiences, which cannot fail
> To please your hostess and amuse the company.

Cited in M. Hayes, *Minority Verdict: Experiences of a Catholic Public Servant* (Belfast: Blackstaff Press, 1995), p. 241.

6 D. Bloomfield and M. Lankford, 'From Whitewash to Mayhem: The State of the Secretary in Northern Ireland', in *The Northern Ireland Question in British Politics* ed. by P. Catterall and S. McDougall (Basingstoke: Palgrave Macmillan, 1996), p. 147.

7 Ibid.

8 P. Hain, *Outside In* (London: Biteback, 2012), pp. 293, 338. Hain used his considerable autonomy to introduce a scheme that would make available complementary medicine facilities, which had been frustrated by the civil service when it had been discussed in Great Britain.

9 Bloomfield and Lankford, 'From Whitewash to Mayhem', pp. 146, 148.

10 J. Prior, *A Balance of Power* (London: Hamish Hamilton, 1985), p. 183.

11 D. Hurd, *Memoirs* (London: Little, Brown, 2003), p. 296.

12 Ibid., p. 297.

13 M. Mowlam, *Momentum: The Struggle for Peace, Politics and the People* (London: Hodder and Stoughton, 2002), xv.

14 Ibid., p. 18.

15 Ibid., p. 32. See also P. Bew and P. Dixon, 'Labour Party Policy and Northern Ireland', in *The Northern Ireland Question: Perspectives and Policies* ed. by B. Barton and P. Roche (Aldershot: Avebury, 1994).

16 M. Rees, *Northern Ireland: A Personal Perspective* (London: Methuen, 1985), p. 3.

17 Prior, *A Balance of Power*, p. 258. Prior had publicly stated that he was not keen on the Northern Ireland post, as part of the internal politics within the Conservative Party in the speculation surrounding a Cabinet reshuffle in 1981. Nonetheless, Mrs Thatcher was not dissuaded, and he eventually accepted the job.

18 Hayes, *Minority Verdict*, p. 259.

19 R. Mason, *Paying the Price* (London: Robert Hale, 1999), p. 161.

20 Hayes, *Minority Verdict*, p. 246.

21 Bloomfield and Lankford, 'From Whitewash to Mayhem', p. 151.

22 Mowlam, *Momentum*, p. 53.

23 Ibid., p. 265.

24 P. Mandelson, *The Third Man: Life at the Heart of New Labour* (London: Harper Collins, 2010), p. 285.

25 Mowlam, *Momentum*, p. 281.

26 Mandelson, *The Third Man*, p. 285.

27 Ibid., pp. 287–8.

28 Ibid., p. 288.

29 It is perhaps instructive to compare the attitude of previous Labour SOSNI to the use of Hillsborough Castle as an official residence. Merlyn Rees refused to countenance living in the splendour of what had been the Governor-General's residence; he argued that it was too closely identified with the *ancien régime*, and that it would send out the wrong message in terms of the alleged neo-colonial attitude of the UK government to the province. On the other hand, of the 'New Labour' SOSNI, Mowlam, Mandelson and Hain all make reference in their memoirs to their enjoyment of the palatial environment and the luxurious rooms at their disposal. When the PM offered Hain the SOSNI post, he 'sugared the pill' by adding, "'You know you will have your own castle!'" (Hain, *Outside In*, p. 310.)

30 Mowlam, *Momentum*, p. 297.

31 *Belfast Telegraph*, 3 September 1985 (cited in Bloomfield and Lankford, 'From Whitewash to Mayhem', p. 151.)

32 Prior, *A Balance of Power*, p. 197.

33 Hurd, *Memoirs*, p. 296.

34 Hayes, *Minority Verdict*, p. 257.

35 Bloomfield and Lankford, 'From Whitewash to Mayhem', p. 155.

36 W. Whitelaw, *Memoirs* (London: Aurum, 1989), p. 106.

37 Rees, *Northern Ireland*, p. 69.

38 Ibid., p. 31.

39 Mason, *Paying the Price*, p. 12.

40 Ibid., p. 10.

41 Mowlam, *Momentum*, pp. 133–4.

42 Prior, *A Balance of Power*, p. 183.

43 Whitelaw, *Memoirs*, p. 144.

44 Ibid., pp. 128–9. There are several conflicting accounts of these talks in the memoirs of key protagonists: see, for example, G. Adams, *Before the Dawn: An Autobiography* (London: Heinemann, 1996), pp. 199–206; S. MacStíofáin, *Memoirs of a Revolutionary* (Edinburgh: Gordon Cremonesi, 1975), pp. 278–86. For a more critical account of the republican engagement, see D. Sharrock and M. Devenport, *Man of War, Man of Peace? The Unauthorised Biography of Gerry Adams* (Basingstoke: Macmillan, 1997), pp. 100–5. For a sympathetic view of Whitelaw's involvement, see M. Garnett and I. Aitken, *Splendid! Splendid! The Authorized Biography of Willie Whitelaw* (London: Jonathan Cape, 2002), pp. 127–48.

45 Rees, *Northern Ireland*, p. 33.

46 Mowlam, *Momentum*, p. 71.

47 Ibid., p. 70.

48 J. Powell, *Great Hatred, Little Room: Making Peace in Northern Ireland* (London, Bodley Head, 2008), p. 88.

49 The Price sisters, Dolours and Marion, had been convicted for their roles in an IRA bombing campaign in London in 1973, and sentenced to life imprisonment. They began a hunger strike in support of their demand that republican prisoners should be transferred to jails in Northern Ireland. See Rees, *Northern Ireland*, pp. 115–17; also G. McGladdery, *The Provisional IRA in England: The Bombing Campaign 1973–1997* (Dublin: Irish Academic Press, 2006), pp. 71–2.

50 Needham, *Battling for Peace*, p. 8.

51 Rees, *Northern Ireland*, p. 204.

52 Ibid., p. 215.

53 Ibid., pp. 60–1. See also Mason, *Paying the Price*, p. 125.

54 Hain, *Outside In*, pp. 312–13. For a fuller discussion of Hain's past activism on behalf of 'Troops Out' from Northern Ireland, see P. Dixon, 'Peter Hain, Secretary of State for Northern Ireland: Valuing the Union?', *Irish Political Studies*, 21.2 (2006).

55 Ibid., p. 313.

56 Prior, *A Balance of Power*, p. 187. See also D. McKittrick, S. Kelters, B. Feeney and C. Thornton, *Lost Lives: The Stories of the Men, Women and Children Who Died as a Result of the Northern Ireland Troubles* (Edinburgh: Mainstream, 1999), pp. 886–7.

57 Whitelaw, *Memoirs*, p. 133.

58 Hurd, *Memoirs*, p. 298.

59 Ibid.

60 Mowlam, *Momentum*, p. 115.

61 Hain, *Outside In*, pp. 313–21.
62 Rees, *Northern Ireland*, p. 87.
63 Mowlam, *Momentum*, p. 116.
64 Powell, *Great Hatred, Little Room*, pp. 26, 152.
65 Mandelson, *The Third Man*, p. 293.
66 Powell, *Great Hatred, Little Room*, p. 172.
67 Ibid., p. 157.
68 Mowlam, *Momentum*, pp. 148–50.
69 Ibid., p. 123.
70 Mandelson, *The Third Man*, p. 291.
71 Ibid.
72 Hain, *Outside In*, p. 318.
73 Hain made plain his understanding of the dangers inherent in a split within the Provisional republican movement: 'they [Adams and McGuinness] had to keep their republican hinterland on board, a notoriously difficult task given the long history of splits in the IRA, some viciously violent. Adams was haunted by the memory of Michael Collins.' (Hain, *Outside In*, p. 319). For Mowlam, 'one of Republicanism's founding principles has always been to stay together, stay united.' (Mowlam, *Momentum*, p. 143). Although divisions were apparent in the Provisional movement over the course of the peace process, and indeed there was a significant split with the formation of the Real IRA and the 32 County Sovereignty movement in 1997, it is instructive that neither SOSNI displayed as much sensitivity to the evident splits within the UUP.
74 Hain, *Outside In*, p. 319.
75 Mason, *Paying the Price*, p. 254.
76 Hain, *Outside In*, p. 330.
77 Ibid., p. 318.
78 Ibid.
79 Rees, *Northern Ireland*, p. 136.
80 Ibid., p. 40.
81 Hayes, *Minority Verdict*, p. 206.
82 Hurd, *Memoirs*, p. 308.
83 Mandelson, *The Third Man*, p. 294.

Notes to Chapter 9: Journalists, the Northern Ireland 'Troubles' and the Politics of Memoir-Writing

1 The heading is taken from Anthony Loyd's journalistic memoir of the Bosnian war, *My War Gone by, I Miss it so* (London: Doubleday, 1999).
2 E. Moloney, *A Secret History of the IRA* (London: Allen Lane, 2002); E. Moloney and A. Pollak, *Paisley* (Dublin: Poolbeg, 1986).
3 D. McKittrick, S. Kelters, B. Feeney and C. Thornton, *Lost Lives: The Stories of the Men, Women and Children Who Died as a Result of the Northern Ireland Troubles*

(Edinburgh: Mainstream, 1999).

4 C. Ryder, *The RUC: A Force under Fire* (London: Methuen, 1989); C. Ryder, *The Ulster Defence Regiment: An Instrument of Peace?* (London: Methuen, 1991); C. Ryder, *Inside the Maze: The Untold Story of the Northern Ireland Prison Service* (London: Methuen, 2001).

5 J. Cusack and H. McDonald, *The UVF* (Dublin: Poolbeg, 1997); H. McDonald and J. Cusack, *UDA: Inside the Heart of Loyalist Terror* (Dublin: Penguin Ireland, 2004).

6 S. McKay, *Northern Protestants: An Unsettled People* (Belfast: Blackstaff, 2000); S. McKay, *Bear in Mind These Dead* (London: Faber and Faber, 2008).

7 For a fuller treatment of this topic, see P. Shirlow and B. Murtagh, *Belfast: Segregation, Violence and the City* (London: Pluto Press, 2006).

8 Walter Ellis of the *Sunday Times* is another journalist 'insider' who has written an unusual memoir of his childhood in Protestant East Belfast and his close friendship with Ronnie Bunting, a future Irish National Liberation Army chief of staff. See W. Ellis, *The Beginning of the End: The Crippling Disadvantage of a Happy Irish Childhood* (Edinburgh: Mainstream, 2006).

9 H. McDonald, *Colours: Ireland – From Bombs to Boom* (Edinburgh: Mainstream, 2005), p. 23.

10 Ibid., pp. 19–20.

11 M. O'Doherty, *The Telling Year: Belfast 1972* (Dublin: Gill and Macmillan, 2007), p. 9.

12 M. O'Doherty, *The Trouble with Guns: Republican Strategy and the Provisional IRA* (Belfast: Blackstaff, 1998).

13 O'Doherty, *Trouble with Guns*, p. 11.

14 Ibid.

15 O'Doherty, *The Telling Year*, p. 5.

16 M. Devenport, *Flash Frames: Twelve Years Reporting Belfast* (Belfast: Blackstaff, 2000), p. 5.

17 Ibid., pp. 7, 3.

18 Ibid., p. 3.

19 K. Myers, *Watching the Door: Cheating Death in 1970s Belfast* (London: Atlantic, 2008), vii.

20 Ibid., vii.

21 Ibid., p. 4.

22 Ibid., p. 12.

23 Ibid., p. 3.

24 J. Conroy, *War as a Way of Life: A Belfast Diary* (London: Heinemann, 1988), ix.

25 Ibid., p. 18.

26 Ibid., x.

27 Shirlow and Murtagh, *Belfast*, p. 30.

28 M. Smyth and M.-T. Fay, *Personal Accounts from Northern Ireland's Troubles: Public Conflict, Private Loss* (London: Pluto Press, 2000), p. 133.

29 O'Doherty, *The Telling Year*, p. 56.

30 McDonald, *Colours: Ireland*, p. 32.

31 Devenport, *Flash Frames*, p. 68.

32 Myers, *Watching the Door*, p. 24.

33 Ibid., 26.

34 Ibid.

35 Ibid.

36 Ibid., p. 51.

37 Ibid, p. 59.

38 Conroy, *War as a Way of Life*, p. 45.

39 Ibid., p. 173.

40 H. Zwicker, 'Gerry Adams, Moving Target', *Canadian Journal of Irish Studies*, 27.2/28.1 (2001–2002), 91.

41 Conroy, *War as a Way of Life*, pp. 40–1. He had received a bursary from the Alicia Patterson Foundation in the US in order to write a substantive piece concerning the effects of the Troubles upon the ordinary people of Belfast.

42 M. Breen Smyth, *Truth Recovery and Justice after Conflict: Managing Violent Pasts* (London: Routledge, 2007), p. 72.

43 Myers, *Watching the Door*, p. 136.

44 Ibid., p. 73.

45 Ibid., p. 136.

46 McDonald, *Colours: Ireland*, p. 11.

47 Ibid., p. 12.

48 Ibid.

49 Ibid., p. 20.

50 Ibid., p. 247.

51 O'Doherty, *The Telling Year*, p. 220.

52 Ibid., p. 221.

53 Ibid.

54 Ibid., p. 222.

55 Myers, *Watching the Door*, p. 144.

56 Ibid., p. 200.

57 Ibid., p. 180.

58 Ibid., p. 182.

59 Ibid., p. 204.

60 Ibid., p. 209.

61 Ibid., p. 24.

62 Ibid., viii.

63 Ibid., p. 271.

64 Conroy, *War as a Way of Life*, p. 38.

65 Ibid., p. 40.

66 Ibid., ix.

67 Devenport, *Flash Frames*, pp. 40–1.

68 Ibid., p. 43.

69 Ibid., p. 45.

70 Ibid., p. 60.

71 McKay, *Bear in Mind These Dead*, p. 7.

72 Ibid., p. 7.

73 O'Doherty, *The Telling Year*, p. 216.

74 Ibid.

75 Devenport, *Flash Frames*, p. 224.

76 Ibid., p. 225.

77 Myers, *Watching the Door*, pp. 201–2.

Notes to Chapter 10: Victims and Memoir-Writing: Leaving the Troubles Behind?

1 G. Egerton (ed.), *Political Memoir: Essays on the Politics of Memory* (London: Frank Cass, 1994), p. 344.

2 M. Breen Smyth, *Truth Recovery and Justice after Conflict: Managing Violent Pasts* (Abingdon and New York: Routledge, 2007), p. 74.

3 L. M. Thomas, 'Suffering as a Moral Beacon: Blacks and Jews', in *The Americanization of the Holocaust* ed. by H. Flanzbaum (Baltimore: Johns Hopkins, 1999), p. 204. Cited by M. Breen Smyth, *Truth Recovery*, p. 75.

4 Egerton, *Political Memoir*, p. 348.

5 D. McKittrick, S. Kelters, B. Feeney and C. Thornton, *Lost Lives: The Stories of the Men, Women and Children Who Died as a Result of the Northern Ireland Troubles* (Edinburgh: Mainstream, 1999).

6 G. Dawson, *Making Peace with the Past? Memory, Trauma and the Irish Troubles* (Manchester: Manchester University Press, 2007), p. 9.

7 M. Morrissey and M. Smyth, *Northern Ireland after the Good Friday Agreement: Victims, Grievance and Blame* (London and Sterling, VA: Pluto Press, 2002), p. 7.

8 M. Smyth and M.-T. Fay, *Personal Accounts from Northern Ireland's Troubles: Public Conflict, Private Loss* (London and Sterling, VA: Pluto Press, 2000), p. 133.

9 C. Gébler, *The Glass Curtain: Inside an Ulster Community* (London: Hamish Hamilton, 1991) provides an excellent portrait of community relations in Enniskillen, and Co. Fermanagh. See also, C. Tóibín, *Bad Blood: A Walk along the Irish Border* (London: Vintage, 1994), esp. pp. 79–102.

10 G. Wilson (with A. McCreary), *Marie: A Story from Enniskillen* (London: Marshall Pickering, 1990), p. 7.

11 Ibid., p. 10.

12 For a recent discussion of the significance of the Somme commemoration to Protestant Unionists in Northern Ireland, see R. Graff-McRae, *Remembering and Forgetting 1916: Commemoration and Conflict in Post-Peace Process Ireland* (Dublin and Portland, Or: Irish Academic Press, 2010), pp. 81–113.

13 R. Restorick, *Death of a Soldier: A Mother's Search for Peace in Northern Ireland*

(Belfast: Blackstaff Press, 2000), p. 2.

14 Ibid., p. 197.

15 Ibid., p. 8.

16 Alistair Little, a former UVF man convicted of murder and latterly involved with the Healing Through Remembering group and storytelling/encounter sessions, makes the argument that all 'insiders' in Northern Ireland bear some responsibility for conflict: 'my own story shows how people are deluding themselves if they think their own lack of violent action […] in a time of conflict exempts them from responsibility for the violence within their community.' See A. Little, *Give a Boy a Gun: One Man's Journey from Killing to Peace-Keeping* (London: Darton, Longman and Todd, 2009), p. 11.

17 Healing Through Remembering Storytelling sub-group, *What is Storytelling? A Discussion Paper*, (Belfast: Healing Through Remembering, 2005), p. 1.

18 S. Travers and N. Fetherstonhaugh, *The Miami Showband Massacre: A Survivor's Search for the Truth* (Dublin: Hodder Headline Ireland, 2007), p. 215.

19 Ibid., p. 15.

20 T. Knatchbull, *From a Clear Blue Sky: Surviving the Mountbatten Bomb* (London: Hutchinson, 2009), xii.

21 Restorick, *Death of a Soldier*, p. 2.

22 Ibid., p. 58. Colin Parry also described his burning desire to keep alive Tim's memory: 'Was he to be just one more statistic in the long line of killings arising out of the Northern Ireland problem? Not if I had anything to do with it he wouldn't.' See C. and W. Parry, *Tim: An Ordinary Boy* (London: Hodder and Stoughton, 1994), pp. 101, 130.

23 Restorick, *Death of a Soldier*, p. 164.

24 Wilson and McCreary, *Marie*, p. 48.

25 Ibid., xv. Introduction by McCreary.

26 Restorick, *Death of a Soldier*, p. 122. Colin and Wendy Parry were also touched by the support they received from Gordon Wilson, who visited them in Warrington; see *Tim*, pp. 104, 106–7.

27 See G. Kelly and B. Hamber (eds.), *Reconciliation: Rhetoric or Relevant?* (Belfast: Democratic Dialogue, Report No. 17, 2005).

28 See S. McKay, *Bear in Mind These Dead* (London: Faber and Faber, 2008), p. 232. Aileen Quinton, whose mother was killed in the bombing, objected to Wilson's support for the adaptation of the war memorial in Enniskillen, which omitted the term 'murder': 'To the rest of the world, Wilson represented the spirit of Enniskillen. To some, in his home town, he was a source of resentment – the acceptable face of victimhood, the good victim who made others look bad.' (McKay, *Bear in Mind*, p. 316).

29 Wilson and McCreary, *Marie*, p. 91.

30 Gordon Wilson had said on the evening of the bombing, in an interview with the BBC: 'I have lost my daughter, and we shall miss her. But I bear no ill-will. I bear no grudge. Dirty sort of talk is not going to bring her back.' He also argued

that his refusal to bear any malice 'might be partly a protection on my own part. It would be extremely stressful for me if I were to spend a lot of time thinking of recrimination'. Ibid., pp. 91–2.

31 Ibid., p. 92.

32 McKay reports Wilson's deep sense of frustration after the meeting (*Bear in Mind*, pp. 231–2). See also D. McDaniel, *Enniskillen: The Remembrance Sunday Bombing* (Dublin: Wolfhound Press, 1997), p. 152. Colin Parry stated (*Tim*, pp. 107–8) that he could not envisage meeting with members of the IRA, and certainly not so soon after the murder; he had no confidence that Gordon Wilson would succeed, and 'sadly, as it was to turn out, I was to be right in my pessimistic prediction.'

33 Two of the gang involved were serving members of the Ulster Defence Regiment at the time, and there was also the unexplained presence at the scene of the attack of an officer with an English accent. It has been alleged that this officer may have been Robert Nairac, an undercover SAS agent, later killed in mysterious circumstances; see Travers and Fetherstonhaugh, *Miami Showband Massacre*, p. 265; also see A. Bradley, *Requiem for a Spy: The Killing of Robert Nairac* (Dublin: Mercier Press, 1993), p. 94; for a fictional recreation of the Nairac case, see E. McNamee, *The Ultras* (London: Faber and Faber, 2004).

34 Travers and Fetherstonhaugh, *Miami Showband Massacre*, p. 125.

35 Ibid., p. 126.

36 Ibid., p. 128.

37 For the Craftsman, 'people might say that my life is self-inflicted [...] but we are victims too. I didn't see my sons for the whole time I was on the run.' Ibid., p. 262.

38 Restorick, *Death of a Soldier*, p. 1.

39 Ibid., p. 7. McElroy had stated that 'one of my strongest emotions this morning was shame. I felt ashamed we were going to be tarred with the same brush as the IRA. But they certainly don't stand for any of my family or friends.' It was later reported that Lorraine McElroy had been threatened by the IRA locally, which was particularly angered by her comments because one of her cousins was a volunteer in Newry. The McElroys subsequently moved from Bessbrook. See T. Harnden, *'Bandit Country': The IRA and South Armagh* (London: Hodder and Stoughton, 1999), p. 283.

40 She had been hurt by the remarks of SF President, Gerry Adams, who was asked about the vigil observed by Rita Restorick at Downing Street on the occasion of SF's talks there with Prime Minister Tony Blair, and had replied: 'there are thousands of Mrs Restoricks in Northern Ireland', and that she was not unique in her suffering. Rita felt that this was unfair; she 'had always stressed in interviews that I tried to represent the suffering of mothers in both communities and in the rest of Britain due to the conflict' (Restorick, *Death of a Soldier*, pp. 159–60).

41 Ibid., p. 182. Immediately after the tense but successful negotiation of the political agreement in April 1998, Rita sent an Easter card to the man awaiting trial in the Maze for Stephen's murder, Bernard McGinn, with a message of forgiveness and reconciliation.

42 T. Knatchbull, *From a Clear Blue Sky*, p. 260. See also McKay, *Bear in Mind*, pp. 88–92.

43 As Jim McCabe, the widower of Nora (who had been killed by a plastic bullet fired by an RUC officer in 1981) put it, 'I was occasionally taken out of my little box by certain politicians and journalists and used as an exhibit as to how bad things were. Then I was put back.' McKay, *Bear in Mind*, p. 101.

44 For a recent exception, see C. McCartney, *Walls of Silence* (Dublin: Gill and Macmillan, 2007).

45 See the report of the Consultative Group on the Past (Eames-Bradley), January 2009, and subsequent controversy.

Notes to Chapter 11: Chroniclers of the Conflict

1 C. McGrattan, *Northern Ireland: The Politics of Entrenchment, 1968–2008* (Basingstoke: Palgrave Macmillan, 2010), p. 157.

2 See M. Breen Smyth, *Truth Recovery and Justice after Conflict* (Abingdon: Routledge, 2007), p. 31.

3 E. Longley, 'Northern Ireland: Commemoration, Elegy, Forgetting' in *History and Memory in Modern Ireland* ed. by I. McBride (Cambridge: Cambridge University Press, 2001), p. 231. See also S. McKay, *Bear in Mind These Dead* (London: Faber and Faber, 2008), p. 301.

4 E. Jelin, *State Repression and the Struggles for Memory* (London: Latin America Bureau, 2003), p. 27.

5 K. Morgan, 'An Exemplary Communist Life? Harry Pollitt's *Serving My Time* in Comparative Perspective', in *Making Reputations: Power, Persuasion and the Individual in British Politics* ed. by J. Gottlieb and R Toye (London: I. B. Tauris, 2005), p. 56.

6 Longley, 'Commemoration, Elegy, Forgetting', p. 231.

7 For a thoroughgoing critique of the communal logic of the Belfast Agreement, see R. Wilson, *The Northern Ireland Experience of Conflict and Agreement: A Model for Export?* (Manchester: Manchester University Press, 2010).

8 P. Arthur, 'Conflict, Memory and Reconciliation', in *The Long Road to Peace in Northern Ireland* ed. by M. Elliott (Liverpool: Liverpool University Press, 2002), p. 147.

9 Ibid., p. 147.

10 Jelin, *State Repression and the Struggles for Memory*, p. 33. Jelin borrows the concept of 'memory entrepreneurs' from Howard Becker's 'moral entrepreneurs'.

11 Ibid., p. 139, fn 9.

12 The term 'people's remembrancer' is borrowed from Gwyn Alf Williams, who used it to describe the South Wales miners' leader and memory entrepreneur, Dai Francis; 'Dai Francis, People's Remembrancer', *Llafur*, 3.3 (1982).

Bibliography

Memoirs

Adair, Johnny with Graeme McKendry, *Mad Dog* (London: Blake, 2007).

Adams, Gerry, *Falls Memories: A Belfast Life* (Dingle: Brandon, 1982).

——, *Before the Dawn: An Autobiography* (Dingle: Brandon, 1996).

——, *Hope and History: Making Peace in Ireland* (London: William Heinemann and Dingle: Brandon, 2003).

Barker, Alan, *Shadows: Inside Northern Ireland's Special Branch* (Edinburgh: Mainstream, 2004).

Barry, Tom, *Guerrilla Days in Ireland* (Dublin: Anvil, 1989 [1st edition, 1949]).

Bloomfield, Kenneth, *Stormont in Crisis: A Memoir* (Belfast: Blackstaff, 1994).

Boyce, Eamonn, *The Insider: The Prison Diaries of Eamonn Boyce, 1956–62* (Belfast: Lilliput Press, 2007).

Boyd, John *Out of My Class* (Belfast: Blackstaff, 1985).

——, *The Middle of My Journey* (Belfast: Blackstaff, 1990).

Bradley, Gerry with Brian Feeney, *Insider: Gerry Bradley's Life in the IRA* (Dublin: O'Brien, 2009).

Breen, Dan, *My Fight for Irish Freedom* (Dublin: Anvil, 1989 [1st edition, 1924]).

Brown, Johnston, *Into the Dark: 30 Years in the RUC* (Dublin: Gill and Macmillan, 2005).

Callaghan, James, *A House Divided: The Dilemma of Northern Ireland* (London: Collins, 1973).

Collins, Eamonn with Mark McGovern, *Killing Rage* (London: Granta, 1997).

Conroy, John, *War as a Way of Life: A Belfast Diary* (London: Heinemann, 1988).

Currie, Austin, *All Hell Will Break Loose* (Dublin: O'Brien, 2004).

Curtis, Nick, *Faith and Duty: The True Story of a Soldier's War in Northern Ireland* (London: Andre Deutsch, 2003).

Delbo, Charlotte, *Auschwitz and After* (New Haven, CT and London: Yale University Press, 1995)

Devenport, Mark, *Flash Frames: Twelve Years Reporting Belfast* (Belfast: Blackstaff, 2000).

Devlin, Bernadette, *The Price of My Soul* (London: Pan, 1969).

Devlin, Paddy, *Straight Left: An Autobiography* (Belfast: Blackstaff, 1993).

Ellis, Walter, *The Beginning of the End: The Crippling Disadvantage of a Happy Irish Childhood* (Edinburgh: Mainstream, 2006).

Faulkner, Brian, *Memoirs of a Statesman* (London: Weidenfeld and Nicolson, 1978).

FitzGerald, Garret, *All in a Life: An Autobiography* (Dublin: Gill and Macmillan, 1991).

Gilmour, Raymond, *Dead Ground: Infiltrating the IRA* (London: Little, Brown, 1998).

Hain, Peter, *Outside In* (London: Biteback, 2012).

Harbinson, Roy, *No Surrender: An Ulster Childhood* (Belfast: Blackstaff, 1987 [1st edition, 1960]).

Hayes, Maurice, *Minority Verdict: Experiences of a Catholic Public Servant* (Belfast: Blackstaff, 1995).

Hermon, John, *Holding the Line: An Autobiography* (Dublin: Gill and Macmillan, 1997).

Hume, John, *A New Ireland* (Boulder, CO: Roberts Rinehart, 1996).

Hurd, Douglas, *Memoirs* (London: Little, Brown, 2003).

Knatchbull, Timothy, *From A Clear Blue Sky: Surviving the Mountbatten Bomb* (London: Hutchinson, 2009).

Latham, Richard, *Deadly Beat: Inside the Royal Ulster Constabulary* (Edinburgh: Mainstream, 2001).

Lewis, Rob, *Fishers of Men* (London: Hodder and Stoughton, 1999).

Little, Alistair with Ruth Scott, *Give a Boy a Gun: One Man's Journey from Killing to Peace-Keeping* (London: Darton, Longman and Todd, 2009).

Loyd, Anthony, *My War Gone by, I Miss it so* (London: Doubleday, 1999).

MacStíofáin, Seán, *Revolutionary in Ireland* (Edinburgh: Gordon Cremonesi, 1975).

McCartney, Catherine, *Walls of Silence* (Dublin: Gill and Macmillan, 2007).

McDonald, Henry, *Colours: Ireland – From Bombs to Boom* (Edinburgh: Mainstream, 2005).

McGartland, Martin, *Fifty Dead Men Walking* (London: Blake, 1997).

——, *Dead Man Running* (Edinburgh: Mainstream, 1998).

McGuire, Maria, *To Take Arms: A Year in the Provisional IRA* (London: Macmillan, 1973).

McIvor, Basil, *Hope Deferred: Experiences of an Irish Unionist* (Belfast: Blackstaff, 1998).

McLaughlin, Ray, *Inside an English Jail* (Dublin: Borderline, 1987).

Mandelson, Peter, *The Third Man: Life at the Heart of New Labour* (London: Harper Collins, 2010).

Mason, Roy, *Paying the Price* (London: Robert Hale, 1999).

Morrison, Danny, *Then the Walls Came Down: A Prison Journal* (Cork and Dublin: Mercier, 1999).

——, *All the Dead Voices* (Cork and Dublin: Mercier, 2002).

Mowlam, Mo, *Momentum: The Struggle for Peace, Politics and the People* (London: Hodder and Stoughton, 2002).

Myers, Kevin, *Watching the Door: Cheating Death in 1970s Belfast* (London: Atlantic, 2008).

Needham, Richard, *Battling for Peace* (Belfast: Blackstaff, 1998).

O'Callaghan, Sean, *The Informer* (London: Bantam, 1998).

O'Doherty, Malachi, *The Telling Year: Belfast 1972* (Dublin: Gill and Macmillan, 2007).

O'Doherty, Shane, *The Volunteer: A Former IRA Man's True Story* (London: Fount, 1993).

O'Donovan Rossa, Jeremiah, *Irish Rebels in English Prisons* (Dingle: Brandon, 1991 [revised edition]).

O'Hanlon, Paddy, *End of Term Report* (Newry: Paddy O'Hanlon Publishing, 2011).

O'Malley, Ernie, *The Singing Flame* (Dublin: Anvil, 1978).

——, *On Another Man's Wound* (Dublin: Anvil, 1979 [1st edition, 1936]).

O'Neill, Joseph, *Blood-Dark Track: A Family History* (London: Granta, 2002).

O'Neill, Terence, *The Autobiography of Terence O'Neill* (London: Rupert Hart-Davis, 1972).

O'Rawe, Richard, *Blanketmen: An Untold Story of the H-Block Hunger Strike* (Dublin: New Island, 2005).

——, *Afterlives: The Hunger Strike and the Secret Offer that Changed Irish History* (Dublin: Lilliput Press, 2010).

Oliver, John, *Working at Stormont* (Dublin: Institute of Public Administration, 1978).

Parry, Colin and Wendy Parry, *Tim: An Ordinary Boy* (London: Hodder and Stoughton, 1994).

Powell, Jonathan, *Great Hatred, Little Room: Making Peace in Northern Ireland* (London: Bodley Head, 2008).

Prior, James, *A Balance of Power* (London: Hamish Hamilton, 1985).

Ramsay, Robert, *Ringside Seats: An Insider's View of the Crisis in Northern Ireland* (Dublin: Irish Academic Press, 2009).

Rees, Merlyn, *Northern Ireland: A Personal Perspective* (London: Methuen, 1985).

Restorick, Rita, *Death of a Soldier: A Mother's Search for Peace in Northern Ireland* (Belfast: Blackstaff, 2000).

Sands, Bobby, *One Day in My Life* (Cork and Dublin: Mercier, 1983).

Stone, Michael, *None Shall Divide Us* (London: John Blake, 2003).

Travers, Stephen and Neil Fetherstonhaugh, *The Miami Showband Massacre: A Survivor's Search for the Truth* (Dublin: Hodder Headline Ireland, 2007).

Whitelaw, William, *The Whitelaw Memoirs* (London: Aurum, 1989).

Wilson, Gordon with Alf McCreary, *Marie: A Story from Enniskillen* (London: Marshall Pickering, 1990).

Articles and Books

Adams, Gerry, 'A Republican in the Civil Rights Campaign' in *Twenty Years On* ed. by Michael Farrell (Dingle: Brandon, 1988).

——, *Cage Eleven* (Dingle: Brandon, 1990).

——, *The Street and Other Stories* (Dingle: Brandon, 1992).

——, *Selected Writings* (Dingle: Brandon, 1994).

Aguilar, Paloma, *Memory and Amnesia: The Role of the Spanish Civil War in the Transition to Democracy* (New York: Berghahn, 2000).

Alonso, Rogelio, *The IRA and Armed Struggle* (London: Routledge, 2007).

Anderson, Chris, *The Billy Boy: The Life and Death of LVF Leader Billy Wright* (Edinburgh: Mainstream, 2004).

Anderson, Donald, *Fourteen May Days: The Inside Story of the Loyalist Strike of May 1974* (Dublin: Gill and Macmillan, 1994).

Arthur, Paul, 'The Heath Government and Northern Ireland', in *The Heath Government,*

1970–1974: A Reappraisal ed. by Stuart Ball and Anthony Seldon (London: Longman, 1996), pp.235–58.

——, 'Conflict, Memory and Reconciliation', in *The Long Road to Peace in Northern Ireland* ed. by Marianne Elliott (Liverpool: Liverpool University Press, 2002), pp.143–52.

——, 'Memory, Forgiveness and Conflict: Trust-Building in Northern Ireland', in *Commemorating Ireland: History, Politics, Culture* ed. by Eberhard Bort (Dublin: Irish Academic Press, 2004), pp.68–78.

——, 'Memory and Reconciliation', paper delivered at the conference Pathways to Reconciliation and Global Human Rights, Sarajevo, 2005.

Aughey, Arthur, 'Learning from "The Leopard"', in *Aspects of the Belfast Agreement* ed. by R. Wilford (Oxford: Oxford University Press, 2001), pp.184–201.

——, 'The Art and Effect of Political Lying in Northern Ireland', *Irish Political Studies*, 17.2 (2002), pp.1–16.

Bean, Kevin, *The New Politics of Sinn Féin* (Liverpool: Liverpool University Press, 2007).

Bean, Kevin and Mark Hayes (eds.), *Republican Voices* (Monaghan: Seesyu Press, 2001).

Beattie, Geoffrey, *We Are the People: Journeys Through the Heart of Protestant Ulster* (London: Heinemann, 1992).

Bew, Paul and Paul Dixon, 'Labour Party Policy and Northern Ireland', in *The Northern Ireland Question: Perspectives and Policies* ed. by Brian Barton and Patrick Roche (Aldershot: Avebury, 1994), pp.151–65.

Bloomfield, David and Maeve Lankford, 'From Whitewash to Mayhem: The State of the Secretary in Northern Ireland', in *The Northern Ireland Question in British Politics* ed. by Peter Catterall and Sean McDougall (Basingstoke: Palgrave Macmillan, 1996), pp.143–61.

Bloomfield, Kenneth, *We Will Remember Them* [Report of the Northern Ireland Victims' Commissioner], (Belfast: HMSO, 1998).

——, *A Tragedy of Errors: The Government and Misgovernment of Northern Ireland* (Liverpool: Liverpool University Press, 2007).

Bradley, Anthony, *Requiem for a Spy: The Killing of Robert Nairac* (Dublin: Mercier Press, 1993).

Breen, Suzanne, 'The Many Tales of Gerry Adams', *News Letter*, 2 October 2003.

——, 'Decommissioned: Provos on Scrapheap of History', *Sunday Tribune*, 16 April 2006.

Breen Smyth, Marie, *Truth Recovery and Justice after Conflict: Managing Violent Pasts* (Abingdon: Routledge, 2007).

Bruce, Steve, *The Edge of the Union: The Ulster Loyalist Political Vision* (Oxford: Oxford University Press, 1994).

——, *Paisley: Religion and Politics in Northern Ireland* (Oxford: Oxford University Press, 2009).

Campbell, Brian, 'O'Callaghan – the Truth', *An Phoblacht/Republican News*, 27 February 1997.

Cochrane, Fergal, '"Meddling at the Crossroads": The Decline and Fall of Terence O'Neill within the Unionist Community', in *Unionism in Modern Ireland* ed. by Richard

English and Graham Walker (Basingstoke: Macmillan, 1996), pp.148–68.

Cordes, B., 'When Terrorists Do the Talking: Reflections on Terrorist Literature', in *Inside Terrorist Organizations* ed. by David Rapoport (New York: Columbia University Press, 1988), pp.150–71.

Crawford, Colin, *Inside the UDA: Volunteers and Violence* (London: Pluto, 2003).

Currie, P. M. and M. Taylor (eds.), *Dissident Irish Republicanism* (London: Continuum, 2011).

Cusack, Jim and Henry McDonald, *UVF* (Dublin: Poolbeg Press, 1997).

Dawson, Graham, *Making Peace with the Past? Memory, Trauma and the Irish Troubles* (Manchester: Manchester University Press, 2007).

De Baróid, Ciarán, *Ballymurphy and the Irish War* (London: Pluto, 2000 [revised edition]).

Devlin, Paddy, *Yes We Have No Bananas: Outdoor Relief in Belfast, 1920–39* (Belfast: Blackstaff, 1981).

Dillon, Martin, *Stone Cold: The True Story of Michael Stone and the Milltown Massacre* (London: Hutchinson, 1992).

——, *The Trigger Men* (Edinburgh: Mainstream, 2004).

Dixon, Paul, 'Peter Hain, Secretary of State for Northern Ireland: Valuing the Union?', *Irish Political Studies*, 21.2 (2006), pp.113–36.

Drower, George, *John Hume: Man of Peace* (London: Victor Gollancz, 1995).

Dudley Edwards, Ruth, 'Gerry the Liar', *Spectator*, 27 July 2002.

Edwards, Aaron, *A History of the Northern Ireland Labour Party: Democratic Socialism and Sectarianism* (Manchester: Manchester University Press, 2009).

Egerton, George (ed.) *Political Memoir: Essays on the Politics of Memory* (London: Frank Cass, 1994).

Elliott, Marianne, *The Catholics of Ulster: A History* (London: Penguin, 2001).

English, Richard *Armed Struggle: A History of the IRA* (London: Macmillan, 2003).

Feeney, Brian, 'Adams Calls for Truth but Keeps Past Secret', *Irish News*, 16 August 2007.

Finlay, Andrew, 'Defeatism and Northern Protestant "Identity"', *Global Review of Ethnopolitics*, 1.2 (2001), pp.3–20.

Flackes, W. D. and Sydney Elliott, *Northern Ireland: A Political Directory, 1969–1993* (Belfast: Blackstaff, 1994).

Foster, Roy, *The Irish Story: Telling Tales and Making it Up in Ireland* (London: Penguin, 2002).

Frampton, Martyn, *Legion of the Rearguard: Dissident Irish Republicanism* (Dublin: Irish Academic Press, 2011).

Gailey, Andrew, *Crying in the Wilderness – Jack Sayers: A Liberal Editor in Ulster, 1939–69* (Belfast: Institute of Irish Studies, 1995).

Gallaher, Carolyn, *After the Peace: Loyalist Paramilitaries in Post-Accord Northern Ireland* (Ithaca, NY: Cornell University Press, 2007).

Gamble, Andrew, 'Political Memoirs', *British Journal of Politics and International Relations*, 4.1 (2002), pp.141–51.

Garland, Roy, *Gusty Spence* (Belfast: Blackstaff Press, 2001).

Garnett, Mark and Ian Aitken, *Splendid! Splendid! The Authorized Biography of Willie*

Whitelaw (London: Jonathan Cape, 2002).

Gébler, Carlo, *The Glass Curtain: Inside an Ulster Community* (London: Hamish Hamilton, 1991).

Gillespie, Gordon, 'The Sunningdale Agreement: Lost Opportunity or an Agreement too Far?', *Irish Political Studies*, 13 (1998), pp.100–114.

——, 'Noises Off: Loyalists after the Agreement', in *A Farewell to Arms? Beyond the Good Friday Agreement* ed. by Michael Cox, Adrian Guelke and Fiona Stephen (Manchester: Manchester University Press, 2006), pp.139–51.

Gilmore, Leigh, *The Limits of Autobiography: Trauma and Testimony* (Ithaca, NY and London: Cornell University Press, 2001).

Godson, Dean, *Himself Alone: David Trimble and the Ordeal of Unionism* (London: Harper Collins, 2004).

Graff-McRae, Rebecca, *Remembering and Forgetting 1916: Commemoration and Conflict in Post-Peace Process Ireland* (Dublin: Irish Academic Press, 2010).

Halfin, Igal, *Terror in My Soul: Communist Autobiographies on Trial* (Cambridge, MA: Harvard University Press, 2003).

Harnden, Toby, *'Bandit Country': The IRA and South Armagh* (London: Hodder and Stoughton, 1999).

Harte, Liam (ed.), *Modern Irish Autobiography: Self, Nation and Society* (Basingstoke: Palgrave Macmillan, 2007).

Healing Through Remembering, *What is Storytelling? A Discussion Paper* (Belfast: Healing Through Remembering, 2005).

Hellbeck, Jochen, *Revolution on My Mind: Writing a Diary under Stalin* (Cambridge, MA: Harvard University Press, 2006).

Hennessey, Tom, *The Evolution of the Troubles, 1970–72* (Dublin: Irish Academic Press, 2007).

Herrmann, Gina, *Written in Red: The Communist Memoir in Spain* (Chicago, IL: University of Illinois Press, 2010).

Hopkins, Stephen, 'Fighting without Guns? Political Autobiography in Contemporary Northern Ireland', in *Modern Irish Autobiography: Self, Nation and Society* ed. by Liam Harte (Basingstoke: Palgrave Macmillan, 2007), pp.176–96.

——, 'Review Essay: The Soviet Politics of the Self', *Labour History Review*, 73 (2008), pp.336–47.

——, 'Comparing Revolutionary Narratives: Irish Republican Self-Presentation and Considerations for the Study of Communist Life Histories', *Socialist History*, 34 (2009), pp.52–69.

——, 'Still a Spanish Red? The Communist Past and National Identity in the Writing of Jorge Semprún', *Twentieth Century Communism*, 3 (2011), pp.70–91.

——, 'The Chronicles of Long Kesh: Irish Republican Memoirs and the Contested Memory of the Hunger Strikes', *Memory Studies*, 7.4 (2014, forthcoming).

Jelin, Elizabeth, *State Repression and the Struggles for Memory* (London: Latin America Bureau, 2003).

Johnston, Philip, *The Lost Tribe in the Mirror: Four Playwrights of Northern Ireland* (Belfast: Lagan, 2009).

Keena, Colm, *Gerry Adams: A Biography* (Cork: Mercier, 1990).

Kelley, Kevin, *The Longest War: Northern Ireland and the IRA* (Dingle: Brandon, 1983).

Kelly, Gráinne and Brandon Hamber (eds.), *Reconciliation: Rhetoric or Relevant?* (Belfast: Democratic Dialogue, Report No.17, 2005).

Leahy, Pat, 'Trimble Knows the Old Days are Over', *Sunday Business Post*, 28 September 2003.

Leitch, Maurice, *Silver's City* (London: Secker and Warburg, 1981).

Lister, David and Hugh Jordan, *Mad Dog: The Rise and Fall of Johnny Adair and 'C Company'* (Edinburgh: Mainstream, 2004).

Longley, Edna, 'What Do Protestants Want?' *Irish Review*, 20 (1997), pp.104–20.

———, 'Northern Ireland: Commemoration, Elegy, Forgetting', in *History and Memory in Modern Ireland* ed. by Ian McBride (Cambridge: Cambridge University Press, 2001), pp.223–53.

Lynch, Claire, *Irish Autobiography: Stories of Self in the Narrative of a Nation* (Bern: Peter Lang, 2009).

Lynn, Brendan, *Holding the Ground: The Nationalist Party in Northern Ireland, 1945–72* (Aldershot: Ashgate, 1997).

———, 'Tactic or Principle? The Evolution of Republican Thinking on Abstentionism in Ireland, 1970–1998', *Irish Political Studies*, 17.2 (2002), pp.74–94.

McAllister, Ian, *The Northern Ireland Social Democratic and Labour Party: Political Opposition in a Divided Society* (London: Macmillan, 1977).

McAuley, James, *The Politics of Identity: A Loyalist Community in Belfast* (Aldershot: Avebury, 1994).

McCluskey, Conn, *Up Off Their Knees: A Commentary on the Civil Rights Movement in Northern Ireland* (Dublin: Conn McCluskey and Associates, 1989).

McCreary, Alf, *Gordon Wilson: An Ordinary Hero* (London: Marshall Pickering, 1996).

McDaniel, Denzil, *Enniskillen: The Remembrance Sunday Bombing* (Dublin: Wolfhound Press, 1997).

McDonald, Henry, *Trimble* (London: Bloomsbury, 2004).

McDonald, Henry and Jim Cusack, *UDA: Inside the Heart of Loyalist Terror* (Dublin: Penguin Ireland, 2004).

McGladdery, Gary, *The Provisional IRA in England: The Bombing Campaign 1973–1997* (Dublin: Irish Academic Press, 2006).

McGrattan, Cillian, *Northern Ireland: The Politics of Entrenchment, 1968–2008* (Basingstoke: Palgrave Macmillan, 2010).

McIntyre, Anthony, 'Provisional Republicanism: Internal Politics, Inequities and Modes of Repression', in *Republicanism in Modern Ireland* ed. by Fearghal McGarry (Dublin: University College Dublin Press, 2003), pp.178–98.

———, 'Uncharted Waters', *The Other View*, Autumn 2003.

———, 'The Battle against Truth', *The Blanket*, 19 August 2007.

———, 'And Goodbye Adams?', *Parliamentary Brief*, April 2008.

———, *Good Friday: The Death of Irish Republicanism* (New York: Ausubo Press, 2008).

McKay, Susan, *Northern Protestants: An Unsettled People* (Belfast: Blackstaff, 2000).

———, *Bear in Mind These Dead* (London: Faber and Faber, 2008).

McKearney, Tommy, *The Provisional IRA: From Insurrection to Parliament* (London: Pluto, 2011).

McKeown, Laurence, *Out of Time: Irish Republican Prisoners Long Kesh 1972–2000* (Belfast: Beyond the Pale Publications, 2001).

McKittrick, David, Seamus Kelters, Brian Feeney and Chris Thornton, *Lost Lives: The Stories of the Men, Women and Children Who Died as a Result of the Northern Ireland Troubles* (Edinburgh: Mainstream, 1999).

McNamee, Eoin, *The Ultras* (London: Faber and Faber, 2004).

Maillot, Agnes, *New Sinn Féin: Irish Republicanism in the Twenty-First Century* (London: Routledge, 2005).

Meredith, Fionola, 'Rounded, Intelligent, Articulate, Human and Murderous', *Fortnight*, 412 (2003).

Mitchell, Gary, *Tearing the Loom* and *In a Little World of Our Own* (London: Nick Hern Books, 1998).

——, *As the Beast Sleeps* (London: Nick Hern Books, 2001).

——, *Loyal Women* (London: Nick Hern Books, 2003).

Moloney, Ed, *A Secret History of the IRA* (London: Allen Lane, 2002).

——, *Voices from the Grave: Two Men's War in Ireland* (London: Faber and Faber, 2010).

Moloney, Ed and Andy Pollak, *Paisley* (Dublin: Poolbeg, 1986).

Morgan, Kevin, 'Parts of People and Communist Lives', in *Party People, Communist Lives: Explorations in Biography* ed. by John McIlroy, Kevin Morgan and Alan Campbell (London: Lawrence and Wishart, 2001), pp.9–28.

——, 'An Exemplary Communist Life? Harry Pollitt's *Serving My Time* in Comparative Perspective', in *Making Reputations: Power, Persuasion and the Individual in Modern British Politics* ed. by Julie Gottlieb and Richard Toye (London: I. B. Tauris, 2005), pp.56–69.

Morrison, Danny, *West Belfast* (Cork: Mercier, 1989).

——, *On the Back of the Swallow* (Cork: Mercier, 1994).

——, *The Wrong Man* (Cork: Mercier, 1996).

——, *Rebel Columns* (Belfast: Beyond the Pale, 2004).

Morrissey, Michael and Marie Smyth, *Northern Ireland after the Good Friday Agreement: Victims, Grievance and Blame* (London and Sterling, VA: Pluto, 2002).

Mulholland, Marc, *Northern Ireland at the Crossroads: Ulster Unionism in the O'Neill Years* (Basingstoke: Macmillan, 2000).

Murphy, Michael, *Gerry Fitt: A Political Chameleon* (Dublin: Mercier, 2007).

Newsinger, John, *Dangerous Men: The SAS and Popular Culture* (London: Pluto Press, 1997).

O'Doherty, Malachi, *The Trouble with Guns: Republican Strategy and the Provisional IRA* (Belfast: Blackstaff, 1998).

——, 'Could Gerry Adams be Living on Borrowed Time?' *Belfast Telegraph*, 16 May 2008.

O'Malley, Eoin, 'Populist Nationalists: Sinn Féin and Redefining the "Radical Right"', unpublished paper.

O'Malley, Padraig, *Biting at the Grave: The Irish Hunger Strikes and the Politics of Despair* (Belfast: Blackstaff, 1990).

O'Neill, Terence, *Ulster at the Crossroads* (London: Faber and Faber, 1969).

O'Toole, Fintan, 'The Premature Life of Gerry Adams', *Irish Times*, 28 September 1996.

——, 'The Taming of a Terrorist', *New York Review of Books*, 27 February 2003.

Olney, James, *Autobiography: Essays Theoretical and Critical* (Princeton, CT: Princeton University Press, 1980).

Ormsby, Frank (ed.), *The Collected Poems of John Hewitt* (Belfast: Blackstaff, 1991).

Parr, Connal, 'Managing his Aspirations: The Labour and Republican Politics of Paddy Devlin', *Irish Political Studies*, 27.1 (2012) pp.111–38.

Pascal, Roy, *Design and Truth in Autobiography* (Cambridge, MA: Harvard University Press, 1960).

Patterson, Henry, *The Politics of Illusion: A Political History of the IRA* (London: Serif, 1997).

——, *Ireland since 1939: The Persistence of Conflict* (Dublin: Penguin Ireland, 2006).

——, 'Sectarianism Revisited: The Provisional IRA in a Border Region of Northern Ireland', *Terrorism and Political Violence*, 22.3 (2010), pp.337–56.

Peace Direct, *Unarmed Heroes: The Courage to Go beyond Violence* (London: Clairview, 2004).

Pennetier, Claude and Bernard Pudal, 'Les autobiographies des "Fils du peuple": de l'autobiographie édifiante à l'autobiographie auto-analytique', in *Autobiographies, autocritiques, aveux dans le monde communiste* ed. by Claude Pennetier and Bernard Pudal (Paris: Belin, 2002), pp.217–46.

Rennie, James, *The Operators: Inside 14 Intelligence Company – The Army's Top Secret Elite* (London: Century, 1996).

Ross, F. Stuart, *Smashing H-Block: The Rise and Fall of the Popular Campaign against Criminalization, 1976–1982* (Liverpool: Liverpool University Press, 2011).

Routledge, Paul, *John Hume* (London: Harper Collins, 1997).

Ryder, Chris, *The RUC: A Force under Fire* (London: Methuen, 1989).

——, *The Ulster Defence Regiment: An Instrument of Peace?* (London: Methuen, 1991).

——, *Inside the Maze: The Untold Story of the Northern Ireland Prison Service* (London: Methuen, 2001).

——, *Fighting Fitt* (Belfast: Brehon, 2006).

Scott, Stephen, 'Dead Man Talking', *Guardian*, 31 January 1999.

Semprún, Jorge, *Literature or Life* (New York: Viking Penguin, 1997).

Shanahan, Tim, *The Provisional Irish Republican Army and the Morality of Terrorism* (Edinburgh: Edinburgh University Press, 2009).

Sharrock, David, 'Adams Signs £400,000 Deal for New Book', *Daily Telegraph*, 10 October 2001.

Sharrock, David and Mark Devenport, *Man of War, Man of Peace? The Unauthorised Biography of Gerry Adams* (London: Macmillan, 1997).

Shirlow, Peter, *The End of Ulster Loyalism?* (Manchester: Manchester University Press, 2012).

Shirlow, Peter and Brendan Murtagh, *Belfast: Segregation, Violence and the City* (London and Ann Arbor, MI: Pluto, 2006).

Sinnerton, Henry, *David Ervine: Uncharted Waters* (Dingle: Brandon, 2002).

Smith, M. L. R., *Fighting for Ireland? The Military Strategy of the Irish Republican Movement* (London: Routledge, 1995).

Smyth, Marie and Marie-Therese Fay, *Personal Accounts from Northern Ireland's Troubles: Public Conflict, Private Loss* (London and Sterling, VA: Pluto, 2000).

Spencer, Graham, *The State of Loyalism in Northern Ireland* (Basingstoke: Palgrave, 2008).

Suleiman, Susan Rubin, *Crises of Memory and the Second World War* (Cambridge, MA: Harvard University Press, 2006).

Taylor, Peter, *Provos: The IRA and Sinn Féin* (London: Bloomsbury, 1997).

——, *Loyalists* (London: Bloomsbury, 1999).

Thomas, Laurence Mordekhai, 'Suffering as a Moral Beacon: Blacks and Jews', in *The Americanization of the Holocaust* ed. by Hilene Flanzbaum (Baltimore: Johns Hopkins, 1999)

Thompson, Sam, *Three Plays: Over the Bridge, The Evangelist, Cemented with Love* (Belfast: Lagan, 1997).

Thornton, Chris, 'Vintage Adams: His Life in Books', *Belfast Telegraph*, 29 September 2003.

Toíbín, Colm, *Bad Blood: A Walk along the Irish Border* (London: Vintage, 1994).

Tonge, Jon, '"They Haven't Gone away, Y'Know": Irish Republican "Dissidents" and "Armed Struggle"', *Terrorism and Political Violence*, 16.3 (2004), pp.671–93.

Toolis, Kevin, 'A Prophet from the Darkness', *Guardian Weekend*, 5 April 1997.

Walker, Graham, *A History of the Ulster Unionist Party: Protest, Pragmatism and Pessimism* (Manchester: Manchester University Press, 2004).

Whalen, Lachlen, *Contemporary Irish Republican Prison Writing: Writing and Resistance* (Basingstoke: Palgrave Macmillan, 2008).

White, Barry, *John Hume: Statesman of the Troubles* (Belfast: Blackstaff, 1984).

White, R. W., 'The Irish Republican Army: An Assessment of Sectarianism', *Terrorism and Political Violence*, 9.1 (1997), pp.20–55.

——, *Ruairí Ó Brádaigh: The Life and Politics of an Irish Revolutionary* (Bloomington, IN: Indiana University Press, 2006).

——, 'Provisional IRA Attacks on the UDR in Fermanagh and South Tyrone: Implications for the Study of Political Violence and Terrorism', *Terrorism and Political Violence*, 23.3 (2011), pp.329–49.

Williams, Gwyn Alf, 'Dai Francis, People's Remembrancer', *Llafur*, 3.3 (1982), pp.6–8.

Wilson, Robin, *The Northern Ireland Experience of Conflict and Agreement: A Model for Export?* (Manchester: Manchester University Press, 2010).

Wood, Ian, *Crimes of Loyalty: A History of the UDA* (Edinburgh: Edinburgh University Press, 2006).

Yagoda, Ben, *Memoir: A History* (New York: Riverhead Books, 2009).

Zwicker, Heather, 'Gerry Adams, Moving Target', *Canadian Journal of Irish Studies*, 27.2/28.1 (2001–2), pp.78–95.

Index

Printed and bound by CPI Group (UK) Ltd, Croydon, CR0 4YY

09/06/2025

14685826-0002